SUBSTANCE

SUBSTANCE

Becoming oaks of righteousness in a world of vapor.

Nicola Gibson

All Scripture quotations, unless otherwise indicated, are from:
The Holy Bible, New International Version®. Copyright © 1973,
1978, 1984, 2011 by International Bible Society. Used by per-
mission of International Bible Society.

Italicized text within Scripture quotations indicates emphasis
added.

Find resources for SUBSTANCE at hpcmadison.com/substance.

Developmental and Lead Editor: Cora Pike
Production and Project Editor: John Sekutowski
Cover design and book graphics: Scott Khail

Printed by CreateSpace in the United States of America.

ACKNOWLEDGEMENTS AND DEDICATION

The work of writing clearly and truthfully is demanding and is rarely done alone. It demands a great deal not only from the author, but also from others who read drafts, edit the work's imperfections, design graphics, typeset, and confront the author's vanity. Quite a number of people have contributed to this book. Thanks particularly to Patrick Hlathein, Cassiana Taylor, Doug S., Nathan Sime, Kate Beecken, Hannah Donor, Laura Sheppard, Niccole Khail, Jill Reasa, Bill Taylor, Dave and Laurie Sekutowski, John Sekutowski, Meagan McCormick, Fran and Shirley Diederich, Lucina Gibson, Abigail Posey, and Jianting He. These High Point Church volunteers and staff have greatly improved this book through their labor of copy and content editing, and I am deeply grateful.

Without a staff member whom I'll call Ms. Cora Pike, this book could not have been completed. She would have been credited as a co-author, but instead, I cannot even use her real name. By the time this book is put to use, she will be traveling east to minister in nations that would not like to see her name on such a work. So I have given her the pseudonym of my great, great aunt, who was a missionary with China Inland Mission at the time of the Boxer Rebellion (1899-1901), during which thousands of missionaries were murdered or expelled from China. She, like you, loved not only Christ, but also the people of other cultures for their own sake. She had the courage as a single woman to go to that far away land during troubled times, though her name is known to no one now. Dear Cora, may your name be as unknown to men, while it dances in the undimmed memory of the God who forgets no one. May your journey be blessed by the one whom, in all the carnage of this world, burns into his eternal memory every cup of cold water given in his name, pledging with it his sacred rewards of everlasting joy. You, my little sister, follow this same path in perhaps similarly dangerous times as one of my great mothers, but we must learn with her that there is nothing safe outside the risk of God's will and word. You have not only improved the writing of this book; you have allowed Christ to write its message on your heart and use you to circulate it to the nations. We should imitate ones like you as you imitate him, for no printed book can be a jar of clay who bears afar the very Spirit and Way of Life.

I am grateful also to those who have labored to make these words into an actual book, specifically Jill Reasa, John Sekutowski, and Scott Khail. Your expertise and effort is always rushed by my late deadlines, but you bear that burden cheerfully and are, in the words of John Wesley, "always in haste, never in a rush." Carrie Firman also deserves thanks in this category, having contributed to earlier iterations of art for this book. Her creative work, too, has been a casualty of the writing process, since she paved the way by generating graphics that, because of delays in writing, weren't used in this final version. My thanks also goes to the staff, elders, and friends who have taken up the slack of what I left undone in order to focus on writing. I know it has not been a light thing, and I am grateful to be a co-laborer alongside each of you.

Lastly, I would dedicate this book to no one but the Church through the local church at High Point. To dedicate it to the Church is to offer it for the glory of God and the good of all. This is not to forget my wife and four children. They have made considerable sacrifices for me to serve the local church as a pastor, not least in the writing of this book. Yet, it is one of Alexi's and my great longings that our children would see and belong to a godly church, a church marked by faith, risk, sacrifice, faithfulness, truthfulness, kindness, patience, perseverance, love, and hope—a community deeply transformed by the gospel. With gratitude, I can say that they do. And I pray that all of our children, neighbors, and friends will see and embody this gospel life with increasing fullness and beauty. For truth unlocks and clarifies the mind, but only truth displayed in spiritual and moral beauty can overpower the rebellious will and heart. It is to this end that I have put my hand and commit my heart.

Soli Deo Gloria
Nic Gibson
May 2017

CONTENTS

PREFACE:
HOW TO USE THIS BOOK

Substance is designed to help us become more spiritually substantive people. It is designed to help normal Christians grow in godliness in a culture that is structured to produce the opposite result.

I have told many people that the only intent of this book is to remind the church of something it has always known: the pursuit of holiness. Older generations (along with the Bible) called this sanctification. It is the path of faithful striving in Christ, through which the Holy Spirit makes us like Jesus. Godliness is an integral part of God's great gift of liberation and freedom. It is his dismantling of sin's slavery. It is the unshackling of every person who will trust that, in Christ, God has given us "everything we need for life and godliness" (2 Peter 1:3, NIV 1984).

Structure

The book is divided into three parts.

Part 1 outlines the main problem this book is designed to address—our confusion, shallowness, and fragility—and makes a case for why we need to do something about it.

Part 2 paints a picture of spiritual substance and outlines what it looks like to seek that substance through faith in Jesus. This section is organized around four characteristics that are evident in people of substance. I call them the four marks of spiritual substance:

1. Self-Sacrificial Love
2. The Mind of Christ
3. Virtuous Freedom (Parts 1 and 2)
4. In Step with the Spirit

Virtuous freedom is covered in two chapters rather than one, because I expect this to be the mark that most modern American Christians have heard and thought about the least. I encourage readers to spend extra time in this section. The importance of the truth it contains could hardly be more critical in our cultural moment.

Part 3 is about pursuing these four marks through faith. It focuses on how we can pursue these marks of spiritual substance while not forgetting that, ultimately, we receive them as gifts in Christ. Many more chapters could have been included in this section, but I've tried to select only those topics that are presently most overlooked, ignored, or out of proportion among Christians and churches. As with the chapters on virtuous freedom, the "Welcome to the Ordinary" chapter is more extended than the others. Again, this is because more than simply overlooking its truths, we often believe the exact opposite of them to our great confusion and unhappiness. These truths may make you uncommonly free. Understanding how to exult in the ordinary without being typical is at the heart of escaping worldliness and finding godliness in Christ.

Features

Lastly, the abundance of ***footnotes*** will be very obvious to most readers and seem strange or burdensome to some. This was a deliberate and serious decision on the part of those involved in producing this book. We wanted to produce a book that would be accessible to all, but we also recognized that some readers would want to make more connections, have more citations, and understand why certain ideas are included. The footnotes are intended to serve that purpose. You will also find occasional *sidebars* expanding on ideas in the main text. As with the footnotes, they're not essential to understanding the chapters. Read whichever footnotes and sidebars interest you, or feel free to skip all of them, especially in your first reading. They are a resource and a reference for those who want them.

For those who are new to biblical topics and other subjects included here, we have included unabbreviated Bible references and defined key terms. In Appendix A, you can find a *glossary* of key terms organized alphabetically. The first time these words are used in the text of the book, they will be **bolded** for easy recognition. Even if you are familiar with a term you encounter, I encourage you to glance at the definition provided to be sure that you and I are using the word in the same way.

A word for your journey

This book is the product of many people's time and energy over more than a year. I hope it serves you in walking with the Spirit toward the character of Christ. May this promise from Christ fill you with expectancy and perseverance as you journey through this book and beyond in your pursuit of Christ:

> Blessed are those who hunger and thirst for righteousness, for they will be filled.

Matthew 5:6

INTRODUCTION

Come to me, all you who are weary and burdened, and I will give you rest. Take my yoke upon you and learn from me, for I am gentle and humble in heart, and you will find rest for your souls. For my yoke is easy and my burden is light.

Matthew 11:28-30

Many Christians—perhaps most Christians—secretly feel like their faith isn't working. They aren't "living the dream," feeling rest in their soul, or experiencing Jesus' burden as light. Many more have tried Christian faith and say it didn't work for them. Others feel spiritually stuck or torn. Many Christians, if they were totally honest, would say they feel a little (or a lot) resentful toward God for his standards and for his silence in their confusion. And all of these groups might tell you they don't know why they feel the way they do, but they count it as evidence that Christian faith is well-meaning but probably false. How about you? If you're a Christian, how do you really feel about your life with God? Do you...

- feel choked and smothered?
- feel fearful, anxious, or worried?
- feel resentful toward God or faith?
- feel worn-out, fragile, or ready to explode?
- crave novelty, delicacy, amusement, or the exotic in order to be happy?
- feel a lack of fulfillment in regular tasks, responsibilities, and roles?

- feel constantly distracted, like your attention is fractured?
- sense that you've become burrowed into your preferences?
- feel like your friendships are shallow, and few people really know you?

People who feel these things often think people like me (pastors) are just going to tell them, "You need to try harder and really make a commitment." Do you need to believe deeper? Try harder? Do more? Does the thought of hearing that make you feel choked, smothered, or attacked?

In fact, that is not what I would say to most people. I wouldn't say it, because it's not what Jesus said. Jesus said the reason so many of us are unproductive or terribly discouraged in our faith is that our faith is being strangled. Our real faith is being slowly choked by a second religion we believe in as devoutly as we believe in Christ, one the Bible calls "worldliness."

We'll discuss this idea at length in this book, but the basic reality of worldliness is that it makes creation, as opposed to its Creator, our primary focus and an end in itself. This distortion has disastrous effects on every part of life, and in our present secular culture, it's growing and mutating. Meanwhile, American Christians have come to ignore the whole phenomenon. To many, lamenting worldliness sounds fundamentalist and embarrassingly unsophisticated. Yet Jesus treats the world's version of sophistication as evasion, not growth. It is a predictable human self-deception, which is itself, ironically, a form of worldliness.

Jesus pulls no punches about worldliness. Worldliness is choking us, and it is the source of all the feelings of dissatisfaction and fear we listed earlier, along with a hundred more. In Mark 4, Jesus talks about a field in which good seed is planted and is growing healthy plants. Some of the seed gets eaten by birds and never grows. Some of it sprouts but because it is planted in gravel, it withers away immediately. Still, about half the seed grows into real plants. These plants represent people who have put their faith in him. Why doesn't the other half produce any fruit, though? Here's what Jesus tells us:

> Still others, like seed sown among thorns, hear the word; but the worries of this life, the deceitfulness of wealth and the desires for other things come in and choke the word, making it unfruitful.
>
> **Mark 4:18-19**

Jesus says, "the worries of this life, the deceitfulness of wealth and the desire for other things come in and choke the word..." That is a perfect description of worldliness: the thing that is choking our faith. This is the cause of many of the symptoms that plague us. The problem isn't with the faith or the Savior. The problem is that the good plant in us is getting strangled. Jesus is getting at the conflict all of us face every day, the conflict between gospel faith and worldliness.

Most people know Jesus is against legalism and man-made religion. We're against those things too, so that's obvious to us. What people often miss is that he says even more about worldliness.[1] He doesn't just tell us the symptoms and results (choking and unfruitfulness); he tells us the true cause and cure.

---

[1] This is in large part because legalism/moralism is a kind of worldliness. It is the conservative and morally-focused kind, but it is still a kind of worldliness—a love of the world. See Luke 15 where the dutiful older brother is angry that the younger son has come home and the father has been generous with him and honored him. He objects, "Look! All these years I've been slaving for you and never disobeyed your orders. Yet you never gave me even a young goat so I could celebrate with my friends" (Luke 15:29). His reaction shows that he doesn't love his father or the loving and truthful way the father runs his household. He is angry that he isn't getting what he wants after he's played by all the rules. That's worldliness. He was as in love with the world (in the negative sense) as his libertine brother. He's just trying to get what he wants through legalism and morality instead of through rebellion and lawlessness. He favors self-righteousness over unrighteousness, but he is no less an idolater.

In Jesus' most famous sermon[2] he talks about the root of the conflict:

> No one can serve two masters. Either you will hate the one and love the other, or you will be devoted to the one and despise the other. You cannot serve both God and money. Therefore I tell you, do not worry about your life, what you will eat or drink; or about your body, what you will wear. Is not life more than food, and the body more than clothes? Look at the birds of the air; they do not sow or reap or store away in barns, and yet your heavenly Father feeds them. Are you not much more valuable than they? Can any one of you by worrying add a single hour to your life? And why do you worry about clothes? See how the flowers of the field grow. They do not labor or spin. Yet I tell you that not even Solomon in all his splendor was dressed like one of these. If that is how God clothes the grass of the field, which is here today and tomorrow is thrown into the fire, will he not much more clothe you—you of little faith? So do not worry, saying, "What shall we eat?" or "What shall we drink?" or "What shall we wear?" For the pagans run after all these things, and your heavenly Father knows that you need them. But seek first his kingdom and his righteousness, and all these things will be given to you as well. Therefore do not worry about tomorrow, for tomorrow will worry about itself. Each day has enough trouble of its own.
>
> **Matthew 6:24-34**

The point of this whole text, with all its emphasis on trusting God and not worrying, is bound up in the first verses. The rest is all commentary on one simple sentence: "No one can serve two masters." This is, essentially, the main focus of *Substance*.

---

2   This body of teaching is called "The Sermon on the Mount." Versions of it can be found starting in Matthew 5 and Luke 6. Jesus probably gave this sermon in different forms many times to different crowds. It appears to be his main sermon, the starting point of his teaching explaining the "kingdom of God" and how he was fulfilling the covenants and promises of the Old Testament but changing them into a message of redemption to include all people.

We have volunteered ourselves for dehumanizing servitude to a master who has no claim over us, and it is keeping us from being fully alive and free under the reign of our true and good master: God.

This book is about seeing with eyes wide open, facing beasts within and without, and finding the true freedom for which we were lovingly and joyfully created.

An engine will not run without fuel. In our confusion and pain, we assume that our tank is empty and resent Jesus for not filling it. But our problem is not that our engine is empty. Our problem is that we're mixing God's fuel with the water of worldliness. Gas mixed with water doesn't burn. It offers no power, only a choking sputtering that leaves the driver angry, frustrated, and confused. Drain the tank and refill it with pure fuel, and she'll burn.

Jesus is calling us away from being fragile, brittle, and diminished, and to something else. He is calling us to substance. We are burdened not by his invitation to godliness, but by our own worldliness. Our backs have been broken not by God, but by our own idols, and these idols have left us tired, broken, and diminished. They keep us in a state of conflicted-ness in our devotion to Jesus, aggravating our anxieties and banishing any peace. It is to us in this state that Jesus says again,

> Come to me, all you who are weary and burdened, and I will give you rest. Take my yoke upon you and learn from me, for I am gentle and humble in heart, and you will find rest for your souls. For my yoke is easy and my burden is light.
>
> **Matthew 11:28-30**

"Come to me," he says, "and reject your false slavery to the world. Come out of the choking stranglehold of worldliness that makes you thin, fragile, and brittle." He promises rest for your soul, an easy (or well-fitted) backpack, and a seemingly light load.

He doesn't say it here, but he makes his yoke light by making us strong. Once we are no longer being choked, we can flourish in fruitful substance. We will grow to be more than spindly stalks. He will make us into vines so robust that we will not break even under the weight of a hundred-fold increase of fruit. Have you heard what the prophet Isaiah said salvation would do to broken and fragile people? Through Isaiah, God promises to "bestow on them a crown of beauty instead of ashes, the oil of joy instead of mourning, and a garment of praise instead of a spirit of despair. They will be called oaks of righteousness, a planting of the LORD for the display of his splendor" (Isaiah 61:3). He didn't just say Jesus would save us from our choked and fragile condition. He said redemption would make us "oaks of righteousness." To a mature oak tree, every burden is light. This book is meant to follow the path laid out in Scripture leading to the fulfillment of this promise.

Once bitten, twice shy

Before we get started, I want to anticipate briefly two objections. First, you may be thinking that it can't be this simple. You think, "Really? That's the answer? Kill worldliness and become substantive. Haven't I been doing that all along? I've heard a hundred versions of this in church. Just repent and trust God, and things will get better." Honestly, I've thought the same thing before. I'm skeptical too. I feel once bitten, twice shy toward every "this is going to be great" Christian push and church campaign. But in praying and thinking about this for a few years now in my own life, I've continually bumped up against the same unavoidable fact: *This is what Jesus says the issue is.* The Bible tells us that whenever our Flesh is allowed to live, it will invite love of the world back in through some form we don't want to notice. Before we know it, it's choking us again, and we can't figure out how it happened.

The problem isn't that the path out is complicated. The problem is that admitting our fragility when we're supposed to be mature is humiliating. We are not nearly as sophisticated as we think we are. If we believe in Jesus, we probably *have* grown in maturity over time. The problem is that our maturity is uneven. And, as we'll see in chapter ten, wherever we aren't being vigilant, that's where we will be conquered by worldliness. Thorns and weeds are always regrowing in a new spot. Worldliness will rush in while our own Flesh holds open the door. Is facing worldliness and growing in spiritual substance a simple answer? Yes. Is it simplistic? No. Simple doesn't mean easy, obvious, or reductionist, and sometimes the simple answer may seem impossible.

That brings us to the second possible objection. One might wonder: If we have not yet rejected worldliness, why do we think this book will make any difference? Sure, worldliness may be choking us, but the world has provided us with a lot of comfort, excitement, and enjoyment. Jesus says we can somehow find rest for our soul, but we already know exactly where to find a pumpkin spice latte, nice fitting jeans, exciting video games, and indoor plumbing. Maybe the tension between worldliness and Jesus is just a tension we have to manage. Maybe they just need to be a little compartmentalized.

That notion rests on a confusion between the idolatry of worldliness and the good of creation. Through substance, God gives us a creation to steward and enjoy. Worldliness uses and perverts creation. Worldliness isn't science, it's cooking meth. Worldliness is not the enjoyment of creation and creativity. Worldliness is making these things primary and an end in themselves. Making anything in creation an end in itself puts a burden on it that it was never designed to bear. In the end, we ruin the thing and ourselves.

My prayer for this book is that God will use it to reveal to us the slavery we've inflicted on ourselves and renew our hunger for the things of God—virtue, substance, true freedom, genuine fellowship with God and man, and love in its truest, most breathtaking fullness.

PART I

THE CHANGING WORLD AND A CLEAN BREAK

1

WORLDLINESS
IN A CHANGING WORLD

Brothers and sisters, I could not address you as people who live by the Spirit but as people who are still worldly—mere infants in Christ.

1 Corinthians 3:1

Let's play a game. Can you guess who said the following quotes and when?

The children now love luxury. They have bad manners, contempt for authority, they show disrespect to their elders... They no longer rise when elders enter the room. They contradict their parents, chatter before company, gobble up desserts at the table, have immodest posture, and are tyrants over their teachers.

The young people of today think of nothing but themselves. They have no reverence for parents or old age. They are impatient of all restraint. They talk as if they alone knew everything and what passes for wisdom with us is foolishness with them. As for girls, they are forward, immodest and unwomanly in speech, behavior and dress.

I see no hope for the future of our people if they are dependent on the frivolous youth of today, for certainly all youth are reckless beyond words... When I was young, we were taught to be discreet and respectful of elders, but the present youth are exceedingly wise in their own eyes and impatient of restraint.

Give up? The first and second are attributed to Socrates as loose paraphrases, which puts them in the fifth or fourth century BC.[1] The third is attributed to Hesiod, a great author of the eighth century BC. But they could just as easily have come from a contemporary blog lamenting the millennial generation, right? Worrying about young people and changing times has occupied human psyches for as long as humans have been around. Middle Easterners in 1000 BC apparently used to complain, "Why were the old days so much better than these?" We know this because Israel's wisest king, Solomon, seems to have heard this enough to prompt him to write these words in his old age:

Curmudgeonliness isn't a virtue. Wisdom is.

> Do not say, "Why were the old days better than these?" For it is not wise to ask such questions. Wisdom, like an inheritance, is a good thing and benefits those who see the sun [who are alive]. Wisdom is a shelter as money is a shelter, but the advantage of knowledge is this: Wisdom preserves those who have it.
>
> **Ecclesiastes 7:10-12**

Curmudgeonliness isn't a virtue. Wisdom is. The question is not, "Are the times changing?" Of course they are. They always do, though now the rate of change is admittedly accelerating. Nor is the question, "Are these days better or worse?"

---

1   The first two quotes in full are disputed by classicists, but their components can be found in Aristophanes' play *The Clouds*. Whether or not Socrates said them doesn't diminish the main point here, namely that someone in his time—and probably in every other time—did.

They are probably both, but the answer doesn't really matter if it leads us to nostalgia or triumphalism.

Wisdom asks, "What is changing, why is it changing, and how will it affect us? What is the spirit of the times? What is behind the changes people are bemoaning or celebrating? How do we respond and prepare ourselves? What will be the unintended consequences when these changes meet with our human condition?" Understanding our moment and knowing what to do with that understanding is called **discernment**, and we'll talk about it in the next chapter.

The Bible passage above says that the actions of the wise are like a shelter in terrible weather. Shelter doesn't change the weather, but it protects us from the elements. Survival experts always say that shelter is the highest priority when we're lost in the wilderness. We can go days without water, and weeks without food. But we often won't last the night without shelter. It buys us time and preserves our lives. God says that discerning wisdom, like shelter, can preserve your life.

CHANGE THAT CHANGES US: THE NEW RISE OF WORLDLINESS

So what do we need to be wise about? What changes do we need to understand? The main change is this: the world has become more **worldly**. I don't mean the world has become more *sinful*, though our cultural emphasis on virtue has definitely declined.[2] The world has always been brutal, selfish, and envious (Titus 3:3), while virtue has ebbed and flowed. Whether or not our culture is more *wicked* than our ancestors', it is definitely more *worldly*. We've increased our focus on getting more out of creation with less interest in the Creator. "Secularism" is the term we have given for severing the vital relationship between the sacred and the secular, the creation and the

---

2   See James Davison Hunter's *The Death of Character: Moral Education in an Age Without Good or Evil.*

Creator, the world and the kingdom, matter and meaning, the City of God and the City of Man.[3]

Not all forms of secularism[4] are bad. Properly ordered, secularism can embrace both understanding creation (science) and harnessing creation (technology) without denying God his place as creator and ruler over that creation.[5] But our modern American version of secularism takes it to a different level. It is intentionally designed to drive thought of God and abstract things such as spirit and meaning[6] out of our minds, pursuits, and conversations. Secularism shouldn't be a bad word, but the way we have practiced it in our culture has made us increasingly worldly. This form of secularism[7] has twisted and mutated our relationship to the world in three key ways.

1. Secularism separates creation from the Creator.

As a cultural system, secularism actively disregards anything that is not material. It treats spirit as irrelevant or non-

---

3   In this book, I'll also refer to our present culture as "secular modernity."

4   Better forms of secularism existed during the Reformation, Age of Reason, and Scientific Revolution (c. 1430-1750 AD). People now refer to the entire early modern period as part of the Enlightenment, but this is mistaken. Many movements had secular effects while still being deeply and profoundly Christian. They included a profound interest in things of this world (i.e. created things, the natural world) without rejecting or minimizing the place of the Creator. Many early theorists in politics, science, classics, history, and other fields sought to understand and investigate the world non-superstitiously through empirical methods without seeing any conflict between that method and their deep Christian faith. In fact, for many, the rediscovery of Christian Classics and early Christian texts led to a deeper understanding of Christian faith, which in turn fed revolutions in the humanities and the sciences.

5   Charles Taylor has distinguished between three possible kinds of secularism. While all secularisms lead away from superstition, modern secularism falls in his third category, seeking to wipe away anything non-physical, resulting in relativism and scientism (the belief that only scientific knowledge is knowledge, and only that which the sciences can study is real).

6   By "meaning" here I am not referring to subjective felt meaning (anything can mean anything to you), but to metaphysical meaning (meaning things have whether we believe them or not).

7   Probably the best book for evangelicals to read about secularism is James K. A. Smith's How (Not) to Be Secular: Reading Charles Taylor. It is a reflection on Charles Taylor's much larger tome, A Secular Age.

existent and claims that science is the only avenue of thought pursuing what is realistic or practical. It changes the very language we use to the point where we explain our lives in biological terms, because it makes us feel more enlightened. Joy is a rush of dopamine, and anger is what happens when one's amygdala hijacks the cortex.[8] Our version of secularism cuts our minds off from considering our Creator, King, and

SHRINKING THE WORLD

The particular form of secularism that disregards anything but material is sometimes called "materialism." It marginalizes anything that cannot be studied by the physical sciences. This leads to a terrible shrinking of the world, since the non-physical world is made up not only of spirits, but also of abstract things like math, philosophy, morality, ethics, and feelings. For example, a proposition like, "Torturing babies is wrong," is an extremely basic moral idea, but it cannot be investigated by the sciences. Medical science can investigate the results of torturing babies, but it can't tell us that it is objectively and metaphysically wrong to do such a thing. This is one of the reasons why secular people can often have a difficult time with the question of abortion. The question cannot be answered without reference to human dignity, which is a notion one cannot derive from the sciences.

Savior. It also diminishes the depth and scope of our focus on morality and meaning. It puts God and the deeper things of life out of sight and out of mind. The god of **Mammon** wants no competitors, and our **Flesh** is happy to oblige him. In a structure that blocks out every potential rival, Mammon

---

8   I'm not saying that these biological hacks aren't helpful in understanding and managing ourselves. My problem with them is that they're reductive; there is so much more going on in us than can be reduced to basic biochemistry. If that weren't the case, we would be determinists. If you can hack your biochemistry with insights, then you, as a thinking being, can override your brain chemistry. When we reduce our behavior to biochemistry, we let our conscious mind off the hook, and our chemistry talk becomes a self-fulfilling prophecy. It makes us passive about our own minds, thinking that our responses and thoughts are happening *to* us. We become spectators to our own mind and thoughts.

thrives unchecked.[9]

2. Technology gratifies our visceral desires in constant and immediate ways.

The sensory stimulation our technologies deliver is constantly grabbing our attention. They please our sensory drives and offer us an immediate payoff of feeling good. But this good feeling isn't a deep and rich enjoyment engaging our whole selves. When our senses are gratified, we experience a tiny chemical release in our brains that isn't joy, but it is addictive. The result is that the technologies and conveniences of our lives are actually addicting us to the shallowest experiences of human instinct and self-gratification. Before we know it, we are looking at our phone every time it beeps and snacking in the kitchen without knowing why. We play video games and watch TV instead of talking to friends, spouses, or children. We do this without even realizing how our sensory addiction is shrinking our being. The magnitude of our gratifications is minimizing our lives.

> The magnitude of our gratifications is minimizing our lives.

These addictive gratifications distract us from developing our higher, less **visceral** gratifications.[10] They cut us off

---

9   In Greek mythology, the figure of Daedalus is a warning to us about the unintended consequences of our own creations. Daedalus was a master craftsman, but he crafted things that led increasingly to his own entrapment and loss. He is famous for enabling the birth of the half-bull, half-man minotaur, then being imprisoned, designing a labyrinth to imprison the minotaur, devising a way to kill it, and designing wings for him and his son to escape their own imprisonment. All of this eventually led to the death of his son, Icarus. Just as Daedalus built his ruin with his own hands, our construction of secularism has empowered the beast of Mammon and is leading us to our own destruction, our own dehumanization.

10   By "higher" I mean that they: (1) are more in keeping with what is special about bearing the image of God, (2) derive pleasure from meaning, not only feeling or instinct, (3) are not extractive—taking pleasure in using others (i.e. promiscuous sex as opposed to covenantal marriage), and (4) do not diminish human productivity. The designer of a farming game, for instance, might make the game more nurturing of human flourishing if the game taught people about the realities of growing things, rather than

from the higher gratifications of character and virtue that find wholesome delight in truth, goodness, and that which God loves. These are the pleasures that enrich our lives and others' and give context and meaning to our visceral drives. But why cultivate a garden when you can play a farming video game? Why cultivate friendships when you can stream all the high-lights of friendship through scripted sitcoms online? To put it simply, why wait and toil for the real, when a rush of lesser pleasure can be had at the press of a button? To harness these things as blessings rather than being enslaved to them, we must actively escape diversion (chapter nine) and embrace discipline (chapter ten) in a culture of formation (chapter eleven).

3. We don't correct course, because we've silenced our warning sirens.

God created the world in such a way that pain would be the natural consequence of our vice.[11] This was both a judicial and loving action. In the Bible, God uses that pain to count-er human selfishness and stubbornness. Secular modernity has channeled much of our human creativity into developing systems and technologies designed to save us from the natu-ral consequences of wickedness and foolishness. Alleviating self-inflicted suffering can produce a brutal unintended con-sequence: it can shield us from the wake-up call pain offers. It hides the relationship between our actions and their conse-quences. We still reap what we sow. We just don't always reap it in the moment; the natural warnings are silenced, allowing us to trespass further and further into our own ruin (Galatians

---

being just a system of virtual achievement pleasure payoffs.

11   Ancient peoples needed a deep understanding of human nature, because noth-ing stood between them and the consequences of foolishness and self-deception. They had few technologies or structures to protect them from the consequences of living against nature and truth. Understanding reality and humanity as they really are was absolutely essential for ancient people. Consequently, much of the ancient wisdom about humans is significantly more insightful and instructive than the brain hacks we find in modern pop psychology books.

6:7-10).

This worldly form of secularism has made us more interested in self-esteem, sensual gratification, social engineering, personal dreams and visions, unrestrained consumption,[12] our projected image, and the governmentalization of life (see sidebar for an explanation of what I mean by governmentalization). Correspondingly, our culture has become less concerned with faith, virtue, wisdom, self-discipline, productivity, perseverance, godliness, fraternity, humility, cheer, hope, prudence, and self-sacrificial love. With all the gains of science and technology, something fundamental to our spirituality and our humanity has correspondingly declined. We have cast off substance in favor of the allure of subsistence.

The Bible calls this predictable human phenomenon **worldliness**, and repeatedly warns *believers* about its choking effect, especially in times of increasing prosperity. It has always plagued humanity, but it has been intensified and mutated in our time. Therefore, we need to listen with more attention than any generation in history to the Bible's teaching on worldliness—how it functions and how it is overcome.

The problem with worldliness isn't just that it's sinful, nor is it just that worldliness makes us feel stuck and frustrated in our faith in Christ. Like the plant in the parable in Mark 4, the choking thorns of worldliness crush our life and our humanity.[13] Worldliness always creates a crisis of substance. It makes us shallow, vaporous, unstable, and brittle. It predictably leads

---

12   People often think of consumerism (society built on consumption) and socialism (governmentalization of life) as opposite phenomena, but they aren't. Once we see the overarching theme of worldliness as expressed in secularism, we can see that both are forms of gratification and security. They both arise from good human impulses that are bent and twisted by worldliness. They deny the wholesomeness of how God has arranged human living and responsibility, misunderstanding the effects of the human condition.

13   I'm speaking developmentally here. Literally the biggest problem with worldliness is that it robs God of his deserved glory and mistreats him as a perfect being. The loss of possible joy for ourselves is incalculable.

WHAT IS GOVERNMENTALIZATION?

Governmentalization is a word I'm using to refer to the retreat from civil society and its reliance on culture and voluntary cooperation, and placing the roles of civil society (church, family, friendship, voluntary organizations, commerce, neighborhood cohesion, etc.) within the realm of government institutions and the state. It rejects a right understanding of social justice, one that says the problems of our society are rooted in our personal responsibility and immediate social responsibility to our neighbors. It fails the subsidiarity principle test (handling things on the most local level possible), because it constantly sends responsibilities up the authority chain to where they are more likely to be left undone, done poorly, or done tyrannically. This, in my understanding and in that of the evangelical American founders, is a rejection of God's intent to create a people who were free *because* they were governed by righteous law rather than human government.

Through the prophet Samuel, God warns his people about turning to the state for leadership instead of relying on self-government through law, morality, and culture through the application of the subsidiarity principle (1 Samuel 8). This passage includes the phrase "he will take..." six times. This stands as a severe warning to a free people who were meant to govern themselves based on law rather than on centralized human authority that would inevitably extract their goods and their very lives. God tells them that in asking for a king to substitute for their virtuous dependence on him, they have rejected faith, freedom, and him.

to misery. Even the visceral pleasures of the body—pleasures we were designed to enjoy—become deranged and unsatisfying as they are separated from their created purpose.

We, Jesus' Church living in modern secular culture, are suffering terribly from this crisis of substance. The threat is not only that we are being strangled. We are not becoming the oaks of righteousness we were made to be (Isaiah 61:3).

SEEING OUR
ENVIRONMENT WITH FRESH EYES

So what is the first step of faith out of this predicament? Before we can thrive, we must reckon with the *environmental* cause of our lack of substance, specifically among American- ized Christians like you and me. Namely, we have to see the unseen effect of our culture in shaping our character and how modernity can hollow us out even while filling us up. We have to see not just how modern secularism affects our visceral hu- man *desires*. Even more importantly, we have to see how it af- fects our human *condition* and human *nature*.

Modern Christians must somehow embrace creation through human creativity and productivity in a way that causes a flowering (not a forgetting) of love and devotion to our Cre- ator and his ways. There is an- other way to be modern—a way of fulfillment and substance. It is possible to receive fully God's gift of creation without worship- ing it as Mammon. We can receive God's physical gifts through science and technology without losing that same Creator's gifts of spiritual substance through faith and virtue. Thankfully, we

> It is possible to receive fully God's gift of creation without worshiping it as Mammon.

worship the God who is spirit, yet became flesh. We follow the Creator who entered creation. We know the news of the one who hates worldliness, yet "so loved the world" that he gave his life to save it and to give it life (John 3:16).

But is Jesus really enough? What if it feels like trusting him isn't working?

DESIRE, CONDITION, AND NATURE

It's important to understand the difference between human *desires,* the human *condition,* and human *nature.* Our *nature* is what makes us human, without which we are not human. It is our created, unchanging nature. The human *condition* is the state we are in as people bearing a human nature that is bent and twisted by the Flesh or "the sinful condition," the out-of-whack-ness of our present state and world. In this human condition, our human *desires* are poorly regulated, unfocused, and out of proportion. When this is true, romantic desire easily becomes lust. The desire to enjoy food becomes gluttony. Just anger becomes wrath and revenge, and so on. If we understand human *nature,* we can distinguish between our created nature and our Flesh in our present *condition.* This will help us understand how we should regulate our human *desires* through faith and virtue, which will lead to a reordering and enjoyment of our desires by bringing them in line with our nature, rather than our desires following our depraved condition.

OUR SECRET FAITH

Many Christians recognize at some point that their faith isn't working. They aren't experiencing the transformation they see promised in the Bible or talked about in church. Some quit. Some feel deeply disillusioned. Some just feel stuck, like they aren't growing. The reason our faith isn't "working" usually isn't what most people think. It's not because the gospel isn't true. It isn't even that we don't believe it. The gospel isn't transforming us because we believe in a second religion. It's mostly unconscious, yet forms what we think is real even more deeply than Christ does.[14] This second, subconscious religion is worldliness.

In the introduction, we looked at Jesus' warning, "No one can serve two masters... You cannot serve both God and money [*mammonas*]" (Matthew 6:24).[15] What's not working is that we're trusting in Jesus and in worldliness at the same time. We tend to dismiss this answer. We can't have fallen into something that simple, that obvious! But we have. And we do. How did this happen? We never accepted

> The gospel isn't transforming us because we believe in a second religion.

Mammon as our Lord and Savior, did we? So how can we have two faiths? Two religions? The answer for many of us is that while we *confessed* one, we *absorbed* a second.

Absorbed before confessed

We believe in Jesus. We're trying to learn the Bible. We want to be good parents, friends, and spouses. We want to honor God rightly, walk in the Spirit, and feel his purpose in our lives. No one wants to be fragile or shallow. Having come to trust the crucified, risen, and returning Jesus, this is the faith we confess. Even if you aren't a Christian, you want on some level to be loving, joyful, and dutiful in what is right.

Yet all the while, beneath the surface, we are being persuaded of a completely different vision of reality. How? It is not happening in the form of an open argument or public explanation. We're not being persuaded of it by logic and

---

14 The technical term for this is our *plausibility structures*, the structures of our assumptions that determine what we think is plausible or not, and therefore motivate or demotivate our willingness to believe in them.

15 When the Gospel writers refer directly to money, they usually either use the word for its denomination like denarius or talent, or they simply use the word for silver. Here, however, Matthew uses the word *mammonas*, which was translated as Mammon in older English. It seems to refer to all that can be pursued in the world for our own wealth and well-being. It is, in short, worldliness. Therefore, worldliness and Jesus cannot both be your master.

facts. We absorb it through the environment of our culture. This faith comes into our hearts unhindered by our conscious thought, being absorbed through the technologies, institutions, and structures of modern secular life. We aren't drinking it in a shot glass. We are breathing it in every day. Like a heavy mist, it has gradually soaked us to the bone. This is the faith we absorb.

Worldliness persuades us through saturation in an environment full of cars, roads, shopping malls, disposable commodities and trash removal, birth control, electricity and indoor plumbing, schools, restaurants, grocery stores, pharmaceuticals and hospitals, professional sports and traveling children's sports teams, five-day workweeks, Photoshop, washing machines, mortuaries, data streaming, and global travel, to name a few. These technologies and structures, though immensely enriching, also have the cumulative effect of persuading us of a competing vision of reality without ever saying a word. This vision tells us we are first. We are safe. We ought to be comfortable. Life should be convenient. Things we don't like or that aren't working are disposable. Reality can be edited. A doctor can fix unhealthy living. Love, sex, and children are disconnected. We don't have to look death in the face, and so on. We don't have to submit to reality if we can control it.

It is critical to understand that we *absorb* this second faith, which we believe at least as deeply as the other one about Jesus. The key difference is that because we *absorbed* this one, it feels more real, and therefore makes Jesus seem a little imaginary. My wife said once, "When the world has formed you, you just feel like it knows you. When it has deceived your heart, it feels like it's the only one speaking your heart language when it talks. And so it steals your trust." That's a critical insight. It never argued with us. It persuaded us without actually telling us what it wanted us to believe. As a result, when we hear its explanations, we think it has found our hearts. It sounds so reasonable, so insightful. In truth, worldliness' message matches our hearts because it has been secretly reprogramming them for some time. Having found a voice that satisfies us, we are left feeling like the voice of our Creator is foreign, and he doesn't really know us. We feel he and his message are out of touch and unbelievable. He is right in front of us, but we don't recognize him. That sounds an awful lot like a verse in the Bible about Jesus: "though the world was made through him, the world did not recognize him" (John 1:10).

> Worldliness' message matches our hearts because it has been secretly reprogramming them for some time.

Not only have we been absorbing worldliness through our environment, but secular modernity is structured to sustain worldliness and deliver it to us in every sphere of life. When left unexamined, it's typically a much bigger influence on us than a thousand sermons. It's like Jesus is radio, and our culture is an immersive virtual reality experience. If our culture is increasingly worldly, then isn't it likely we are more worldly than we have yet dared to imagine?

Consequently, in our emotions, perceptions, and choices, our culture is overcoming our confession. But it doesn't have to be this way. The deformational culture is most powerful when it is most unseen, so the first step in escaping it is to bring it to light.

FORMATIONAL AND DEFORMATIONAL CULTURES

Why call our culture deformational rather than just evil? No human culture is all evil or all good. They're all made up of a mixture of **common grace** and worldliness. The discerning question is, what happens when our human condition is set loose in a given culture? Does the culture's structure serve to develop virtue, wisdom, and faith? Or does it offer an alternative to faithful, virtuous dignity while gratifying our Flesh? And how does its structure affect our formation in faith, virtue, and substantive discipleship? Is the gospel's relevance displayed or obscured by our culture?

Defining deformational culture

Any culture that tends strongly to obscure the gospel and exacerbate the Flesh can be referred to as a deformational culture. And our culture doesn't just *tend* toward deformation; it is *designed* to gratify our Flesh (to be worldly).[16] It is designed *to provide substances for* humans, not *to produce substance in* humans. Secular modernity is designed to support human desires (our dreams, our consumption, our projected image, and our self-esteem), not to evaluate, develop, or regulate them. *It doesn't build substantive character, because it isn't designed to.* The human need for spiritual and moral transformation is not the problem it

---

16 That the culture is designed to be worldly doesn't mean that it's wholly ungodly. If the designers ignore God or have rejected him, they will just seek to make a culture without reference to God. Common grace ensures that this culture will not be *entirely* ungodly. It will all be worldly, but only a portion of it will be intensely and intentionally ungodly.

> The tragic irony of secular modernity is that, in the very way it gratifies our visceral longings, it eviscerates our longing for grace. As it feeds our Flesh, it hollows out our spirit.

was designed to solve. We have crafted it to ensure the gratification and expression of our human *desires*.[17] The tragic irony of secular modernity is that, in the very way it gratifies our visceral longings, it eviscerates our longing for grace. As it feeds our Flesh, it hollows out our spirit.

According to Jesus, the evaluation, reordering, and regulation of our desires is the formation we need most. In fact, substance is a *prerequisite* for great human expressions of passion and emotion. Jesus has come to show us how our desires have gone wrong (evaluation/conscience), what the right objects for our desires are (reordering/conviction), and how to express them rightly (regulation/persevering self-control). This isn't stuffing or repressing our desires and emotions; it is preparing them for beautiful and constructive expression. God has created a formational counter-culture (the Church/Body of Christ) to help us break free from the worldliness that disorders and deadens our desires.[18]

The Body of Christ is a gospel culture with a system of beliefs, relationships, connections, commitments, technologies,

---

17   Therefore secular modernity is as good as the desire any of its particular systems are meant to support. It is good to the extent that it doesn't aggravate something else in human experience, desire, or action that is counterproductive. So, television may be a positive expression of feeding a human desire for inspirational stories, which leads to a personal response of living with inspirational beauty in our own lives in response to good art. However, the form of television also has a pacifying effect, which predictably increases humanity's sloth and passivity (among other things). So every system and product of modernity can be judged on these two criteria: (1) Does it support a good human desire based in our creation, and (2) does it aggravate some sinful disposition in the present human condition of depravity?

18   In *The Abolition of Man*, C.S. Lewis says of modern men that our desires have not been made out of control by modernity, but that modernity deadens the deep and sublime passions and joys of human existence. As a teacher, Lewis found his job was "not to cut down jungles but to irrigate deserts" of emotional deadness.

structures, and institutions designed to help us become what we are meant to be in Christ and to overcome the deformational culture of secular modernity in which we are living. Look at how Peter describes it in 2 Peter 1:3-9 (the passage from the introduction):

> His divine power has given us everything we need for life and godliness through our knowledge of him who called us by his own glory and goodness. Through these he has given us his very great and precious promises, so that through them you may participate in the divine nature and escape the corruption in the world caused by evil desires.
>
> For this very reason, make every effort to add to your faith goodness; and to goodness, knowledge; and to knowledge, self-control; and to self-control, perseverance; and to perseverance, godliness; and to godliness, brotherly kindness; and to brotherly kindness, love. But if anyone does not have them, he is nearsighted and blind, and has forgotten that he has been cleansed from his past sins.
>
> **2 Peter 1:3-9, NIV 1984**

Peter emphasizes both the negative and positive application of trusting in Jesus to become substantive disciples: escaping worldly corruption and making every effort to grow in godliness.

He leads with what may sound like overly spiritual wording in verses 3 and 4, because it's essential that we not fall into the conservative form of worldliness: legalism and moralism. We normally think of worldliness as being liberal and lawless. But curing lawlessness with legalism is no gain, and isn't God's goal.[19] He wants to cure all worldliness, not just half of it. He

---

19 "Liberal" is a bias for change, generosity, and loosening things up. "Conservative" is a bias for conserving what is tested, raising standards, using discipline, and upholding order and civilization. Whether one should be liberal or conservative in any given situation is relative to that situation. One should not be liberal with toddlers

wants to bring us into full remission. (We'll talk about this in depth in chapters five and six.) So he starts with the gospel: God, because he is glorious and good, has used his *divine power* to give us everything we need for life and godliness in the crucified and risen Christ. All of the divine resources we need for knowing God and escaping the corruption of worldliness are given in Christ as a sheer gift through faith. Our next questions are ones of application: What are we told to do with these gifts, and how do we "participate in the divine nature"? We'll look at these questions in parts two and three of this book.

The word translated "evil desire" in 2 Peter 1:4 means "craving" or "lust," referring to a desire that's out of place and out of control. Cravings and lusts are strange paradoxes, because they are, like a river's rapids, intense yet shallow. Rapids are not just shallow and fast; they are full of hazards covered over with an insubstantial froth of bubbles in the fast water. Therefore, in the quick and shallow water lie hazards that will wreck you—hazards that wouldn't threaten you in deeper water. That is what our corrupted, evil desires make us: intense yet shallow, forceful yet fragile, utterly committed yet completely fickle, and therefore utterly self-destructive and dangerous. When they have their way, they make our minds foolish and our emotions erratic. We are thrown around between fear, anger, pride, boredom, anxiety, diversion, resentment, wrath, lust, sensuality, envy, amusement, sloth, ridicule, fickle affection, thoughtless gossip, and a hundred vaporous froths of our moral weightlessness. Corruption, then, is the effect of anything used to fulfill and confirm these cravings,

around cliffs. A man should not be conservative in expressing love when he is proposing marriage to a woman, nor she if she responds with "Yes!" Some independent standard is necessary in order to know whether it is time to loosen up or tighten up, change or conserve. Otherwise both the liberal impulse and conservative impulse can become monstrosities. In 1924, G.K. Chesterton said, "The whole modern world has divided itself into Conservatives and Progressives [liberals]. The business of Progressives is to go on making mistakes. The business of Conservatives is to prevent mistakes from being corrected" (*Illustrated London News*, 1924).

even good things like food, sex, art, technology, or any of the blessings of modern subsistence or convenience.

What makes secular modernity so deformational is not that its structures are inherently bad, but that when it's applied to our evil desires, it's like sugar to a diabetic or a perfectly innocent cocktail to a raging alcoholic. It terribly exacerbates the sinful condition, and if we're honest, that's why we like it. Like licking a wound, it cools the momentary itch of our condition, yet replaces the discomfort of actual healing with a deeper festering infection.

> Like licking a wound, it cools the momentary itch of our condition, yet replaces the discomfort of actual healing with a deeper festering infection.

Deformational culture morally affirms our evil desires. It mitigates the natural consequences of our foolishness while normalizing our perversity and gratifying our evil desires, strengthening them into habits. It makes godliness seem foreign, illogical, surreal, and judgmental. It frames evil as good, ugliness as beauty, and falsehood as truth. The more it influences us in our sinful condition, the more deformed we become. The less we realize our absorption of it, the more rapid, powerful, and complete its effect.

Defining formational culture

While the deformational culture intensifies these evil desires—partly innocently and partly by design—knowledge of Christ reframes and renews our desires in relationship to the truth in the culture of Christ. This is possible through union with Christ. The passage quoted earlier from 2 Peter is especially instructive. When Peter exhorts Christians to "make every effort to add to your faith goodness," he doesn't mean add to Christ's death and resurrection in terms of what saves us. He means trusting in Christ for forgiveness and, adding to that, trusting him in everything else. Faith can become faithfulness and spiritual substance when we apply this truth. This requires intentional departure from deformational community and engagement in the formational culture of Christ. It means first believing that, with Christ's divine power in you, you really do have everything you need to find substance. Then, based on that belief, it requires exerting every effort you can possibly muster to apply that faith to spiritual formation.

You are not applying faith to participate in the divine nature and escape the corruption of the world unless you are making every effort to embrace the formational culture of Christ (described in verses 6 and 7). This is what Christians have called *discipleship* for a couple thousand years. Discipleship is the gospel response to the frothing worldliness of our broken desires, whether they are legalistic or lawless. Discipleship is a path of God's power and generosity—a gift. But it is also an intentional path of effort—every effort.

This formational culture of Christ is described in different ways in the Bible. The passage in 2 Peter shows us a progression:

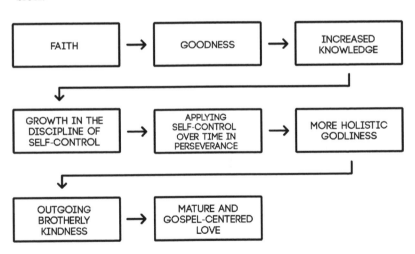

By ending with love, defined so deeply in relationship to these seven steps of spiritual maturity, Peter shows how completely our passions need to be redefined and reordered. In the end, this discipleship is meant to unleash true, passionate love. Seeing mature love as the end goal ought to prove to us that substantive godliness is not the denial of desire, but the transformation of our desires into their most substantive, vibrant, and beautiful forms. Its

> Substantive godliness is not the denial of desire, but the transformation of our desires into their most substantive, vibrant, and beautiful forms.

goal is to express passion in a way that is consistent with the passion of the divine nature, the same passion that created and redeemed the world. In part two, we'll look more deeply at what this love is.

In this chapter, I've attempted to present the problem of our love affair with worldliness and its most devastating consequences. In the next chapter, we'll look at how the Bible calls us to respond when we are sobered by the realization that we've traded substance for subsistence, love for lies.

SUGGESTED BIBLE MEMORIZATION

His divine power has given us everything we need for life and godliness through our knowledge of him who called us by his own glory and goodness. Through these he has given us his very great and precious promises, so that through them you may participate in the divine nature and escape the corruption in the world caused by evil desires.

For this very reason, make every effort to add to your faith goodness; and to goodness, knowledge; and to knowledge, self-control; and to self-control, perseverance; and to perseverance, godliness; and to godliness, brotherly kindness; and to brotherly kindness, love.

2 Peter 1:3-7, NIV 1984

REFLECT AND RESPOND

1. Christians in the past have talked a lot about "discernment." What is your experience with it, or how have you grown in it? Have you known someone particularly discerning? What was special about him or her because of this virtue?

2. What is one effect of the deformational culture you can see affecting you? How did you absorb it?

3. Do you think you believe the Scriptures when they say God's power has given us "everything we need for life and godliness"? What evidence in your life supports your answer? What evidence do your family and friends see? (Ask them, and beg them to be honest with you.)

2

SAYING GOODBYE

I have given them [the disciples] your word and the world has hated them, for they are not of the world any more than I am of the world. My prayer is not that you take them out of the world but that you protect them from the evil one. They are not of the world, even as I am not of it. Sanctify them by the truth; your word is truth. As you sent me into the world, I have sent them into the world. For them I sanctify myself, that they too may be truly sanctified.

John 17:14-19

It's been popular for many years to say things like, "all roads lead to heaven" or "any road will get you there," but doesn't that overlook the nature of a fork in the road? The only thing one *cannot* believe about diverging paths is that they aren't really parting. Different paths exist because they lead to different places. Taking Jesus' path of substantive discipleship means saying goodbye to another path. We have to leave the path of insubstantial worldliness behind. Decisively.

In the last chapter, we considered the dangers of our deformational culture in contrast to the kind of formational culture we need and ought to cultivate. Escaping worldliness means seeing the deformational culture for what it is and saying a decisive goodbye. What does that really mean? Does it mean we are going to leave all the structures of secular modernity behind? Are we going to form rural communes without internet or plumbing or burritos? My wife's response was, "Only if it's a Chilean mountainside. You know, so there's still coffee."

The reality is that we can't leave the world, and God wouldn't want us to if we could. Rather, we need to learn to discern the real from the counterfeit and say a decisive goodbye to the worldliness that keeps us addicted to lesser things while numbing our craving for greater things. In this chapter, we'll consider what it means to say goodbye to *worldliness* while wholeheartedly embracing that Jesus has sent us to *the world*.

NO PERFECT ENVIRONMENT

There is no distinct City of God on Earth. No social situation or structure produces spiritual substance in the way modern secularism produces worldliness. In Proverbs 30:8-9, King Agur says, "…give me neither poverty nor riches, but give me only my daily bread. Otherwise, I may have too much and disown you and say, 'Who is the LORD?' Or I may become poor and steal, and so dishonor the name of my God."

Of course, being a king, Agur had more than daily bread. The point of the proverb is that the sweet spot where spirituality is supported by the right natural tension is razor thin. What environment is most conducive to godliness? Apparently, it is above starvation and below having food in your cupboard for tomorrow. That's a pretty narrow window. The logic is that we'll be more likely to trust God if we recognize that we're dependent on him for surviving the next twenty-four hours. Everything else is "poverty [or] riches," both of which carry their own sets of inherent temptations. Generations of men and women in every corner of the world have had to deal with the spiritual trial of poverty (among other trials). And for now, many of us face the spiritual trial of wealth, especially its sin of self-sufficient pride that denies God's authority in everything (saying, "Who is the Lord?").

No environment can exist that perfectly builds our faith and removes temptations unless it is built entirely in faith exercised in discernment and vigilance. God is saying that every earthly environment has serious worldly temptations. We can't run from the worldly environment to a fully godly one. There is no such place in our current world. And even if there were, we aren't supposed to retreat to it.

SENT TO A WORLDLY WORLD

You may have heard that Jesus said we are to be in the world while not being of it, but he actually takes it one step further. He doesn't just say we are in the world. The fuller version of what he says is:

> I have given them [the disciples] your word and the world has hated them, for they are not of the world any more than I am of the world. My prayer is not that you take them out of the world but that you protect them from the evil one. They are not of the world, even as I am not of it. **Sanctify** them by the truth; your word is truth. As you sent me into the world, I have sent them into the world. For them I sanctify myself, that they too may be truly sanctified.

> **John 17:14-19**

Did you see it? We are not just in the world. Instead, like Jesus, we are "*sent into* the world," and we are here for a specific purpose. That is why we cannot leave it and still be his disciples any more than the Son could have avoided coming to earth and still have been its savior. But, of course, there is a difference between being sent to a farm and rolling around in its mud. Jesus says this is why he sanctifies himself: for the specific purpose "that they too may be truly sanctified." To be sanctified is the opposite of being worldly, but while still in the world.

Jesus' specific (sanctified) purpose and identity is that he is the Christ, the anointed Savior. Everything he did and is doing fits perfectly with that identity, whether performing miracles, preaching, judging unrighteousness, or joking around with little kids. He was set apart for that purpose, and everything he does is part of his sacredness.

Part of Jesus' purpose in sanctifying himself was that *we* would do it. He showed us what it looked like to be sent into the world, yet not be of the world—how to love the world while being hated by it (verse 14). Sanctification is the Bible's word for spiritual substance. It means to be completely set apart from the world in godliness, while being entirely imbedded in the world for its redemption. To be substantive, sanctified Christians, we have to say goodbye to the world (worldliness) without saying goodbye to the world (creation).

SHARPENING YOUR ZOMBIE RADAR: THE IMPORTANCE OF DISCERNMENT

My son, preserve sound judgment and discernment, do not let them out of your sight; they will be life for you, an ornament to grace your neck.

Proverbs 3:21-22, NIV 1984

Can you tell the difference between a real and a counterfeit dollar bill? Why does all police shooting training include pictures of good guys mixed in with bad guys? Why can't military pilots be colorblind? Why do graphic designers think there are forty-seven different shades of blue? These and a hundred other possible examples show how incredibly important it is to be able to tell the difference between things in life. The spiritual process of formation, sanctification, requires a process

> The spiritual process of formation, sanctification, requires a process of learning what we should receive, what we should reject, and what we should redeem.

of learning what we should receive, what we should reject, and what we should redeem. This is called discernment, and it's not an optional virtue for a person of spiritual substance. Without discernment, we will not be able to tell the difference between being in the world we are sent to and being captured by worldliness.

But how do we acquire discernment? How do we sort through the entire culture of secular modernity and understand exactly what we should be receiving, rejecting, and redeeming? Isn't that going to be infinitely complex? Or won't we become prone to default to either "yes" (liberal) or "no" (conservative), ultimately dividing us all into two camps of lawless libertines and fundamentalist protectionists?

We can avoid that fate if we let the gospel show us how to say goodbye to worldliness and develop discernment, responding to God's revelations with conviction. This requires being "transformed by the renewing of [our minds]" (Romans 12:1-2) and receiving the "mind of Christ" (1 Corinthians 2:16). Remember, God has given us everything we need to become discerning people (2 Peter 1:3).

Our evil desires and the idols that gratify them are twisted versions of good desires and their God-gifted enjoyment. Evil is not the opposite of good; it is the degradation of something good in itself or in relation to other goods. Evil cannot create; it can only twist and derange. Think of evil as a virus like rabies. Rabies can't create a dog. It can only infect and distort your childhood puppy into

> Evil cannot create; it can only twist and derange.

an enemy. But the tricky thing is that idols look and sound so much like the good things they have twisted. They're like the zombie versions of God's truly good design, but zombies with really good makeup—or at least it looks that way to us when we have such poor eyes.

That's why, without gospel discernment, worldliness can

hide in plain sight and define our lives, even while we try desperately to devote our hearts to Jesus. Without discernment, we don't see how our lives have been warped and bent into grotesque versions of the good things God created as gifts. Gospel discernment enables us to recognize zombies as what they are, allowing us to say goodbye to the counterfeit and joyfully embrace and enjoy the wholesome creation original. It clears away the fog of confusion that keeps us trapped in misunderstandings about God, his goodness, and the true distortions and enslavements of worldliness. Discernment is the first step in allowing the lethargy of idolatry to become the vigor of worship.

Evil desires can corrupt creation by twisting something in itself, which is sin or by making a good thing absolute or independent, which is idolatry. The following are examples of good desires gone bad that have created idols that make us shallow and fragile. They are exercises in discerning the deformation of God's good creation and recovering its wholesome original. Only when we can discern the original from the counterfeit can we say goodbye to the path of worldliness by rejecting or redeeming what we cannot receive in its present state.

Example 1: Dreams and visions

If you want to become the villain in a room of modern secular people, say this: "Kids don't need dreams! They need responsibilities." The modern obsession with pursuing dreams, especially for children, would have seemed insane two generations ago and back to, well, the beginning of recorded history. Still, something about the claim that people should have dreams comes from a genuine insight about creation. *That's why we find the idol plausible in the first place.* Dreams emerge from imagination, and imagination opens the mind to possibilities.

> Our problem isn't that we don't dream big enough. Our problem is that we can't dream strange enough.

But this is the rub of the idol: Kids (and we) don't need specific dreams; they need well-developed imaginations.

Our problem isn't that we don't dream big enough. Our problem is that we can't dream strange enough, because our imaginations can't make more than a couple moves into the future. Imagination works best as a faculty creating possibilities that can be easily discarded. When we treat the products of our imagination like stone tablets, which is how many of us approach dreams, we hamper the next moment's imagination, and we become terrified to let go of obsolete dreams.

A gospel-driven imagination can accept providence, creation, limitations that come from being finite, and misfortune while still accommodating the imaginations of others. Personal dreams not forged by the gospel become calcified idols that bind our personal worth to a view of ourselves stuck in situations, roles, and accomplishments that almost certainly are not part of our real future. Imagination allows substantive people to apply themselves to the improvisational present without being angered by things they could never control. They can make the most of the present, since they feel no debilitating sense of loss from "losing their dreams." Lastly, teamwork, friendship, romance, and community require constantly reimagining life with new and eccentric characters and events we could have never anticipated. Substantive people have the character and imagination to constantly write a new story with the ending unknown. Static dreams, no matter how big, make us narrower and more fragile. They make us less likely to accomplish a worthwhile dream.

> Substantive people have the character and imagination to constantly write a new story with the ending unknown.

You might not think that sounds very Christian. Maybe you have heard people reference this verse: "Where there is no vision, the people perish" (Proverbs 29:18a, KJV). I've heard a number of fiery sermons about how we all need dreams like Joseph, the dreamer of the Bible.[1] But these biblical examples actually make my point perfectly.

Interestingly, the word for "vision" in this proverb is actually the word for "prophetic revelation" (i.e. God's word), not a plan for the future or a personal dream.[2] The second half of the verse clarifies, "but blessed is the one who heeds wisdom's instruction" (Proverbs 29:18b, NIV). So the point of the verse is that when no one knows or speaks God's truth, people do whatever they want, and it's terrible. Conversely, the person who knows and does God's commands is blessed. That is, you don't need a dream; you need to know and obey God's revelation. You need a character formed by God's universal revelation, not your own subjective, personal dream. The verse means literally the opposite of what many quote it to mean.

Take, for example, Joseph. First, *God* gives him a dream (literally, a dream that comes to him in his sleep). Second, note

---

1   See Genesis 37 and following. Joseph's story is one of the most famous and important in the Bible.

2   Many more recent translations have preferred "prophetic vision" or "revelation" to the term "vision," which gets closer to the original intent and avoids confusion in the way we use the word "vision" today.

that the dream came from God, not from Joseph's own imagination. Third, by directly applying the dream and telling people, he got in a lot of trouble. Fourth, the dream was fulfilled through providential events over which he had absolutely no control and in ways he could never have anticipated. Joseph did nothing strategically to make his dreams come true.[3] Lastly, *God used Joseph's character* to bring about the dream. Joseph is one of only a few biblical figures about whose character nothing negative is said. He was a man of substance. God and godliness brought him to the realization of his dream.

Our dreams emerge from who we already are. So the most important preconditions of a great dream or vision are substance, character, and godliness. We don't need a special dream to become a person of substance, but substantive people produce the best dreams. Let the dreaming go, and really follow Proverbs 29:18—learn to follow God's word by the Spirit. The deeper you go, the more the gospel will expand your imagination. Dreams and visions you currently have may fall away, but more beautiful (and potentially wilder) ones will emerge from a more spiritually substantial you.

Our dreams emerge from who we already are.

Dreams and visions are good exercises, but bad gods. Without profound substance, they tend to be unrealistic, narcissistic, self-important messes of idealism run amok that disappoint us, debilitate our expectations, and hurt others. Ironically, they can cripple and narrow God's good creation of our imagination. They tempt us to take shortcuts into sin and worldliness to bring them about. Yet, when our vision comes from God's

---

3   Note how we conflate the two meanings of "dream," and how that contributes to our misunderstanding of both. An experience during sleep and a personal goal rooted in a visual imagination are not the same thing. One we experience or receive passively, and the other we actively create. In Joseph's case, not only with his first dream, but with all his subsequent dreams, he was a passive recipient. He didn't envision a future for himself; he walked into the one God imagined for him.

revealed truth (vision) and a gospel-filled imagination, then our dreams emerge from the solid source of substance.

Example 2: Self-esteem

It took modern science decades to realize that the self-esteem fad was a huge mistake. Yet, our culture is so committed to it that it still infects our self-understanding, our institutions, and our debilitated parenting models. By 2003, the research was already available: Self-esteem may increase happy feelings and initiative, but it also has a pile of major liabilities. It tends to increase in-group favoritism, also known as prejudice or discrimination. Some kinds of self-esteem correlate with the highest levels of lying, stealing, and narcissism. One paper summary notes: "The lowest *and highest* rates of bullying and cheating are found in different sub-categories of self-esteem."[4] Self-esteem, as a general idea, does virtually none of what we have been told it would do for two generations. It turns out that the *kind* of self-worth we have, how we acquire it, and the kind of character to which it is bound determine whether self-esteem will be a balm or a blight.

> It turns out that the *kind* of self-worth we have, how we acquire it, and the kind of character to which it is bound determine whether self-esteem will be a balm or a blight.

The problematic effect of modern self-esteem on substance is that we want it to *precede* solidity of merit and character. But, stable and secure self-worth is the *result* of moral formation, personal discipline, and real achievement, and is developed within secure relationships. When our method of imparting self-esteem is common pseudoscientific flattery, we ask people

---

4   R. F. Baumeister, J. D. Campbell, J. I. Krueger, K. D. Vohs, "Does High Self-Esteem Cause Better Performance, Interpersonal Success, Happiness, or Healthier Lifestyles?" *Psychological Science in the Public Interest*, vol. 4, Association for Psychological Science, https://www.ncbi.nlm.nih.gov/pubmed/26151640 (accessed 23 May 2017). Emphasis added.

to build their worth on dishonesty and insubstantial things. This fiction predictably results in people who are entitled and yet insecure, the very definition of a tyrant.[5] Such self-value has its feet planted in midair, and deep down we know it. This is why those with sky-high self-esteem can be among the most insecure people. In treating self-esteem as primary, we have tried to create self-worth by inflaming vanity with flattery. Worse, we have done it especially to the young, those least able to understand its devastating effect on them.

The substantive message of Christ tells us self-worth must come from a larger truth about both selves and worth. We must already know what human selves are and what they're worth within creation and redemption. Substantive human worth is a moral value based on truths about our creation, redemption, purpose, relation to God, and ultimate destiny. That is, accurate and solid self-worth comes from our being (in God's image), purpose, and relationship with other things. Therefore, self-worth is a classic dependent thing.[6] It depends not only on other character qualities, but also on other truths—spiritual and moral ones.

Moral substance has always situated our sense of self-worth alongside the value of everything else. You are worth a great price—shown both in creation and redemption—and so is your neighbor who you dislike. So is the person of a different race or creed. So are the environment, truth, virtue, courtesy, covenants, and community. Jesus tells us that we are of incredible value, but that our value comes from many other values and priorities in the cosmos to which we are related. It is only in seeing our value situated alongside all other right values and goods that we can see ourselves as worthwhile while being in-

---

5   By "tyrant" here I mean anyone who exerts his or her will on others in order to extract an outcome to his or her own benefit without regard for God or virtue.

6   C.S. Lewis gives a good description of the difference between dependent and independent things in his essay *First and Second Things*.

credibly humble, honest, thankful, self-sacrificial, loving, and worshipful.

Put self-esteem before substance, and we lose the latter and deform the former. Focus on substance and we get self-worth for free. Focus on self-esteem, and we pay a terrible price in the long run in both happiness and goodness. We must learn to discern the right kind of self-worth from its distorted counterfeit, then pursue the real and abandon our obsession with the imposter.

THE POINT OF GOODBYE

We could dig into the worldly understandings of image,[7] approval, humor, consumption,[8] and comfort in the same way and come up with similar results. When we only care about these things because of how they gratify our fleshly desires, we sever them from the values and truths of God's creation and

---

7   Image is the perception others have of you. Images are managed for the approval of others. The pursuit of a good image, if not pursued by having substantive character, is necessarily pursued in a way that undermines substance. No one can both protect their image and build their character. To protect your image, you have to be flexible in ways a solid character is not. To consistently gain the approval of others, you cannot singly pursue the approval of a morally serious God. It is much easier to create technology used to promote our image than make substantive disciples. Each of us will ultimately decide whether to manage an approved image or develop character that deserves approval. When we prioritize our image over our godliness, real substance is always a casualty. When our image isn't backed by the density of substance, it tends to be vaporous—like our self. Caring about the truth about ourselves more than about how we are regarded by others is at the heart of a healthy sense of image and desire for approval.

8   Debt is one of the greatest norms and deepest pains of modernity. The heart of debt is that we consume more than we produce. One of the quickest and most predictable releases of pleasure and relievers of stress is buying something. Looking at any of our cities, it becomes obvious that consumption is one of our greatest pursuits. Consumption itself takes many wholesome forms. When we take more joy in consumption than in production, however, we have perverted enjoyment. Substantive faith takes satisfaction in producing *and* consuming, both in proper proportion and in proper orientation to God. A central aspect of our bearing the image of God is that we create and produce. Our disordered longing to devour yields only scarcity and the most brutal and menacing competition. Consumption in proper relationship with productivity has inherent beauty.

redemption, outside of which they can't really exist. When our evil desires latch onto how they can gratify us, these good creations are corrupted and deformed.

It is only by saying a decisive goodbye to worldliness and pursuing substance in Christ by his power that we can become discerning. Only in a decisive goodbye can all of these creation gifts come back to us in good health and in their right place. That's not self-help manipulation. Jesus said this is how creation works. We see this in Matthew 6:31-33:

> So do not worry, saying, "What shall we eat" or "What shall we drink?" or "What shall we wear?" For *the pagans run after all these things,* and your heavenly Father knows that you need them. But *seek first his kingdom and his righteousness, and all these things will be given to you as well.*

This comes just a few verses after Matthew 5:6:

> Blessed are those who *hunger and thirst for righteousness,* for they will be filled.

Do you see the difference between the "pagans" (worldliness) and the "blessed" (godliness/substance)? The kingdom of God and his righteousness are to be pursued *directly.* They are the things that ground everything else. When they are in place, everything else can fall into place. Those with spiritual substance hunger and thirst for righteousness more than their inner "want-er" drives them to food, drink, and clothes (and lattes, heated seats, great vacations, and so on). For the one who hungers and thirsts after righteousness (substance), God makes two promises:

1. You will be filled (with substance).
2. God knows about your other needs (for subsistence).

To say it another way, *the difference is between what we must actively pursue and what will take care of itself.* Worldliness has these backward. It entices us to pursue everything except Christlikeness and his kingdom—God himself—when in reality, only this single-hearted pursuit can release us from the fear of scarcity.

Many Christians are familiar with the part of Matthew 6 that says, "But seek first his kingdom and his righteousness, and all these things will be given to you as well" (verse 33), but they don't know the larger context of that verse. Taken as part of this larger passage, it is clear that "all these things" refers to food, clothes, and all of our tangible needs. It might not normally occur to us, but seeking God's kingdom and righteousness is more in our control than buying bread or a shirt. A decision or action is something you can do, while getting results in even the smallest task requires things outside our control, things under God's providential rule. God knows we have needs and that many things are out of our control. Yet if we seek God's kingdom and righteousness, we move with him toward everything we need. When we pursue the way God has promised to work (his kingdom and righteousness), God works for us in our character and in situations we can't control. We place ourselves in a position in which God's work to reveal his own glory includes him working for our good (see also Romans 8:26-39).

Jesus has called us to spiritual substance (sanctification) and has demanded we pursue godliness in the world to which we have been sent (John 17). Doing this requires discernment that can only be developed by pursuing godliness as a hunger and a thirst. Do you thirst for Jesus, his spiritual substance, and escape from the corruption of worldliness? If we seek these, God promises that all the other things we require will be added to us as well.

When we are "transformed by the renewing of [our minds]" (Romans 12:2) in Christ and the gospel, we can discern the purpose and use of all the gifts of creation. We can understand the purpose, meaning, and duties of our lives. Once the ultimate things are present, they can support the things that depend upon them.

Therefore, if Jesus is right, we have to say goodbye to our old way of viewing the world and our own way of pursuing our good. One of the most difficult things to do when we are short on substance is to embrace something that is decidedly *not* cool. But discernment recognizes that a new path is waiting, a path that leads to the substance that fills our deepest God-given hunger and thirst. It leads out of the "corruption in the world" and toward "his very great and precious promises" in the gospel (2 Peter 1:4).

THE MARKS OF SUBSTANCE: GOD'S DREAM FOR YOU

So what does substance look like? The Bible shows us four *primary* marks of spiritual substance—four traits that characterize substantive followers of Jesus. We could easily come up with at least fifteen, but if we understand these four marks, we will have a very biblical and helpful sense of the what spiritual substance looks like. Pursue these, and all the other traits will be added to you. Plus, Jesus said everything else in life will be added to you, too.

1. **Living in self-sacrificial love:** Love is the queen of the virtues, and holy love is the essence of God's character.[9] Outflowing love recognizes that we are **stewards**,[10] and that everything we have belongs to God to be used for his purposes, not for our own comfort, power, control, or approval. It is the enemy of selfishness, ambition, vanity, and conceit (Philippians 2:3). God sends us to love others and demands we trust him for our reward.

2. **Seeking the mind of Christ:** We need a renewing transformation of mind including both a systematic *rejection* of "the pattern of this world" that is worldliness, and a complete *renewal* of our minds in the knowledge of Christ (Romans 12:2). The purpose of the mind of Christ is that we can know God's will and embrace it as living sacrifices who please God, serve others, and are satisfied in God.

3. **Walking in virtuous freedom:** God's ultimate plan for redeemed humans is freedom. We are not meant to be shallow and stupid animals, fenced in by an exhaustive set of rules. Nor are we supposed to be robots who can only

---

9   Holiness (Isaiah 6:1-5) and love have the preeminent place in clarifying what God is like in the Bible. Only holiness is chanted in repetition by angelic beings (Isaiah 6:3; Revelation 4:8), while love is referred to as the greatest of the virtues and as morally synonymous with God's very being (1 John 4:8-16). Since the concept of holiness can easily modify love—while the reverse, loving holiness, is much less clear—we often refer to the quintessential center of God's character as *holy love*. We should hold this lightly as a summary, since summarizing God's character has numerous conceptual dangers.

10   A steward is the manager over some enterprise. It comes from an old English word for "house-ward," meaning the keeper of a house. Stewardship refers to management over something that does not belong to you, but which you are completely responsible to order according to the real owner's will. This role is found many times in Scripture, since it perfectly parallels our lives in Christ and in God's creation. Nothing—not even our own lives—belongs to us, and yet everything in our hands is for us to manage according to the will of the Owner and Master. This concept of stewardship is a one-word definition for the whole of what we are doing in the Christian life. Our job is to be faithful stewards.

execute direct commands. God has made us free, creative agents, living by his Spirit on his mission. However, freedom requires virtue and maturity of character.

4. **Keeping in step with the Spirit:** Our bodies are to be living sacrifices, not gratification machines. Once we know what God's will is, we have to combine the knowledge (2 Peter 1:3) and the mind of Christ (1 Corinthians 2:16) with the discipline to follow the Spirit rather than our sinful desires until our desires align with the Spirit more and more. Keeping in step with the Spirit is the application of the gospel through faith, in all the improvisational choices and situations of each day.

We should be eager to see ourselves growing in these four marks of substance, knowing that they are signs that we are becoming increasingly substantive disciples and, ultimately, becoming more like Christ. The spiritual character resulting from pursuing these four marks will completely change our inner lives. In them we will know how to use our freedom without indulging our sinful desires (Galatians 5:13). It will liberate us from the anxiety and restlessness that come from worldliness, the boredom we feel in repetition, the smothering of our faith, and our resentment toward the God who won't tolerate our love of Mammon. We will no longer be fragile creatures grasping at shallow pleasures. We will have the substance to find and take satisfaction in all of our toil (Ecclesiastes 3:11-13). We will find peace, pleasure, and significance in the roles, rhythms, repetitions, and responsibilities (what I call "the Four Rs") of ordinary life. In all of this, we will find our hearts enlarged and filled with a deeper love. Deep love that imitates God's love is like a liquid inside the vessel of human character. A vaporous character cannot contain love. Only a solid vessel—even a vessel that is plain and chipped—can be filled with love and of use in pouring it out (2 Corinthians 4:7).

That can be you. We can be a people characterized by deep love, satisfaction, solidity, peace, and pleasure as we pursue God and his kingdom first, trusting him to supply the rest.

In part two of this book, we'll examine each of these four marks in more detail.

SUGGESTED BIBLE MEMORIZATION

Blessed are those who hunger and thirst for righteousness, for they will be filled.

Matthew 5:6

So do not worry, saying, "What shall we eat?" or "What shall we drink?" or "What shall we wear?" For the pagans run after all these things, and your heavenly Father knows that you need them. But seek first his kingdom and his righteousness, and all these things will be given to you as well.

Matthew 6:31-33

REFLECT AND RESPOND

1. Imagine we (authentic Christians) could create a place to live that was separate from the worldliness of the world, but we weren't allowed to. Would you be upset that you couldn't live in such a place, or would you be relieved that you wouldn't have to?

2. Does Jesus' promise in Matthew 5:6 do anything inside you?

3. Do you need to say a more decisive and complete goodbye to worldliness? Why, and in what way(s)?

FOR FURTHER READING

When I Don't Desire God: How to Fight for Joy by John Piper

The book focuses on how to build hunger and thirst for God when we don't feel it. Though hunger and thirst are feelings we're used to experiencing passively, there are things we can do to increase our spiritual hunger and thirst.

PART II

THE MARKS OF SUBSTANCE

3

SELF-SACRIFICIAL LOVE

You, my brothers and sisters, were called to be free. But do not use your freedom to indulge the flesh; rather, serve one another humbly in love.
Galatians 5:13

A new command I give you: Love one another. As I have loved you, so you must love one another. By this everyone will know that you are my disciples, if you love one another.
John 13:34-35

No one has ever seen God; but if we love one another, God lives in us and his love is made complete in us.
1 John 4:12

What does substantive discipleship really look like? When we try to assemble something, we almost always have a picture, plan, or model. For example, puzzles are much easier with the box cover. So, what is the box cover of substantive spirituality? What is the image to which we should look?

The obvious answer is that a substantive disciple looks like Jesus. But that only gets us so far. It assumes you already have an accurate idea of what Jesus is like. Understanding what God has shown us in and through Jesus is itself something of

the puzzle we are putting together. If you have read the Gospels, you know that it took Jesus' own disciples quite a long time to really figure out what he meant by his teachings, the significance of his death, and the meaning of his resurrection. This is not because Jesus is hard to understand. It's because our worldliness makes it hard for us to understand him.[1]

Jesus is constantly mischaracterized and misunderstood, even by Christians and churches. When we're captured by worldliness, we make Jesus look like us while saying we are becoming more like him. If we are worldly, then it's likely our picture of Jesus is much more worldly than we want to admit.[2]

> **When we're captured by worldliness, we make Jesus look like us while saying we are becoming more like him.**

---

1   One of Jesus' favorite sayings was, "Whoever has ears, let them hear" (Matthew 11:15; 13:9, 43; Mark 4:9, 23; Luke 8:8; 14:35; Revelation 2:7, 11, 17, 29; 3:6, 13, 22; 13:9). He's talking about attitude and disposition—"to the one willing or inclined to hear, to the one willing to change his mind and be challenged by what I really mean..." This is Jesus' way of telling us that if we don't understand him, it's because we aren't really listening, not because what he's saying is all that hard. The problem is worldliness.

2   Remember, worldliness isn't the *opposite* of godliness. If it were, it would be easy to recognize. It's not as though the Bible says, "Thou shall not murder," and so worldliness says, "No, you definitely *should* murder." Nor does it paint a picture of Jesus with horns and a pitchfork. Its deceptions are always subtle and framed as things we *want* to believe in. Paul once said worldliness and legalism can have the "form of godliness" while denying and lacking its power (2 Timothy 3:2-5). Because of this, we need a

In fact, our picture of Jesus might be *the very thing we need to fix* in order to have a clear picture of godliness.

Think about it this way: Before sending Jesus, God sent 1,500 years of divine revelation for Jesus to fulfill. And now that he has come, we don't just have the four accounts of his life in the New Testament; we also have twenty-three other books to help us understand what his life and teachings mean. Think also of why God established a chosen people, prophets, and the Covenant. God went to great lengths to keep us from misunderstanding Jesus. The Old Testament books set the context for this coming and tell us what it's supposed to mean. The New Testament books theologically interpret the meaning of his life, death, and resurrection for us. Even the Gospels themselves—the four books that record the life of Jesus—were written not only as records of events, but as guides for understanding the significance of Jesus' life and work.

BEING GODLY ≠ BEING SAVED

Before we go too far, it's important to remember that we are talking about a picture of *godliness*, not the *gospel*. If you confuse the gospel (how we are saved and changed) with godliness (what we're changed to be and why), then the beauty of grace and divine generosity is deformed. Trying to earn godliness neither gains forgiveness nor is of any use in the deep transformation of the heart.

The simplest summary of the gospel is in 1 Corinthians 15:3-5:

> For what I received I passed on to you as of first importance: that Christ died for our sins according to the Scriptures, that he

---

clearer definition, a higher resolution picture to empower our discernment. We need the ability to see Jesus clearly as he is in the whole of the Bible, framed by all of revelation and the whole story of redemption. This allows God—not our culture—to control the picture and meaning of Jesus. It allows Jesus to speak to us about godliness rather than us putting words in his mouth to affirm our worldliness.

was buried, that he was raised on the third day according to the Scriptures, and that he appeared to Cephas [Peter], and then to the Twelve.

That is, the Christian gospel (which means good news) is the fact that Jesus has died to pardon your sins and has risen from the dead. His rising demonstrates he has accomplished God's design and defeated sin and death with their guilt, shame, alienation, and punishment. You can receive all these liberating benefits of his victory through faith. That is, faith is repentant (meaning it admits wrongdoing), rejects the old way of rebellion, and turns to Christ to receive everything we need. These acts together are often summarized as *repentance and faith.*

With this forgiveness comes new spiritual life. When we are in Christ, God is with us (John 14:16-17). He will transform us into what he has declared us to be in Christ. He will first make us righteous in Christ through faith, and then, he'll make us godly through Christ by that same faith. The question of this book is, what does that look like? What is God transforming us into? How can we know, so that out of joy, faith, hope, and thankfulness we can throw our full strength into cooperating with him?

DEFINING SPIRITUAL SUBSTANCE

The Bible defines godliness on every page, in multiple cultures, and on different continents. Its definition can be seen through biography, narrative, and teaching, and supremely in the Savior, Jesus himself. Taken together, the Scriptures all weave a rich and full picture of God's character and how we are called to be like him. So one solution to defining godliness is to read the whole Bible, but that could take a little while. We need to get started faster than that.

A few parts of the Bible are especially concise in their attention to godliness, and they serve as puzzle box covers for understanding what godliness looks like. We'll look at a few key examples:

After a long section on the true nature of love in 1 Corinthians 13, the apostle Paul gave this summary: "...these three remain: faith, hope and love, but *the greatest* of these is love"[3] (verse 13). In Romans 13:8-10, he summarizes it this way:

Let no debt remain outstanding, except the continuing debt to love one another, for *whoever loves others has fulfilled the law.*[4] The commandments, "You shall not commit adultery," "You shall not murder," "You shall not steal," "You shall not covet,"[5] and whatever other command there may be, *are summed up* in this one command: "Love your neighbor as yourself."[6] Love does no harm to a neighbor. *Therefore love is the fulfillment of the law.*

In Galatians 5, Paul argues that **virtue** and spiritual freedom come from Christ and the Spirit through faith. These aren't for indulging the Flesh. Virtue and spiritual freedom should produce serving love. He says:

For through the Spirit we eagerly await by faith the righteousness for which we hope. For in Christ Jesus neither circumcision nor uncircumcision has any value. *The only thing that counts is faith expressing itself through love...* You, my brothers and sisters, were called to be free. But do not use your freedom to indulge the flesh; rather *serve one another humbly in love.* For the *entire law is ful-*

---

3   All of 1 Corinthians 13 is an exposition on the character of love and is therefore a good summary in itself.

4   Here Paul is referring to the Law given to ancient Israel through Moses, which can be found in the books Exodus, Leviticus, and Deuteronomy. In other places, biblical authors are referring to a more general idea of law. While the original Greek and Hebrew don't use capitalization to distinguish between these two uses, in this book I use "Law" and "law" to clarify which use is intended, based on the surrounding context. In this instance, Law is left lowercase because that is how it appears originally in the quoted text.

5   See Exodus 20:13-15, 17; Deuteronomy 5:17-19, 21.

6   See Leviticus 19:18.

filled in keeping this one command: "Love your neighbor as yourself."
Galatians 5:5-6, 13-14

In each of these passages (and others), Paul is quoting Jesus' teaching on the most important command of God, recorded by three of the Gospel writers: *"Love the Lord your God with all your heart and with all your soul and with all your mind.'* This is the first and greatest commandment. And the second is like it: 'Love your neighbor as yourself'" (Matthew 22:37-39).[7] In Matthew's account, he adds this statement: "All the law and the Prophets hang on these two commandments" (Matthew 22:40).

Do you get it? By saying that love fulfills the Law, he's implying that the Law is a summary of love. Love fulfills the Law, and the Law fills out love. Love is not an open category for us to define as we feel or like. Love may be complicated, but God's commands make it concrete. Remember that Jesus also said:

> Do not think that I have come to abolish the Law or the Prophets; I have not come to *abolish* them but to *fulfill* them. For truly I tell you, until heaven and earth disappear, not the smallest letter, not the least stroke of a pen, will by any means disappear from the Law until everything is accomplished.
> **Matthew 5:17-18**

The Law is an expression of God's moral character.[8] It is a

---

7   See also Mark 12:29-31; Luke 10:25-28.

8   This refers to the Law as a whole. Since all laws are created in specific situations for specific people, they will include some concessions to the foundational assumptions and situations of life at that time. In a fallen world, nothing is as it should be, even the commands of God, since they have to take into account what humans presently are. Therefore, some commands will have in them what theologians call divine concessions. These are cases in which God gives the command most in keeping with his character given what humans are in their fallen state, in the limitations of civilization within that moment, and in their place in salvation history, among other considerations. The Law as

summary of what God is like. In it, God consistently says, "be holy, because I am holy" (i.e. Leviticus 11:44-45). That is, "I'm telling you about my character, what I'm like morally. You should be like this too." The part of the Law that gives us God's commands may not tell us the story of how and why he created us, makes us his people, forgives us, and changes us. Those are revealed in gospel, not Law (even though these can be found in the books of the Law).[9] Love and the Law are both summaries of God's moral substance—his virtue and character. Love is the most general reference to the whole, and the Law the most specific by example. When we put together the summary of knowing God's character of holy love, it lays out something like this:

1. God's character is morally perfect, holy love.
2. Godliness is being like God in his character, also called holiness.
3. The Law is a summary of that character.
4. Love is a summary of the Law.
5. Therefore, holy love is a biblical summary of godliness.

Holy love is the substance of the character of God. It is displayed most completely in the life and virtue of Jesus. And it is made concrete and specific for us in God's commands, so that we can only deceive ourselves so far about love. If we start thinking something selfish and fleshly is love, we won't get far before we bump into a command that is there to help us by giving us a reality check.[10]

---

a whole is a reflection of the character of God, but that reflection is still partly connected to the people to whom he is reflecting it. For an example of Jesus' teaching about divine concessions in the Law, see Matthew 19:8.

9   This can be a little confusing, because the gospel is found in the books of the Law themselves (Genesis, Exodus, Leviticus, Numbers, and Deuteronomy). But the laws regulating behavior are an embodiment of God's holiness, because they are expressions of love.

10   An easy example of this would be leaving one's spouse if one feels unhappy in

BEARING THE IMAGE OF HOLY LOVE

God's character is holy, and from the holy love in his virtuous character, his love flows out into action. We are not supposed to try to recreate God's outflowing works of creation, salvation, and redemption. Those are free gifts. He does not demand that faith make us god-lings (little gods), but that it make us god-ly (holy, because he is holy). We are called to pursue lives flowing out in works of similar character. Godliness means imitating his outflowing holy love through all the ways we bear his image.[11]

> Godliness means imitating his outflowing holy love through all the ways we bear his image.

Although we can't be creators of a universe, holy love can motivate an outpouring of creativity and productivity. We can't sacrifice ourselves to purchase forgiveness for any part of humanity, but holy love pours out sacrificial forgiveness toward those who commit offenses against us. We can't redeem the world's guilt, but we can be redeemers who claim back people, relationships, land, and much of life from degradation and destruction. In fact, all the actions of the outflowing life are sacrificially generous, especially to the undeserving. God does not function out of a mindset of scarcity or based on what

---

a marriage where there is no physical abuse or infidelity. People often think that the loving thing for everyone, including their children, is to divorce. With enough suffering, almost anyone will be seriously tempted to come to this conclusion. But God's Law forbids divorce in any other case but those mentioned above. This law may seem harsh, but only harsh things can ground people in the midst of their weakness, anger, pride, bitterness, fear, and pain. The Law objectively tells us that divorce is not compatible with God's holy love. Nor is doing nothing. Holy love will drive us forward, but in a new, God given direction—usually one simultaneously harder and better. Harder for a while, but often wonderful in the long run. Without the command, we would have given up. I see this dynamic constantly in pastoral ministry, and I experience it personally every single day.

11   Many of our faculties that are not reflections of God's character are still part of his image, but their significance is bound to moral character. Virtue is what gives them their good unity and makes gifts like life, reason, will, and emotion beautiful and good rather than corrupted and damnable. Virtue generates holiness.

people deserve. God's holy love is gracious—freely generous. Jesus told his disciples, "Freely you have received; freely give" (Matthew 10:8).

When we give, there is something we do without. Our sacrifice is usually related to the reality of scarcity. Is God's love sacrificial? He doesn't experience scarcity. But then again, much of our scarcity is the result of sin, not simple limitations of creation. God sacrifices when something is either/or— when logic itself dictates you can't have both. For example, whenever the glorious, holy God loves rebellious humans, that love always requires his forbearance toward their constant and countless insults against his divine majesty,[12] which is a continual sacrifice on his part. Then, in order for God to be just toward sin's crime and also redeem us, sacrifice was necessary in Jesus (Romans 3:26). So, even God, who lacks no resources, must still choose to sacrifice some things in order to gain others. Even God sacrifices to be generous. Holy love gives to create and gives sacrificially to redeem. This is what we emulate.

Therefore, godliness looks like outflowing, self-sacrificial, generous, holy love expressed through God's image in us. Love is the queen of the spiritual pursuits that produce spiritual substance, because it is itself spiritual substance. It is the first pursuit, because it is also the central goal. Holy love is at the white-hot center of the character of God, and it is the part of his character he has commanded us to imitate. This is how we bear his image. This is what it means for us to be like God (godliness).

> Holy love is at the white-hot center of the character of God, and it is the part of his character he has commanded us to imitate.

Knowing Love for what She is: The company Love keeps

We started on this path of defining love because we want-

---

12 Or dignity—see Romans 3:25.

ed a clearer understanding of substance than "be like Jesus."
Yet, is it really any clearer to say, "be loving"? Not unless we

take things a step further. The
word love can be distorted even
more easily than the character of Jesus. We already hinted
at the answer to this question

> Love is known by the company she keeps (virtues) and the house she lives in (God's commands).

above: Love is known by the company she keeps (virtues) and
the house she lives in (God's commands). Just as you can know
someone by the company they keep, so you can know the true
nature of Love. Let's look at these two companions to Love:
virtue and God's commands.

First, there are many examples of Scriptures presenting
Love in the company of her sister virtues. Paul is known for
speaking of faith, hope, and love together. In Galatians 5, love
is in the company of the "fruit of the Spirit" (Galatians 5:22-
23) and opposed to the "acts [vices] of the flesh" (Galatians
5:19-21). In Philippians 2, love is accompanied by humility,
tenderness, compassion, desire for unity, and other virtues that
display the nature of love. Above all, we know Love in relation

to her twin sister, Humility, since self-forgetfulness is the other side of seeing and remembering others. Love's nature is clearest when surrounded by these accompanying virtues.

In this way, we can imagine Love as a queen with amnesia, not sure where she came from or who she is. She might be persuaded she is a bar maid, thief, or slave. We see this when selfishness and sin of all kinds are passed off as love. But when Queen Love is in the presence of her sisters, the virtues, she remembers herself and her dignity. In this illustration, we are actually the ones who forget the face of the queen. When she's surrounded by her sisters, we see her for who she is. In the Scriptures, Love is always shown in the company of her companion virtues, because they are also the company she keeps in all of life—in God's kingdom and righteousness here and now.

Second, many Scriptures also test our love against our obedience to God's objective commands. If God's commands are examples of his holy love, then they are all examples of right answers to the question, "What is loving?" In Romans 13:8-10, Paul shows that all of the Old Testament laws are examples of what it means to love (all 613 of them). Jesus said, "*all* of the law and the Prophets" hang on the command to love God and love your neighbor (Matthew 22:40). God's laws are the ethics of real love.

Take just the Ten Commandments as an example.[13] People who love God don't give their allegiance to other gods and don't take his name lightly (in vain).[14] People who love their neighbors don't minimize God, use his name vainly, work people when they should let them rest, humiliate the dignity of

---

13   See Exodus 20; Deuteronomy 5.

14   That is, the name of God should only be used when referring to God. Referring to God should always have an air of reverence about it. One example of this would be not swearing, and not even saying, "Oh my God," as a reaction to something that is surprising or unsettling, unless it is really addressed to God. By not throwing around God's name lightly, it keeps us more constantly mindful of the weightiness of God, so we don't become profane and flippant about him, our neighbors, or ourselves.

parents, murder people, steal from people, commit adultery with other people's wives or husbands, or covet others' property. The things God commands are always loving, and their inverse is always unloving. In this sense, every biblical command gives us part of the definition of love worked out in practical situations. They comprise the solid house in which Love lives.

Therefore, if someone calls something love that violates a commandment, then we can know that something is distorted; it is not truly love. "Love does not delight in evil but rejoices with the truth" (1 Corinthians 13:6). The whole Bible helps us check our definition of love. Every verse tests our summary of godliness, correcting the distortions of temptation, worldliness, and the Flesh. Love is always in the company of God's revealed laws and virtues.

Love's true nature: A feeling or an action?

So let's summarize this first of the four marks of spiritual substance: substantive spirituality is best displayed in virtuous, self-forgetful, self-sacrificial, holy love.

Everywhere you look in the Bible, these characteristics always accompany Love. They are her closest sisters. Love is always *virtuous*. Love does not contradict the right application of the other virtues. She is always in loving harmony with them, since every virtue is a means of love. Love is always humble and *self-forgetful*, because only this view of ourselves opens us fully to love, joy, wonder, and thankfulness. Only humility can make us outflowing people. In being outflowing and generous, love is always *self-sacrificial*.[15] Love sacrifices for the good of oth-

---

15 This is true even if love brings back to you more than you sacrifice. In fact, God promises this will be the case (Mark 10:28-31). Love will bring back to us an exponential ton of blessing. However, God seeks to keep the sacrifice and the blessing separate, so the blessing is never our motivation for love. Love must flow out toward the value of the other, the holiness and glory of God, and the inherent worth of love itself. Only then can it be self-forgetful, virtuous, and truly self-sacrificial. When this virtuous motivation comes together with knowing that love produces blessings for all, love produces joy. Love's pleasures, when motivated by virtue and humility, multiply joy

ers, and does so out of its own resources. Finally, love is always *holy*, taking its character from the character of God.

When we understand love in this way, we will never argue again about whether love is a feeling or an action. It is neither, and it always produces both. People who love others will have affection or compassion, which are loving feelings. Love will always motivate a response, whether service, enjoyment, sacrifice, or a hundred other expressions.

> When we understand love in this way, we will never argue again about whether love is a feeling or an action. It is neither, and it always produces both.

So what is love? Is it too abstract to nail down? Is John's summary, "God is love," (1 John 4:8b) the best thing we can say? We could try to describe it artistically as something like, "Love is the effluence[16] of truth, goodness, and beauty enjoying each other in eternal radiance." That might work, but at its base, love is an attribute of being, which we call a virtue. Love *produces* feelings. Love *motivates* actions. But ultimately, love is a feature of our character, which is the frame upon which our being is built.

Once we see this, we can see that love is the moral energy that animates the expression of truth, goodness, and beauty in the world. When the divine power of the Holy Spirit applies the divine character of holy love in us through faith, the result is ten thousand expressions of spiritual substance embodied in self-forgetful, self-sacrificial, virtuous human action. And these sublime divine actions gush forth in utterly practical incarnations: planting, cleaning, repairing, ordering, defending, comforting, nurturing, forming.

---

between many people, and never extract pleasure, leaving nothing in return.

16   Effluence is that which flows out of something else.

Love on Monday

One of the strangest things about love is that we can't unleash its spiritual greatness without our bodies. For all our fantasies, we are not merely psychic beings. Love has to come out of us through speech, embrace, work, listening, waiting, suffering, cleaning, and cooking. We have a sauce spoon at our house that is inscribed with the words, "Cooking is love made edible." One could adapt that saying to myriad different activities.

So what does mature love in a substantive disciple look like in physical demonstration? What does practical, ordinary love look like? The first step is looking past our distorted view of romance. So much of our romance is hateful rather than loving. But even at its best, romance is only a tiny sliver of the opportunity for love in the world. Let's look at three very practical categories of mature love:

1. **Counting the ordinary:** Substantive discipleship starts with the absolute embrace of the ordinary as our primary context for love.

   The eighth chapter of this book is dedicated to this, so I won't talk much about it here. However, learning to love in and through embracing every ordinary moment in the present is critical to both real love and true contentment in an anxious and resentful world.

2. **Making people our business:** God's image bearers are the primary application of love. God loves people incredibly.[17]

---

17 That does not mean he loves people more than he loves truth or goodness. God loves people because of his own character, just as his own character and being was the basis for him to create and redeem us. God's character and being are always primary. Therefore, how he loves us is based on his being and character. The one comes from the other, and therefore the two cannot be in contradiction. This is why Jesus became the Christ, to bring together God's just character and to allow God's mercy for sinners to be just (Romans 3:21-26). If we won't receive mercy, we receive damnation,

Jesus makes no secret of the fact that he came primarily to redeem people (Mark 6:34; Luke 15; 19:9-10; John 13:35). I suspect it is because humans are the only moral beings that must cooperate with redemption. He can recreate and redeem all of the rest of creation without

> We must make people our business. Making redemption our business means making people our business.

its consent. It seems that only humans bear his image in knowledge and life. Only we are moral and everlasting beings. Apparently, this requires us to be redeemed in a different way than everything else. We must be saved through revelation, sacrifice, repentance, faith, and transformation.

For this and other reasons, we must make people our business. This is not an extrovert versus introvert question, nor is it a task-oriented versus people-oriented question. I am a task-oriented introvert. My hunting buddies call me the "lone wolf," because I can spend days alone in the woods and like it. I don't feel the need for people, and I prefer to do my work alone. Yet, people are God's goal. Jesus said, "Come, follow me...and I will send you out to fish for people" (Matthew 4:19; Mark 1:17). One can seek a lost coin (Luke 15:8-10) or fish for people in a thousand human ways. Many of those ways can be with a few people doing tasks that help others. But if heaven really rejoices more over one person who is found than over ninety-nine who don't need to be found, then making redemption our business means making people our business.

Over time, we'll see that sharing our faith, expressing hos-

---

because one of God's characteristics cannot overrule another. His love will not violate the rest of his being, character, and name.

pitality, carrying other's burdens, developing friendship, seeking intergenerational and multiethnic unity, and including dysfunctional people are all part of love, specifically by making other people our business. They are the basics of love moving through a human body. They are also the starting point for the next category.

3. **Social justice:** Love in the larger family.[18]

We have responsibilities to people outside our family. The term "social justice," born out of Catholic thought, was meant to signify the virtue of giving to society what we justly owe it through the mechanisms of civil society (all institutions between the individual and the government). All of our just responsibilities to others comprise the demands of social virtue. Fulfilling the social virtues is to live according to social justice. This is a thoroughly biblical and Christian notion.

However, the meaning of social justice has been tortured and twisted to refer to political human goals chasing the myth of progress. The term is more commonly used now to refer to a goal to be pursued through the state that we must all support in order to be good people. The political use of the word is almost always a misuse of its biblical meaning and should be resisted by Christians. Christians should desire the largest civil society possible, since God's creation institution, the family, and redemption institution, the Church, are part of that sphere. We should also desire a large civil society because virtue requires voluntary association (civil) rather than coerced association (State). Christian faith demands we, and all humans, should act

---

18 Further reading: Michael Novak and Paul Adams, *Social Justice Isn't What You Think It Is* (New York: Encounter Books, 2015).

according to conscience. Both anarchy and statism destroy the fabric of human cooperation that must function on the basis of personal trust, mutual understanding, and love. Wide liberty is the only environment in which virtue can thrive. And since social justice is a virtue, it relies on liberty, which relies on civil society being larger than government or independent individuality.

Therefore, in order to understand love, we must understand what justice requires of us toward our neighbor, and through what means. This includes generosity, work that enriches others, taking responsibility for care of family, fighting in just wars, paying just taxes, honoring public officials and institutions, voting, using land and resources in environmentally sound ways, and other tasks. Social justice, when understood correctly, is a major part of real and practical love.

Love or nothing

Love is worth the difficulty. It is hard because it is complex and full and can take so many forms. Nor is it natural for us. In our sinful condition, we are all prone to redefine love or to avoid our responsibility to it in different ways. Our world is full of love confusion. Yet, Holy Love is the beating heart at the center of human purpose and redemption. She is the foretaste of eternity, the medicine and nourishment prescribed for creation. She is the first mark of godliness and God's summary of his character embodied in the Law. Love is the spinning hub of spiritual substance, the queen of the virtues, and the binding tie between them. Love is the most important aspect of our redeemed character, and she must be our greatest pursuit. The Scriptures tell us that without her, though we might do everything, we have nothing:

If I speak in the tongues of men or of angels, but do not have love, I am only a resounding gong or a clanging cymbal. If I have the gift of prophecy and can fathom all mysteries and all knowledge, and if I have a faith that can move mountains, but do not have love, I am nothing. If I give all I possess to the poor and give over my body to hardship that I may boast, but do not have love, I gain nothing.

1 Corinthians 13:1-3

SUGGESTED BIBLE MEMORIZATION

For through the Spirit we eagerly await by faith the righteousness for which we hope.

Galatians 5:5

You, my brothers and sisters, were called to be free. But do not use your freedom to indulge the flesh; rather, serve one another humbly in love.

Galatians 5:13

LONGER PASSAGES TO MEMORIZE
1 Corinthians 13

Philippians 2:1-16

REFLECT AND RESPOND

1. If it is easy to misunderstand Jesus and mis-define love, how do we get clear on what spiritual substance looks like?

2. Saying that the Law exemplifies love makes some people nervous. Without specific definition, "love" could mean anything and essentially, therefore, become meaningless. How does the Law continue to help us understand love?

3. What is the relationship between love and virtue? Why does it matter for becoming people of substance?

4. Who or what is close to you that you should love but have a hard time loving? Why do you think that is?

FOR FURTHER READING
Social Justice Isn't What You Think It Is by Michael Novak and
Paul Adams

4

THE MIND OF CHRIST

The mind governed by the flesh is death, but the mind governed by the Spirit is life and peace. The mind governed by the flesh is hostile to God; it does not submit to God's law, nor can it do so. Those who are in the realm of the flesh cannot please God.

Romans 8:6-8

Therefore, I urge you, brothers and sisters, in view of God's mercy, to offer your bodies as a living sacrifice, holy and pleasing to God—this is your true and proper worship. Do not conform to the pattern of this world, but be transformed by the renewing of your mind. Then you will be able to test and approve what God's will is—his good, pleasing and perfect will.

Romans 12:1-2

"Who has known the mind of the Lord so as to instruct him?" But we have the mind of Christ.

1 Corinthians 2:16

DOING IT OURSELVES

I have four children. I cannot tell you how many times I have heard them tell me, from toddlerhood to the present, "I'll do it myself." When you're a kid with no responsibilities, control feels attractive. Kids want to take control and prove themselves. This doesn't really change in adulthood, and it is one of the greatest strengths and weaknesses of the human race. Through bearing God's image, we are capable of amazing things, and God wants us to do those things with independence (like any parent would). Yet in our sinful condition of depravity, we often say, "I'll do it myself!" for the wrong reasons. We say it out of a desire for control or to win power or approval. When this is motivated by a selfish and untrusting pride or fear, it is sinful. The result of this sinful sort of independence is worldliness.

Two areas where humanity is prone to wrongly tell God, "I'll do it myself!" are moral knowledge and spiritual understanding. The Bible tells us that God's loving gift of knowledge was the point at which our relationship with him first broke apart. What was the first sin? Adam and Eve tried to steal the knowledge of good and evil[1] (Genesis 3). It was forbidden fruit for a good reason; it wasn't just that God was saving it for his lunch.

Sometimes people think that God wanted to keep humanity dumb and innocent in that garden forever. If not, why wouldn't he have given them that tree already? How could God think people could be happy having everything except knowledge? Many ancient mythologies include tales in which the gods are holding out on humans, not giving them good things. In Greek mythology, for example, Zeus punished the Titan Prometheus for stealing fire (which many believe signified knowledge) to bring it to mankind. The gods were stingy and jealous.

But in the Bible, the man and woman got the idea that God was stingy from the snake Satan's false accusation, and we've

---

1   What the Bible calls "the knowledge of good and evil" (Genesis 2:9) means more than just basic morality. It is essentially the meaning and significance of everything—what things mean, how they fit together, how they are to be used, and why they matter. It encapsulates everything that is beautiful as opposed to ugly, wise as opposed to fleshly, good as opposed to evil, and so on.

been buying into the snake's logic ever since. We are prone to believe that God was withholding that knowledge from humanity because he was jealous and threatened by what we would become. The serpent said, "For God knows that when you eat from it your eyes will be opened, and you will be like God, knowing good and evil" (Genesis 3:5). This claim wasn't just false; it was a profound perversion and reversal of the truth. In reality, it was God's design all along that we would be like him in this way. The purpose of creation and redemption was always for us to receive the very thing the snake claimed God was withholding. Even the doctrine of damnation assumes we are meant to embody God's moral knowledge and are created for everlasting life. Paul said it this way:

> You were taught, with regard to your former way of life, to put off your old self, which is being corrupted by its deceitful desires; to be made new in the attitude of your minds; and to put on the new self, *created to be like God in true righteousness and holiness.*
>
> **Ephesians 4:22-24**

He's saying that the point of redemption was re-creation—to get us back to our original created purpose. That purpose is that we were created *to be like God in righteousness and holiness* (in knowing how to distinguish between good and evil).

So why didn't God just give us that knowledge right away? The answer requires a distinction that the snake was side-slithering (side-stepping for the rest of us). To God, knowing doesn't mean just to be aware of something. It is more than familiarity. It means having something in the bones of your character, attitude, and behavior. That kind of knowledge takes time. A human body can be created in a moment or in nine months, but character needs to be forged over time. Just as humans develop character through their lives, it apparently needed to be developed in Adam and Eve. The first step of fashioning godly character is trust, and teaching trust was the reason God withheld a single tree while giving them access to everything else.

GROWING IN THE GARDEN

After God's initial creation of the world, the Bible shows his relationship with humanity continuing to develop. In Genesis 1, God makes men and women in his image and gives them his whole creation to subdue and rule over. Yet in the next chapter, God suddenly narrows the scope to something tiny by comparison. He makes a garden for them. We already know from chapter 1 that this isn't some permanent zoo exhibit. Humanity is meant to dig in and cultivate life, and God is preparing them to spread out and do so all over the world. We are meant to see the garden as an environment for the process of development. It's what people would later call a home. In this home, God makes the man out of the dirt. He gives the man a job (subduing), and teaches him to name things (taking dominion). He lets the man sense his need for a different kind of companion. Only then does God make the woman, and the man rejoices over her with all her similarities and differences. Then, before they are sent to tend the world, they are to tend together this special garden God planted. God is walking them through a process of learning, growing, and developing. It's a process with change, responsibility, practice, authority, and relationships.

This is how we get to the tree. God created[2] the world and fashioned it through a process in the first chapter of Genesis, then the second chapter shows him creating and developing[3]

---

2   Genesis 1 uses a few different words for God's act of creation. One, *bera*, seems to signify outright creation. Another verb, *asa*, is used in a number of places. It means "to fashion" and is a word one might use in relation to a craftsman. So the rhythm of Genesis 1 is creating and fashioning. It's possible that these different verbs are just literary differences so the author didn't have to use the same word every time, but on close reading this seems unlikely.

3   St. Augustine believed that God planned to teach the humans the knowledge of good and evil in a particular order, in a certain way, over time.

humans. The man has been working and has taken his place of leadership in creation by naming all the animals. God has created the woman for the man and made a true complimentary union to rule and bless the world. Now has come the time for God to reveal his character to mankind, and he begins with the most basic revelation: You must trust the Trustworthy One. Without trust, truth is either lost

> Now has come the time for God to reveal his character to mankind, and he begins with the most basic revelation: You must trust the Trustworthy One. Without trust, truth is either lost or misused.

or misused. God tells them explicitly that the result of stealing the fruit will be certain death (Genesis 2:17). The humans can either steal the knowledge of good and evil, or trust God to give it in his own time and in his own way. This is where the serpent comes in. Humanity's first parents chose to steal that knowledge, and knowledge without trust has been poisoning us ever since.

Adam and Eve were already doing science. Adam was learning and recognizing all the plants and animals and coming to understand the world of God's creation. As soon as they created the first family, they were doing sociology. But when it came to spiritual and moral knowledge, God demanded that they trust him to supply it. Though the basic moral truths of the world are burned into our consciences, human beings can never be fully formed in righteousness and holiness without this trust, no matter how much knowledge we acquire. As a result, we now exist in a state in which we cannot see the beauty of God's moral and spiritual truths, yet we're haunted in our conscience by the guilt of those truths we can't *not* know. When it comes to the knowledge of good and evil, it turns out we can't acquire or invent it by ourselves, and we were never meant to. This knowledge comes only through trusting God and knowing him down to our bones by believing his revelation.

THE MIND OF CHRIST

In 1 Corinthians 2, the apostle Paul says something about Christians that can be kind of confusing, but is really quite direct: "we have the mind of Christ" (2:16b). What does that really mean, and why is it so important? He is contrasting the gospel with what he calls "eloquence or human wisdom" (2:1). That is, he is contrasting the mind of Christ with "the wisdom of this age or of the rulers of this age, who are coming to nothing" (2:6). He starts the passage with a very simple argument: Did any of them recognize Jesus as the rightful ruler and as God's wisdom? No. None of them did. Not the religious leaders, not the professional academics, not the political leaders. They all participated in crucifying him.

Jesus' work—in the cross and resurrection—is what Paul is talking about in the famous verse, "'What no eye has seen, what no ear has heard, and what no human mind has conceived'—the things God has prepared for those who love him" (2:9, referencing Isaiah 64:4). The thing God has prepared for those who love him is the eternal Son who became the man Jesus; the One who was killed on a cross and buried, but who rose to life and ascended. There is a reason they didn't recognize him: blinding people to truth is God's response to their unwillingness to know him through trusting his revelation. Paul says a few verses earlier, "For since in the wisdom of God the world through its wisdom did not know him, God was pleased through the foolishness of what was preached to save those who believe" (1:21). This is God's wise way of dealing with foolish people who think they can be wise on their own, which is all of us.

He built certain basic moral truths into our consciences, so there are things we can't *not* know. That way, we can never plead ignorance. Conscience is enough for us to know that we are guilty, and enough for us to know many things that we should do rightly. Scripture even says all humanity knows enough to know that there is a Creator to whom we should be thankful (Romans 1:18-20). However, even when humanity puts together all its mental and moral resources, it still doesn't believe and trust God. Without that trust, it cannot recognize what the only wise God does. Consequently, it cannot recognize Christ who is the wisdom of God (1 Corinthians 1:24).

Just as the worldly thinkers and rulers didn't anticipate or recognize *Jesus* as king when he displayed and spoke real wisdom, so now the world does not see or recognize the *gospel* as the ultimate revelation of the wisdom of God. Christ is the embodiment of that wisdom (literally), and believing in him and in the gospel is what Paul calls "wisdom among the mature" (1 Corinthians 2:6). Therefore, in order to know the wisdom of God, we have to recognize Jesus and the gospel as the power and wisdom of God. Jesus is what "God has prepared for those who love him" (2:9). Or to summarize as he does in the final verse of the chapter, we need to "have the mind of Christ" (2:16b). It is the only way we can experience God re-creating and redeeming us into Christ's righteousness and holiness, which is what God intended for us from the start (Ephesians 4:21-24). It is the only way we can receive the knowledge of good and evil into our character by trusting him.

A SPIRIT WITHIN US

So, why can't the worldly really *know* God's wisdom on the level of spiritual substance? Why can't we really *know* these truths (the knowledge of good and evil) by ourselves? We get two answers in 1 Corinthians 1-2. First, there is a morality to knowing. In fact, the Bible argues that the biggest problem with humans failing to know the truth is not that we *can't* find it, but that we *don't want* to find it. This is one of the most profound hypocrisies of the entire human race.[4] We say we are seeking the truth, yet we never obey the truth we already have, and we ingeniously avoid the truths we don't want to find. How can we be honestly seeking the truth when we don't even trust the truths we can't avoid? Psalm 19

> **How can we be honestly seeking the truth when we don't even trust the truths we can't avoid?**

says that all of the heavens declare the glory of God. The Bible argues that if we don't know that God exists, it's not because he is profoundly hidden. It's because *we don't want to know* that

HOW WE KNOW

Worldliness assumes that human knowing moves from epistemology (figuring out what you know) ▶ ontology/metaphysics (what is there) ▶ morality (what is good and evil). The Bible and the gospel teach that this is naive. That's why the Bible talks of our sinful depravity and our unwillingness to know God. Knowing God is actually first a moral problem: Moral unwillingness to know ▶ the epistemological problem of not knowing what can be known ▶ ontological/metaphysical confusion (not believing in what is there) ▶ moral confusion (not having the direction of true metaphysics to show us the way morally).

God exists. *We don't want to know* that he deserves our thanks. *We don't want to know* that we are created in his image and are therefore responsible to live in accordance with the spiritual and moral beauty of that image. And *we don't want to know* that if we reject these truths, we can and must be held dramatically accountable for refusing them, because we bear his divine im-

---

4   This is equally true of both religious and irreligious people. For religious people, we avoid the truth by embracing nominalism (believing in the faith in name only, as if claiming membership means everything) or moralism/legalism (as if following rules means everything). Irreligion has the same phenomenon. Instead of nominalism, the irreligious use the "wisdom of the world" to accomplish the same 2 options: salvation through freedom of expression or successful performance. The justification is in different terms—but both phenomena obscure what humans must come to know in Christ to receive their creation dignity as agents of good and evil, the trait that makes them perhaps most like God.

age. We can't consciously find and love a truth that we are also semi-consciously avoiding so intensely.

Most importantly, though, we can't have spiritual substance without the mind of Christ, because the mind of Christ isn't a *philosophy;* it's a divine *mentality.* It isn't like knowing God's attributes or tendencies; it includes an understanding of God's purposes and his will. Knowing God is knowing a personal being who chooses and acts. It's one thing to understand human biology. It's another thing to be able to tell what another person is thinking or to recognize his handiwork. Similarly, it's one thing to philosophize something about God's being, and another to think you know what he's thinking, what he likes, and why he does what he does.

To know what someone is thinking, feeling, or planning, you have to be inside his or her head. But how could you possibly get inside God's head? Paul's answer: God's Spirit is in his head, and he reveals the mind of Christ to us:

> …these are the things God has revealed to us by his Spirit. The Spirit searches all things, even the deep things of God. For who knows a person's thoughts except their own spirit within them? In the same way, no one knows the thoughts of God except the Spirit of God. What we have received is not the spirit of the world, but the Spirit who is from God, so that we may understand what God has freely given us.
>
> **1 Corinthians 2:10-12**

This is the point: God has revealed himself. That revelation is the only way to know the mind of God. It is the only way to know good and evil, how they function in the world, and how God is acting to bring redemption to us and to all of creation. He has *already* spoken in his written word. He has *already* displayed his mind in the life, death, and resurrection of Jesus. And by his Spirit, he has overcome our denial of their true meaning. All of these things—written revelation, the history of salvation among the Jews, the coming and work of Christ, and the present spiritual revelation of God's Spirit to ours—are God's free gifts to a humanity that wants to do it themselves but can't.

THE SPIRITUAL MIND
AND THE MIND OF CHRIST

Paul ends 1 Corinthians 2 like this:

> The person with the Spirit makes judgments about all things, but such a person is not subject to merely human judgments, for, "Who has known the mind of the Lord so as to instruct him?"[5] But we have the mind of Christ.

1 Corinthians 2:15-16

For those who have received the Spirit's revelation of God's wisdom in Christ, everything has changed. We can know what to do ("[make] judgments") in any situation. But since our judgments are based in a knowledge the world can't know without the Spirit revealing Christ, they are not subject to the world's approval ("not subject to merely human judgments"). They will consider our actions foolish and often wicked, but they are not in charge of judging us anymore.[6]

The second part of this verse is built on a double meaning of the word "mind." Have you ever heard someone say, "I have a mind to..."? The word "mind" can refer to someone's will, or to everything they know, or simply to their ability to be conscious. The prophet Isaiah was right: no one can possibly

---

5   See Isaiah 64:4.

6   Paul does not mean that if we are Christians, we don't have to listen to anyone. Only one page later in chapter 5, Paul will instruct the church that they must judge those within the Church on the basis of the mind of Christ. The particular example is a man involved in sexual immorality. The apostle's point is that those who have the mind of Christ must judge to some extent the actions of those who claim to be spiritual men and women. But they are not to judge those who do not claim to have the mind of Christ, those outside the Church, in the same way.

know the whole mind of the Lord and therefore be able to correct and instruct God. Neither a spiritual man nor a worldly one can do that. But we can know, by the Spirit, what God *has a mind* to do, what his character is like, and what the gospel of Christ really means. That is, we can understand good and evil in a way that changes us and enables us to apply it as wise and righteous stewards of God's world. Christ "has become for us wisdom from God—that is, our righteousness, holiness and redemption" (1 Corinthians 1:30). Through revealing this Christ to us, the Spirit re-creates us to "be like God in true righteousness and holiness" (Ephesians 4:24b). We can know his wisdom. We can have the mind of Christ. We can find the true knowledge that forms the spiritual substance for which we were created and redeemed.

A SPIRITUAL FLOP

Do you know what comes right after this deep theological explanation in 1 Corinthians 1-2?

> Brothers and sisters, I could not address you as people who live by the Spirit but as people who are still worldly—mere infants in Christ. I gave you milk, not solid food, for you were not yet ready for it. Indeed, you are still not ready. You are still worldly. For since there is jealousy and quarreling among you, are you not worldly? Are you not acting like mere humans?
>
> **1 Corinthians 3:1-3**

That doesn't sound good. These are folks who have received Christ's Spirit, but they aren't really looking all that spiritual. What they look like is worldly. There is terrible and bitter arguing. There is leader favoritism. There is sexual immorality. People are suing each other. Leaders are too tolerant to confront open sin. People are getting trashed at church dinners, and the middle class and wealthy are doing things that humiliate the poor. Some Christians are eating feasts venerating pagan gods at the pagan temples. They're misusing the spiritual gifts, using them to show off rather than to love and strengthen people. Some people are forbidding marriage, and men are going to prostitutes like they always have. Others think they shouldn't give financially to support world missions.[7] This spiritual church is incredibly worldly.

> It turns out *having Christ in mind* isn't the same thing as *having the mind of Christ.*

So how is this possible if they have the mind of Christ and the Spirit? These people believed in Jesus. They loved Paul and had a church. What gives? It turns out *having Christ in mind* isn't the same thing as *having the mind of Christ.* We can change our minds about Christ in an instant, but it takes time for Christ to transform our minds to think like his. That process was God's intention in creation. So how does this happen? How can we grow in substance by being transformed in the mind of Christ?

A TRANSFORMATION OF THE MIND

By far, the most well-known Bible verses on this subject are Romans 12:1-2:

> Therefore, I urge you, brothers and sisters, in view of God's mercy, to offer your bodies as a living sacrifice, holy and pleasing to God—this is your true and proper worship. Do not conform to the pattern of this world, but be transformed by the renewing of your mind. Then you will be able to test and approve what God's will is—his good, pleasing and perfect will.
>
> **Romans 12:1-2**

The process of transformation starts with worship. When we trust in God's good and truthful mercy, we will offer our whole selves to him. That is worship. We want to offer our bodies as

---

7   These issues are all covered in detail in 1 Corinthians 1-14.

living sacrifices to please him. But sacrifices in the Old Testament were for specific things and had to be offered in carefully prescribed ways. They had to be offered according to his instruction, in line with his will, and on the basis of his commands. He

The process of transformation starts with worship.

was teaching the people what he was like, about his holiness, and therefore what pleased him. So if we are to offer our bodies as living sacrifices, how do we do it in a way that we know is truthfully and trustfully spiritual? How do we learn what is holy and therefore pleasing to God? What is our target? At what are we aiming?

These verses say holy worship aims at two things:

1. Stop conforming to the world.
2. Renew our minds to understand God's will.

First, we need to stop allowing ourselves to be conformed to the culture of the world. It has a predictable pattern in all its ways and institutions, a system of conformity. We need to understand that pattern and see how it opposes Christ while capturing us. We need to rebel firmly against it in the right kind of disciplined way. We have to be liberated from its hold, and we have to do this actively.

Second, we also need to have our minds renewed, so that we can test, know, and personally approve of God's will. We can't just believe in God. We have to learn to appreciate deeply the goodness of his mind, the beauty of his plan, and the nobility of all his work. We need to feel a deep and devoted approval toward God's will. We need not only to see it, but to love it.

Practicing the mind of Christ

How do we get there? Do we just try to open ourselves to the Spirit and worship God? Yes. Should we just try to please God? Right, except without the word "just." Worship helps us actively trust God with our minds—the first lesson of human formation in the knowledge of good and evil. Obedience forces us to face whether we really believe what we say we do. Obedience is also a process of discovery. Some things make more sense when we do them and taste their fruit through many years (John 7:17).[8] Yet, this is not the main work God has given to us concerning the transformation of our minds.

The mind of Christ develops when we think on Christ and the message of the gospel. This is the focus of the rest of 1 Corinthians. Paul takes all of the worldly dysfunctions of that church and shows us how to rethink them in relation to Christ and the gospel.[9] Similarly, the famous passage from Romans

---

8   The example I always give for this truth is that my wife and I struggled mightily to be chaste in our three and a half years of dating. During that experience, it seemed like an unnecessary trial in some ways. We knew the health and pregnancy reasons that supported God's commands, but we didn't see nearly all of the reasons this was so important. We didn't see that married life didn't allow for many intimate escapades, and that life together could not be built on sex. We also didn't realize that chasteness in our dating era became the basis for our confidence in each other for these last twenty years. For if we could restrain ourselves in the throes of youthful passion for the one we would choose to make our lifelong love, then we could trust each other to be faithful in the temptations of marriage. My wife has said that if we had not forged this trust in those days, my travel and ministry in very large groups of people would have been a horrible recipe for jealousy and fear. We didn't see that we were giving each other this gift when we were just trying to obey God's sexual commands.

9   For example, 1 Corinthians 6:12-20 refers to men going to prostitutes, and Paul quotes their use of a proverb: "Food for the stomach and the stomach for food." The meaning of the proverb is that the body has sexual organs and desires sex, and so therefore sex is for the body. It's not a moral thing; it's just an appetite thing. Therefore, they reasoned that it was fine for them to go to prostitutes even as Christians, as they no doubt had from their youth. Men going to brothels, even married men, did not have much of a stigma then, if any. Paul argues on the basis of our union with Christ, "Do you not know that your bodies are members of Christ himself? Shall I then take the members of Christ and unite them with a prostitute? Never!" Within this argument, Paul references the teaching in Genesis that in sexual intercourse, two people become "one flesh." Therefore, if there is an intimate mystical union between Christ and our body, and if sex produces an intimate mystical union between two people who have sex, can it possibly

12:1-2 comes after twelve chapters about Jesus and what his work as the Christ means in the universe and for us. In a different letter, Paul says it this way:

> Since, then, you have been raised with Christ, set your hearts on things above, where Christ is, seated at the right hand of God. Set your minds on things above, not on earthly things. For you died, and your life is now hidden with Christ in God.
>
> **Colossians 3:1-3**

In shooting, to hit anything you have to be oriented to a very specific target. To aim your character at something is to "set your [heart]" on it. It's to aim your mind, will, and strength at a specific goal. Here, Paul is explaining *how to get* the mind of Christ. You have to actively and consistently "set your [heart]" and "set your [mind]" on Christ and the things with him that are your life, while being dead to worldliness. This is the target, the prize, the summit, the goal—the focus of all our spiritual

---

be reasonable for someone who belongs to Christ to create that union with a practicing prostitute? The point is that by thinking through Christ and what we have in him through the gospel, many things in life must be judged very differently than the world judges them. The example of sexuality is just one among many. To have the mind of Christ, this logic must be primary in all our judgments.

attention. In another letter, while he is talking about humility, love, compassion, and the virtues of spiritual substance, he says:

> Therefore if you have any encouragement from being united with Christ, if any comfort from his love, if any common sharing in the Spirit, if any tenderness and compassion, then make my joy complete by being like-minded, having the same love, being one in spirit and of one mind. Do nothing out of selfish ambition or vain conceit. Rather, in humility value others above yourselves, not looking to your own interests but each of you to the interests of the others. In your relationships with one another, have the same mindset as Christ Jesus...
>
> **Philippians 2:1-5**

Paul starts and ends the verses with Christ, his character, and the effects and meaning of his salvation. He talks about our spiritual union with Christ, then talks about Jesus' attitude at the end. The verses that follow are all about considering Jesus' example—how he made himself nothing, obeyed the Father, emptied himself of his rights, suffered on the cross, and created reconciliation for everyone—and that this humility and service is why God the Father exalted him to the highest place (Philippians 2:7-9).

Do you see that? How should we think about unity, love, reconciliation, ambition, and humility? We do it by setting our minds and hearts on what it means to be united with Christ and his Spirit and on the humility of Jesus in his life and death—on the rightness, nobility, and beauty of these things. We see and believe that this is why the God of true righteousness and holiness exalts anyone and why Jesus himself did this work with joy.

We can't do it by ourselves. The mind of Christ can only come by God's generosity—by grace.[10] Only the Spirit of God

---

10 Grace is unearned generosity. Whenever we are given something we don't deserve, that is grace.

knows the mind of God and is able to make it known to us in Christ. We are invited to a work that God will not allow to fail. He will not just support *your* purpose in it. Don't forget, this was always *his* purpose. He has desired to teach us real wisdom since creation. He always wanted to give us knowledge of good and evil. Embracing the practice of setting our minds and hearts on Christ is the means he has appointed to show us. This is how we offer our hearts, minds, and bodies to him as spiritual sacrifices (Romans 12:1). All we need in order to have the mind of Christ is present in Jesus. He shows us the meaning of all of creation, all the knowledge of good and evil. It is all there, everything we need to be like God in true righteousness and holiness. Or to say it another way:

> My goal is that they may be encouraged in heart and united in love, so that they may have the full riches of complete understanding, in order that they may know the mystery of God, namely, Christ, in whom are hidden all the treasures of wisdom and knowledge. I tell you this so that no one may deceive you by fine-sounding arguments.
>
> **Colossians 2:2-4**

He is not saying that all real knowledge is religious knowledge. He is saying that seeing Christ allows us to see everything else as it is—to have the "full riches of complete understanding."

God wants us to see all that is in creation through the mind of the redeeming Creator King. He wants the wealth of our wisdom to be "full" and "complete." This canopy of wisdom is not just a shelter that preserves our lives,[11] or a force that makes us loving toward our neighbor. It is also the true and dazzling fresco of the universe, a satisfying taste of the true glory of God.

---

11   See Ecclesiastes 7:12.

SUGGESTED BIBLE MEMORIZATION

Therefore, I urge you, brothers and sisters, in view of God's mercy, to offer your bodies as a living sacrifice, holy and pleasing to God—this is your true and proper worship. Do not conform to the pattern of this world, but be transformed by the renewing of your mind. Then you will be able to test and approve what God's will is—his good, pleasing and perfect will.

Romans 12:1-2

The person without the Spirit does not accept the things that come from the Spirit of God but considers them foolishness, and cannot understand them because they are discerned only through the Spirit.

1 Corinthians 2:14

REFLECT AND RESPOND

1. How would you define the mind of Christ in your own words?

2. What are a couple things you tell God you want to do yourself that you shouldn't? What are some things you should do for yourself that you are expecting God to do for you?

3. What are some ways your mind might be conformed to the "pattern of this world"? Which of them are you most afraid to admit (things that will lead to rejection, isolation, disapproval, or persecution)?

4. How does one get the mind of Christ? What do you need to do starting now to get there?

5. What structures or accountability do you need to succeed where you have failed before in seeking the mind of Christ more fully?

5

VIRTUOUS FREEDOM 1: FREEDOM FROM

Tell me, you who want to be under the law, are you not aware of what the law says? For it is written that Abraham had two sons, one by the slave woman and the other by the free woman. His son by the slave woman was born according to the flesh, but his son by the free woman was born as the result of a divine promise. These things are being taken figuratively: The women represent two covenants. One covenant is from Mount Sinai and bears children who are to be slaves: This is Hagar. Now Hagar stands for Mount Sinai in Arabia and corresponds to the present city of Jerusalem, because she is in slavery with her children. But the Jerusalem that is above is free, and she is our mother.

Galatians 4:21-26

By a misfortune attached to the human condition, great men who are moderate are rare; and, as it is always easier to follow one's strength than to check it... It is a thousand times easier to do good than to do it well.

Montesquieu[1]

---

1   Charles de Secondat, baron de Montesquieu, *Montesquieu: The Spirit of the Laws*, ed. Anne M. Cohler, Basia C. Miller, Harold Stone (Cambridge: Cambridge University Press, 1989), 595.

It is a great mercy to be enabled to yield to his will; for every thing,
and every heart must either bend or break before it.

John Newton[2]

FREEDOM'S FORGOTTEN NATURE

Ask ten people if they like freedom, and you'll get nine or more thumbs up. Ask them what it is, and you'll likely get ten different answers. Freedom is one of our most well-loved and poorly-defined ideas. Milton Friedman, the famous economist, continuously reminded Americans of his day that the typical state of humanity has not been the relative freedom of American life. The typical human experience has been tyranny, servitude, corruption, and misery, both historically and globally.[3]

> **The typical human experience has been tyranny, servitude, corruption, and misery, both historically and globally.**

Today, we usually define freedom in one of two ways:

1. Freedom *to*: The absence of external restraints (no physical, moral, legal, or ideological limitations)
2. Freedom *from*: The possession of sufficient resources to live as one pleases (no poverty, poor health, lack of education, etc.)

These popular understandings are partly right and completely misleading. Older generations (older as in the 1700s and before)—ones that paid more attention to the Bible—saw it

---

2   John Newton, *The Works of the Rev. John Newton*, vol. 4 (New Haven: Nathan Whiting, 1894), 200.

3   "Because we live in a largely free society, we tend to forget how limited is the span of time and the part of the globe for which there has ever been anything like political freedom: the typical state of mankind is tyranny, servitude, and misery." Milton Friedman, *Capitalism and Freedom* (Chicago: University of Chicago, 2002), 9.

differently: Freedom is the ability[4] to do good. True freedom includes freedom *to* and *from*, but it is primarily freedom *for*. This is true of both spiritual and civil freedom.

They saw that civil freedom must be built on something deeper, because our slavery is rooted in something deeper. Edmund Burke,[5] an Irish Christian statesman of the 18th century, expressed it this way:

> Men are qualified for civil liberty, in exact proportion to their disposition to put moral chains upon their own appetites; … in proportion as they are more disposed to listen to the counsels of the wise and good, in preference to the flattery of knaves. Society cannot exist unless a controlling power upon will and appetite be placed somewhere, and the less of it there is within, the more there must be without. It is ordained in the eternal constitution of things, that men of intemperate minds cannot be free. Their passions forge their fetters.[6]

Burke is restating the Christian belief that without virtue we

---

4   "Ability" here refers both to freedom from anyone stopping you, and having the internal resources of character to have the will and the strength to carry it out. This may sound like a combination of both definitions, but it isn't. It requires a kind of character and moral purpose that neither definition requires. Its focus is on something completely different. What it requires we be free to and from is different than what definitions 1 and 2 call for.

5   Burke (1729-1797 AD) is considered one of the founders of institutional conservatism: the belief that all institutions and franchises of civil society (everything between the individual and the State) are full of accumulated wisdom and should be the primary institutions of society, mainly the family and the church. He said this about religion in public life: "Religion is so far, in my opinion, from being out of the province of the duty of a christian [sic] magistrate, that it is, and it ought to be, not only his care, but the principal thing in his care; because it is one of the great bonds of human society; and its object the supreme good, the ultimate end and object of man himself" (Edmund Burke, "Speech On a Motion for Leave to Bring in a Bill to Repeal and Alter Certain Acts Respecting Religious Opinions, 1792," *The Works and Correspondence of the Right Honourable Edmund Burke*, vol. 6 (London: Gilbert and Rivington, 1852), 102.

6   Edmund Burke, "A Letter, to a Member of the National Assembly in Answer to Some Objections to His Book on French Affairs, 1791," *The Works of Edmund Burke*, vol. 2 (London: George Bell and Sons, 1901), 555.

cannot be free. Rights[7] are not sustainable in a society without virtue. Virtue is the ability to restrain our appetites and obey the good, the true, and the wise. Without virtue, we will have no internal power to manage our compulsions and will therefore be enslaved to our own passions. This results in people who use their rights to harm rather than bless their neighbor.

Consequently, if we cannot govern ourselves, we require governance from others—parents, laws and regulations, law enforcement, supervisors, licensing boards, presidents, bureaucracies, etc.[8] Freedom isn't just an issue of rights.[9] It's also an issue of trust. Leaving our neighbor to their rights means we trust them not to use their freedoms to do us harm. Without that trust, our fear will tempt us to attack their freedom to protect our own. Therefore, only widespread virtue can sustain the trust necessary for freedom.[10]

Those who live by their appetites are a danger and trial not

---

7   Rights are something we have in our being that must be recognized by others. They are gifts of God tied to what we are. Virtue is something that must be forged in our character. We are capable of being virtuous, but the degree to which we are is in a different state from person to person. Men without virtue will not only refuse to recognize the rights of others through power, but they will also not trust others with their rights through fear—believing unvirtuous men will do them harm with their freedom.

8   This is the basis for the right authority of parents. Children are not able to govern themselves. To the extent to which they cannot, parents are a gracious gift of God, and they must embrace their responsibility to govern their children while empowering them to govern themselves.

9   Rights and virtue are both necessary for freedom. Recognizing rights comes from the recognition of what we are as made in God's image. Virtue is being what we are and what we are meant to be. There is something perverse and unworkable about demanding we be recognized by others for what we are (rights), if we are not also intent on conforming our character and habits to what we are (virtue). This is the truth behind the saying "rights bear responsibilities."

10   For this reason, Christians should be very distrustful of political movements that may have the intentional or unintentional effect of diminishing people's virtue, even to achieve a desirable end. This is one reason many Christians have favored politics organized around personal responsibility or have sought to make charitable programs more focused on work and accountability. It is also why the Bible seems to have a high view of civil authority, from which we get the Western notion of the "rule of law." This does not mean that civil government cannot have some role in helping the weak, but it must take great care not to erode the virtue of its people in the process.

only to themselves but to everyone. The only way to control a person governed by *compulsions* is through *coercion*—some kind of external incentive or threat that demands cooperation. Coercion, of course—whether by good laws or bad tyrants—isn't a real solution. Sinful humans

> "Almost all men can stand adversity, but if you want to test a man, give him power" - Abraham Lincoln

are as bad at governing others as we are at governing ourselves, and when the power to coerce others is laid in our hands, it leads all too reliably to corruption. Notice the progression: compulsion leads to coercion—which leads to corruption.[11]

Most people have heard Lord Acton's famous quote, "Power tends to corrupt, and absolute power corrupts absolutely." Abraham Lincoln claimed power was an even greater trial to character than all forms of hardship. He said, "Almost all men can stand adversity, but if you want to test a man, give him power." Coercing others tends very rapidly toward the slavery of tyranny.[12] Only supreme virtue has a chance at using power justly, so power and coercion can never solve the problem of a lack of virtue.[13] This is why the American founders took such care to divide up power in government. They did not hope in governance to protect our freedom.[14] They knew that wide-

---

11　And corruption leads to the compulsion to use coercion to fix the corruption, which leads to more corruption, which leads to more coercion and more corruption. This is why anarchy always leads to tyranny. It is also why a decline in public virtue also leads to tyranny and hatred.

12　The first slavery is the internal tyranny of the Flesh. The second, which necessarily follows, is the external tyranny and slavery of coercion. It might be the right coercion of law, the broken coercion of human tyranny, or the transactional and evil tyranny of our idols, but they all demand a price in order to receive our gratification.

13　For even if there was one person of great virtue in a declining society, the unvirtuous culture would never intentionally appoint the person of virtue to power. Unvirtuous people never select virtuous leaders. They don't know what to look for and are easily deceived by scoundrels; virtuous behavior seems foreign to them and, therefore, suspect. They will elect the corrupt or the tyrannical, or they will revolt to install him.

14　See chapter 5 of Joshua Charles' *Liberty's Secrets* (Washington, DC: WND, 2015).

spread personal virtue is the only possible basis for civil freedom. In fact, virtue is the only basis on which *any* relationship can proceed with freedom, because it is the only sound basis for trust. It is the foundation of love.

This principle of American civil government was developed from the Bible. This is because the basis of *civil* freedom is the same as the basis for *all* freedom—whether social, spiritual, or moral. All free relationships must have what Lord Moulton called "obedience to the unenforceables"[15] and what Alexis de Tocqueville called "habits of the heart."[16] Virtue must be upheld and developed by an internal impulse causing us to love the good. Reflecting on the work of the founding fathers, Os Guiness includes a third element to accompany freedom and virtue. He describes these three as the "golden triangle of freedom."[17] Without this third element, we are still vulnerable to slavery and tyranny. With it, freedom and virtue can grow—and grow together. This third, necessary component is faith. So how does it work?

THE GOLDEN TRIANGLE OF FREEDOM

God has lovingly shaped the world so that divorcing freedom from virtue cannot produce happiness, gratitude, hope, or justice. Seeking freedom as liberation from moral restraints requires rejecting virtue. This always leads to anarchy,[18] and

---

15 Lord Moulton, "Law and Manners," *The Atlantic Monthly* (July 1924), Iowa State University, http://www2.econ.iastate.edu/classes/econ362/hallam/NewspaperArticles/LawAndManners.pdf (accessed 28 May 2017).

16 Alexis de Tocqueville, *Democracy in America and Two Essays on America*, ed. Isaac Kramnick (London: Penguin, 2003), 336.

17 Os Guiness, *A Free People's Suicide: Sustainable Freedom and the American Future* (Downer's Grove, IL: IVP, 2012), 99.

18 The political and social category of anarchy (meaning "no arche" or "no rule or ruler") has a spiritual and moral equivalent in antinomianism (meaning "against law," that is, lawlessness). Antinomianism claims that there is no such thing as moral or spiritual law; any restraint that contradicts our romantic and emotional impulses is artificial and imposes internal slavery. In relation to Christian substance, the most common form of antinomianism in the American Church is the belief that if salvation is by sheer grace,

anarchy always leads to tyranny and slavery.[19] Liberty, which is the presence of freedom, cannot last without virtue. Conversely, the full practice of virtue requires liberty, because doing something praiseworthy requires that you have the option to do evil or leave the good undone. Liberty and virtue depend on each other.

Yet while these two *depend* on each other, they are powerless to *create* each other. That's why a third thing is needed: faith. Think about it: Freedom is a status, not a direction. Freedom needs something to stabilize and direct it, or it can just as easily be used for evil as for good.

> Virtue has to be forged. But by what? Only faith in something else can forge true virtue.

That stabilizing thing is virtue, which the Bible refers to in various places as godliness, holiness, and righteousness.[20] But where do we get virtue? It's certainly not automatic in humans. Humanity's normal state is more vicious than virtuous. Virtue has to be *forged*. But by what? Only faith in something else can forge true virtue. The American founders applied these biblical principles to the nation, recognizing the following:

---

then living a holy life isn't necessary, since God will forgive all of our sins, even if we continue to sin presumptuously. This chapter attempts to show part of why that is false.

19 The American founders expressed this with axioms like "the fruit of anarchy is tyranny." As Thomas Hobbes argues in the famous work *Leviathan*, humans are governed greatly by fear. So whenever people live without restraint (either internal or external), which is anarchy, people grow afraid and distrusting of each other. This leads them to look for someone who will protect them. They want a king (see 1 Samuel 8). This protector is given all power and authority to protect, and then promptly uses that power and authority to be a tyrant. Anarchy always leads to tyranny, because humans are happy to have someone else be strong and take risks for them.

20 Technically, all of these words emphasize something a little different. Holiness means the good that bears the marks of otherness (from worldliness), purity, and goodness. Righteousness emphasizes true rightness and justice using moral and legal categories. Godliness emphasizes likeness to God and his character. Virtue emphasizes an internal state of character that is stable and reliable. They all refer to the same thing but emphasize a different aspect of it.

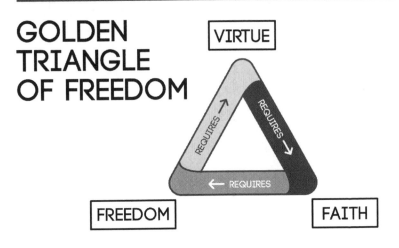

GOLDEN TRIANGLE OF FREEDOM

VIRTUE · FREEDOM · FAITH · REQUIRES

1. Faith (religion) is necessary to create virtue.[21] For virtue to exist, faith is required.
2. Virtue directs and sustains freedom.[22] For freedom to be supported, virtue is required.
3. Freedom is the best environment for sincere faith and healthy religion. For faith to thrive, freedom is required.

The third relationship may not be obvious. Faith, especially Christian faith, thrives in freedom but becomes corrupt when

---

21   Thomas Jefferson said he could never be an atheist. John Adams said to a friend in a letter, "I have never heard of an irreligious character in Greek or Roman history, nor in any other history, nor have I known one in life who was not a rascal. Name one if you can, living or dead." Adams saw science and religion as not only "mutually compatible, but mutually necessary." He called "science, liberty, and religion" the "choicest lessons of humanity" and stressed their "inseparable union." Joshua Charles, *Liberty's Secrets* (Washington, DC: WND, 2015), 83.

22   The American founders believed this because only self-governed people can live in peace without a tyrannical government protecting them from each other. Freedom without virtue quickly descends into the chaos of anarchy. Anarchy never lasts very long, though, because the competing compulsions of people eventually force slavery on others. It is the very nature of anarchy to invite the rise of a superman or tyrant who coerces those who are vulnerable to their mastery, because their compulsions send them hunting for a master who promises satisfaction. Unvirtuous freedom, though liberating for a moment, always leads to a deeper and more complete tyranny, whether in our character or our government.

it is forced or is captured by a culture or state.[23] Religious faith is most sincere and free from corruption wherever it is wholly voluntary and not associated with any governmental power or cultural pressure.[24] This environment leaves only the right elements—truth, beauty, and goodness—as motivations to believe and follow it. It is only with these motivations in place that faith can have the greatest effect on promoting virtue in people and, consequently, maintaining the integrity of our liberty. These three—faith, virtue, and freedom—all require and strengthen each other. Yet it begs a question: faith *in what?*[25] Does the object of the faith matter?

Of course it does. Trusting in sin or idols doesn't forge virtue; it empowers vice. There is a faith that not only saves, but

---

23 This was true in the Constantinian period when the Roman Empire "became Christian." This was one of the worst times of corruption flooding into the Church. State approval meant money and prestige was to be gained in the Church. By the 5th century, urban churches were seeking monks like Gregory of Nazianzus and John Chrysostom to become bishops, because their other candidates were so obviously corrupt. I think this also is becoming evident in people's faith in modern secularism and progressivism. The more power a group of any kind has, the more the truth they claim to believe in tends to suffer. The ideas get co-opted for various ends; both ideas and people tend to become corrupted by power. The same effect plagues any belief embraced with faith or full allegiance of the heart, regardless of whether the belief is true or not.

24 This is one major difference between faith in America and Europe. Both are industrialized and secularized societies, but religion has remained strong in America, while it is disappearing in Europe. The most obvious difference is not that Europe is more secular than America, but that Europe has had state churches, and its religion has not been free for hundreds of years. This led to its corruption and insincerity, its indulgence in the temptation to power, and its ultimate decay. The growing churches in Europe and America are free churches (not connected to the government). You can also see this principle in the growth of the church in China, India, and many other places where churches have thrived even while persecuted.

25 The American founders didn't specify the object of faith or the particulars of the religion. They thought many different beliefs could support virtue, but they mainly had in mind different forms of Christianity. Minimally, they pictured belief in a God to whom we were morally accountable, "for it kept [mankind] morally anchored, never able to escape ultimate justice. It was for this reason that the Founders considered belief in God as the cornerstone of all morality." Without grounding belief in a God of morality and ultimate judgment, "as [John] Adams noted, 'human reason and human conscience... are not a match for human passions, human imaginations, and human enthusiasm'" (Charles, *Liberty's Secrets*, 84-85).

also liberates, both socially and spiritually. It is the good news about Christ. In the previous chapter, we referred more broadly to this faith as having the mind of Christ. To understand how this faith in the gospel uniquely saves and liberates us, we need to understand more of what the Bible tells us about our spiritual slavery.

UNDERSTANDING OUR SLAVERY

In biblical terms, our most basic slavery is that we live dominated by the cravings of the Flesh. Ephesians 2:3 says, "All of us also lived among them at one time [sinful and demonically deceived], *gratifying the cravings of our flesh and following its desires and thoughts*. Like the rest, we were by nature deserving of [God's] wrath." In our typical state, we not only *gratify* the Flesh, but we are *guided* by what it wants. That is, the Flesh dominates our thoughts and feelings, while we gratify its cravings almost compulsively. This enslaves us by controlling us from within, even while we think we're free. Peter said it this way: "[The false teachers] promise them freedom, while they themselves are slaves of depravity—for 'people are slaves to whatever has mastered them'" (2 Peter 2:19).[26]

> **Whatever masters you is your master. If we don't master our cravings and compulsions, they will master us.**

That's the bottom line: Whatever masters you is your master. If we don't master our cravings and compulsions, they will master us. The more we gratify the cravings, thoughts, and desires of our Flesh, the more they tighten their grip on our will and our character—the more they become our master. This is precisely the meaning of Burke's famous line quoted previously. For people dominated by the Flesh, "their passions forge their fetters." Everything that enslaves our character can be

---

26 "Mastered" refers to both internal compulsion and external coercion. See also 1 Corinthians 5.

traced back to obeying the Flesh's appetites and will.

This isn't only true about being mastered by sinful compulsion. Our compulsive passions "forge our fetters"—they make even more layers of chains binding our liberty. Compulsion builds the slavery of habit. It encourages people to control us because they fear our instability. It leads us to the idols of Mammon that gratify our compulsions only if we pay ever-increasing costs that will degrade and impoverish us in every way. In the Bible, God called idolatry a kind of prostitution—selling ourselves for something that degrades and uses us. In every way, those who won't govern themselves will be governed by something else. Their passions form their fetters.

So, if faith is the third part of the Golden Triangle, how does it remedy this slavery?

A question of allegiance

Consequently, before virtue can bear fruit, it must be rooted in faith. Faith is ultimately a question of allegiance. Allegiance is trust in and faithfulness to something or someone. To whom do we belong, if anyone, what are we here for, if anything, and why? In Christian faith, this allegiance is trust and loyalty to God and a vision of reality based on what he has done through Christ in his creation, redemption, and restoration (i.e. having the mind of Christ). The spiritual shorthand for this is allegiance to Christ and his kingdom. Though Jesus is at the center of that vision, our faith must look even further back than Jesus and the cross—further back even than Moses or Abraham[27]—to creation. Jesus completes the "who" of our allegiance, but creation tells us the "what" and the "why."

Creation shows us the supremely important distinction: the difference between the Creator and the created. God is uncreated, perfect, and independent. He is the only being in that category. Therefore, all other beings and objects are created, contingent, subordinate, and dependent.[28] So when God created humans, he made a different kind of thing. He made a created, contingent, subordinate, and dependent creature *in his image*, or *like him*.[29] He put his uncreated, divine likeness into dependent creatures, giving them the authority and responsibility to rule his creation.[30] This is an amazing thing. God gave a created thing the work of creativity; he gave a produced thing the role of producing. He didn't just give us *a* job; he gave us *his* job, a job worthy of God.

> He didn't just give us *a* job; he gave us *his* job, a job worthy of God.

Think about how deeply this reality shapes all of creation. God gives us the entire creation account in the form of a work

---

27 Moses and Abraham represent the first covenant—or the first arrangement—of allegiance and trust God made with people for the redemption of all of creation. This first covenant was fulfilled in Jesus and expanded outward to reach all people and nations, moving from a particular family of people (the Jewish people) to a global Church. For more on this, see Isaiah 49:6.

28 The meaning of these terms is important. For our purposes here, the significance of "created" is that a thing began to exist at some point. "Contingent" means dependent on something else for meaning and existence. A "subordinate" being serves under the rule of a higher authority. The "dependence" I'm addressing here is dependence on something else for identity, purpose, meaning, and significance.

29 See Genesis 1:26-27; 5:1; James 3:9.

30 This bestowal of responsibility can be found in Genesis 1:28 and is referred to as the creation mandate or cultural mandate. See also Psalm 82 and Jesus' teaching on it in John 10:31-39.

week, and then he demands our work week follow his pattern of creation and productivity.[31] Is this a coincidence? No. He is showing us the pattern and dignity of our subordination and dependence on him. He's teaching us how to live in allegiance to him, and therein, how to be like him.

It's popular to insist that being fully alive and realizing our identity means believing we are not subordinate to or dependent on anything else for our meaning or purpose.[32] Not only is that not true, but it's simply not how people behave. People long for meaning, and we find it *in* something. All people live by allegiance. Whether to ideologies, sports teams, children, spouses, vacations, fitness, past pain, ambitions, power, the approval of others, or the cravings of our nervous and digestive systems—everyone's sense of purpose and actual behavior can be explained by a fairly simple set of allegiances. And it turns out that our allegiance and obedience doesn't only affect our actions. In time, we come to resemble the master we obey. All humans have faith in something, and we are all growing in the likeness of our masters.

This is why God did not speak about people mainly in terms of faith and non-faith. He claims we trust either in *him*, the true God, or we trust in other masters, our self-made gods and idols. In ancient times, these referred to specific, named deities, but pagan deities always represented a human desire that we have always had and still have: protection, strength in conflict, fertility, prosperity, good fortune, removal of obsta-

---

31   See Exodus 20 and Deuteronomy 5 for the connection God makes between his work week and ours.

32   It's not always clear what we mean when we use language like this. Are we talking about our *true* meaning or *any* sense of meaning? It's very possible to find a sense of meaning, or what we normally call significance—the feeling that something is meaningful. However, our true meaning is independent of us and doesn't depend on our feelings. It is connected to what we are or aren't in creation. When people say they find meaning in something, they mean they find a sense of significance in it. However, in modern language, the words "meaning" and "significance" are both usually used subjectively to refer to our feelings or sense of meaning.

cles, love and sexual companionship, sense of origin, explaining why the world is like this, making sense of death, handling guilt and shame, and so on. These gods have not really gone away in secular modernity. We have simply traded the old totems of the pagan gods for new totems of modernity. The gods of modernity are just as much idols—the new mutations of Mammon.

We have never stopped looking to things in creation to provide for us, fulfill us, gratify us, empower us, approve of us, or comfort us in our desires, passions, and cravings. We have never stopped and we never will stop looking to something to approve of our pride, to comfort our fears, or to justify our bitterness. Jesus never feared we would serve nothing. He took his time to show and tell us we cannot serve *more than one* thing: "You cannot serve both God and money [Mammon]" (Matthew 6:24). He was warning us that our idols are enslaving, choking, and dominating us, making us work with no rest—unlike the Creator. They are like the Pharaoh of Egypt; always wanting more and giving less. They demand that we make bricks without straw.[33]

---

33 Exodus 5 records the Pharaoh demanding that the Jewish slaves make bricks with-

It is precisely because we don't see ourselves as dependent, contingent, and subordinate image bearers that we are so gullible in our enslavement to the modern forms of idolatry. We are deceived, because we don't see our identity as a question of faith, and faith as a question of allegiance.[34] When we start with creation, we can see that our freedom does not mean independence. It means not giving our allegiance to anything in creation over which God has given us governance. Real freedom is being dependent only on what is *greater* than ourselves; namely, the Independent One.

The great irony, so lost on modern humanity, is that we can only find freedom when we see that we belong to God, and we give him all of our allegiance. This becomes clearer when we think about allegiance in relation to the all-important Creator-creation distinction. Ultimately, we have three options for objects of our allegiance. Our identity, character, and purpose will be radically different based on where our allegiance falls.

3 Objects of allegiance based on the Creator-creation distinction:

OBJECT OF ALLEGIANCE	ALLEGIANCE RESULTS IN
1. Creator (God) ——————→	1. Conviction (truth and right authority)
2. Human power (including ourselves) ——————→	2. Coercion (inflicting or submitting to tyranny)
3. Created things (the pleasure we gain from them) ——————→	3. Compulsion (living for the Flesh)

out providing straw, a necessary ingredient. I recommend that you read the whole chapter in light of this topic. The Jewish people's slavery in Egypt is held up as a holistic type for all people's slavery to our tyrannical false gods. Their demands progressively increase while they give us less and less in return. The striking difference between our slaveries and theirs, however, is that ours are typically self-inflicted.

34 This should begin to clarify why the notion of worship is critical to freedom. Worship distinguishes what is equal to or below us from what is above us, drawing our devotion to the latter, namely, God and his ways. This gives our faith direction. This faith can define and form virtue, and virtue can direct the use of our freedom.

Allegiance to the Creator-God results in right convictions, which guide right human authority in love and justice. This allows us to be productive, creative, and enjoy creation without craving or hating it.

Allegiance to human power leaves us in a state of self-deception about God, misunderstanding of ourselves, and rejection of God's authority. In this state, we lose our identity, provoke God, and consequently tyrannize and are slaves of one another, compelling us to compete ruthlessly to possess the pleasures and power in creation, multiplying hatred and conflict.

Allegiance to the pleasures and comforts of created things causes us to be driven by our compulsion and craving for gratification. As a result, we value people and structures for their ability to give us what we crave, and we therefore consume and defile what God has given us for creativity and productivity.

Only by putting our faith fully in God can we learn what freedom and virtue should look like in this world. If we put our faith in ourselves or other humans, we will wrongly inflict or submit to human tyranny. If we put our faith in creation and the pleasure it brings us, we will be mastered by our Flesh and become slaves to our compulsions. It is only when we put our faith in God and give him our full allegiance that we can live free of *compulsion* and *coercion* while being formed by *convictions* flowing out of his truth and goodness.

> We experience virtuous freedom to the degree that our hearts' allegiance to Christ is pure and undivided.

It should be clear to us that we almost always harbor some mix of these three in our hearts. Even if we want to say our allegiance is to God alone, we can see the effects of compulsion and coercion at work. Can't you? Seen this way, their presence is not evidence that our faith is false, but that worldliness is present, and our allegiances are still divided. We are trying to serve both God and Mammon. Jesus is onto us, and he wants to free us. We experience virtuous freedom to the degree that our hearts' allegiance to Christ is pure and undivided. It is for freedom that Christ has set us free (Galatians 5:1), so virtue and freedom come down to a question of faith.

Idols and the Flesh: The snowballing and the crash

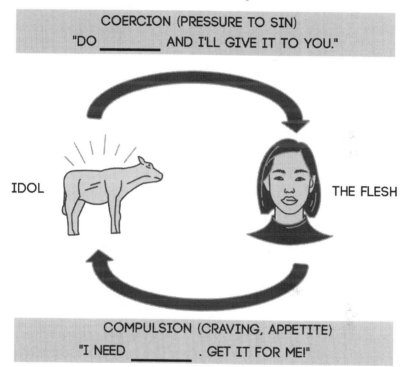

COERCION (PRESSURE TO SIN)
"DO _____ AND I'LL GIVE IT TO YOU."

IDOL

THE FLESH

COMPULSION (CRAVING, APPETITE)
"I NEED _____ . GET IT FOR ME!"

We've talked about how the Flesh makes us slaves to our cravings and compulsions, and idolatry is always the result of misplaced and divided faith. The third thing to understand about our slavery is this: The compulsion of the Flesh and the coercion of our idols feed into each other in a snowballing effect. The more the cycle loops, the more binding it becomes, and the more resilient it becomes against anything that would divert energy or attention from it.

Our Flesh and our idols will always tell us they're acting in our best interest—for our happiness. They aren't. They are working a fixed system against us. They have a scam going. Since the Flesh's cravings can't be gratified by God, it can only turn to idols for gratification. But since idols can only offer the kind of counterfeit and diminishing pleasures that leave us perpetually hungry, they won't point to anything higher than the Flesh. They are the perfect match made in hell.

This is our self-imposed slavery. Our fleshly compulsion drives us toward the idol. The idol coerces us to pay the price of our gratification, but the gratification it offers doesn't lead to gratitude or satisfaction; it leads back to craving. We crave again, and again, and again. Around and around we go, from compulsion to coercion to compulsion to coercion, sometimes satiated, but never satisfied. Often gratified, but never grateful.

> Around and around we go, from compulsion to coercion to compulsion to coercion, sometimes satiated, but never satisfied. Often gratified, but never grateful.

Always doing more and getting less in return. Becoming ever more desperate, proud, fearful, bitter, and self-obsessed. Willing to cross ever more risky boundaries to get the payoff we crave.

Turning to idols for happiness, contentment, humble significance, and joy is like asking your drug dealer to introduce you to your future spouse. He's not in that kind of business. You can tell yourself a drug expands your mind, or a prostitute can tell you she loves you, but the sense of transcendence we find in idols is a deception. All it offers us is a semiconscious fantasy with which we can numb ourselves to the nagging aches of deeper longings. Gratification, like a drug, yields diminishing returns, and the idol's price keeps going up.[35] This is only pos-

---

35 Fleshly gratification actually has diminishing returns for similar reasons as a drug

sible because we believe two lies about our idols:

1. We think we can control them. That's why we chose them over the Creator in the first place. God could ask anything from us, so we think that as long as we pay a fixed fee to our idols, we can have what we want indefinitely without having anything else demanded of us.

2. We think our idols are our ticket to freedom (another way to say "salvation"). We believe they are the only thing that can free us by removing restraints that would hold us back or from a need that might hold us down.

We've been listening to this slander of God for years: He's dangerous. He can't be controlled. He will ask too much of you. He's rigid and controlling. He can't be trusted to liberate you.

In our compulsion for fake liberation, we will do whatever we think we need to do to get whatever we think it is. Worse, since our idols enjoy a monopoly in our minds, they can demand any price from us for the things we crave. (Their fee isn't fixed.) Coercion and compulsion perpetuate each other, trapping us in a never-ending, ever-deepening cycle of slavery.

The result is a loss of our integrity and true identity. We lose our real selves. What tyranny could be greater? We do things that God calls wicked and say, "I had no choice." But that isn't true. *We* gave ourselves to our craving for security. *We* looked to our job, our marriage, or the approval of others for that security. And then *we* felt we had to protect that idol by paying whatever cost it demanded. *We* boxed ourselves into giving the idol a monopoly on providing liberation and sal-

---

does. Bodily pleasures are meant to accompany psychological feelings of joy, meaning, purpose, thankfulness, etc. When these are together, the experience is more pleasureful, and we don't crave it again with the same bodily reflex, because we think of the things as mainly in the emotional experience, not just as a bodily function. This phenomenon is true for sex, entertainment, eating, humor, and many other experiences.

vation. *We* did all this, because *we* decided that God was too risky an option for liberation and salvation. It all comes back to trust—to faith. It's a question of allegiance.

LIBERATION AND SALVATION

We're much more comfortable talking about liberation than salvation today, but they're really the same thing. "Liberation" just sounds more sophisticated. Liberating, whether giving freedom *from* or *to* do something, *is* saving.

We want our idols to liberate us *from* something—usually the limitations of traditional morality—so we are free *to do* as we please. Or we want *freedom from* what limits, hurts, and threatens our happiness, sense of identity, or security (like traditional morality, poverty, or others' power).

When our ideas of *freedom from* and *freedom to* are limited to this, we are saturated in idolatry, and we are looking to our most ruthless enemy for salvation.

The crash

Finally, when we have sacrificed everything for the idol and come to rely on it completely, it crumbles. Our compulsion for a lesser liberation is really bondage, not only to us, but to the idol itself. Most of our idols are good things that have a real purpose in God's creation, but when we make these created things into gods, they can't bear the weight. The more weight we put on them, the more they resist us or begin to crumble. Not only will the idol not deliver as a god, but in the long run, it won't even be able to deliver as what it is. When our idol is a good thing, like children, work, health, love, or leisure, our idolatry will crush and defile it. Our kids will resent us. Our hobbies will feel empty. Work will feel more like a prison than a blessing. Everything bolts, buckles, or bores us under pressure it was never meant to bear. Whenever we put something in creation in the place of the Creator, we ruin it, ruin ourselves, and rob God of his rightful place. The real cost of idolatry is the loss of God, ourselves, and everything in creation.

AN EXAMPLE OF THE CYCLE AT WORK

All people want security. They want to know they'll be okay. God is our security, but he uses means like governments, families, enterprises, and jobs to meet our need for security. However, if your trust isn't convictionally focused on God, you'll begin to see your job not just as God's present *means* of security, but as the *source* of your security. If your job is the only thing keeping you from destitution, your sense of security will be fragile, and you'll crave the security that your job offers without recognizing that your security doesn't depend on the job, but on the One who gave it to you. When you look to your job to give you security, it becomes an idol. You're no longer serving the God who gives you security partly *through* your job. Your job is now the source of your security, and likely your source of approval, power, and significance as well. When your job is the one dispensing your happiness, you'll focus on doing whatever is needed to sustain it rather than focusing on pleasing God.

Idols can demand anything from us in exchange for fulfilling our compulsions. In service to our jobs, we might lie or falsify documents, overwork ourselves or others, refuse to give others credit, or use tricks of power to keep and advance in our job. Creativity and productivity are no longer our focus, and they don't bring us joy. The job isn't just a job anymore; it represents and bestows the security we crave. And if the price goes up, we will pay it, damn the morality or the consequences. Even more hours? Even deeper manipulation? It's all about loyalty. We serve the one who has our allegiance. In this way, a non-living thing can tyrannize us. And it will snowball.

THE GARDEN AND THE MINE

Our idols only have power over us because they gratify cravings that are broken in the first place. When we allow these cravings to drive us to idols, and idols to coerce us into sin, we are walking into the beginning of damnation.[36]

But we do not need to submit to this snowballing and crashing tyranny. It is for freedom that Christ has set us free. We can be free of our craving Flesh and impotent idols. They will still be present, but through faith, our bondage to them can be broken.[37] The Spirit will weaken their influence more and more. God will carry on the good work he began through faith (Philippians 1:6). Philippians 2:12-13 exhorts us to "continue to work out [our] salvation with fear and trembling, for it is God who works in [us] to will and to act according to his good purpose." What began *in* faith proceeds *by* faith. Every advance against the compulsions of the Flesh and toward virtuous conviction is an act of faith; a display of allegiance and loyalty to God as Christ, Creator, and King. Faith in the God of creation and redemption will grow virtue in us. Virtue will direct and sustain liberty, and virtuous liberty is the best environment for the growth and health of deeper faith.

> **What began *in* faith proceeds *by* faith.**

To end this wading through the mud of our slavery, let us remember one truth we often forget: God gives, produces, and cultivates, while sin robs and destroys.[38] Sin is ruthless and bar-

---

36 These early stages of damnation are reversible, but the Bible talks about ways in which God's judgment closes our minds and hearts while we are still living. This is the main reason we should never wait to be saved or hesitate to repent. If we wait, we allow ourselves to be progressively darkened, desensitized to the things of God, and enslaved to the Flesh and our idols (see 1 Timothy 4:2).

37 We will still face compulsion and coercion, but they will no longer be the prevailing desire of our hearts, and their hold on our character and impulses will be continually weakened. As John Wesley said, they "...remain, but no longer reign." John Wesley, "On Sin in Believers," *Wesley Center Online*, Northwest Nazarene University, http://wesley.nnu.edu/john-wesley/the-sermons-of-john-wesley-1872-edition/sermon-13-on-sin-in-believers/ (accessed 17 June 2017).

38 In this section I use the word "sin" to refer to the phenomenon that combines the internal work of the Flesh, our allegiance to it, our actions going along with it, and the presence of our idols in it. It is the most general reference in the Bible for the whole of what separates us from God and his created purpose for us.

ren. It can extract good things, but it cannot make anything. It's like digging a mine into someone else's property, gaining only by stealing. Sin can only enrich us by taking something that's designed for another purpose. Every sin is a perversion of a good in God's creation. It gives a cheap gain by losing almost all of creation's value in the process, like a thief who pawns a stolen ring worth ten thousand dollars for a quick fifty bucks. Sin contrives but cannot create. It's like eating seed corn God has given us to plant. It is an offense, a tragic waste, and a suicide.

Yet, through faith, God's Spirit grows in us the tree of virtuous liberty that slowly bears more and more fruit over time, and from which more and more trees can be planted. From here, we can begin to discover the second half of our freedom. We have been freed *from* the tyranny of sin, death, and our Flesh. In the next chapter, we will examine what it is we were set free *for.*

SUGGESTED BIBLE MEMORIZATION

Therefore, my dear friends, as you have always obeyed—not only in my presence, but now much more in my absence—continue to work out your salvation with fear and trembling, for it is God who works in you to will and to act according to his good purpose.

Philippians 2:12-13

REFLECT AND RESPOND

1. What was the most important idea in this chapter for you? What practical difference does it make in how you see life or what kind of person you are to be?

2. Can you explain in your own words what The Golden Triangle is and why it is important?

3. Are you convinced that liberty cannot thrive without virtue in a society? Why or why not?

4. Can you think of a time in your life you did something for fleshly reasons that caused more problems; a time when your "passions forged your fetters"?

5. Can you identify any of your remaining compulsions or idols? What are you hoping for in them that you don't think God can be trusted to supply?

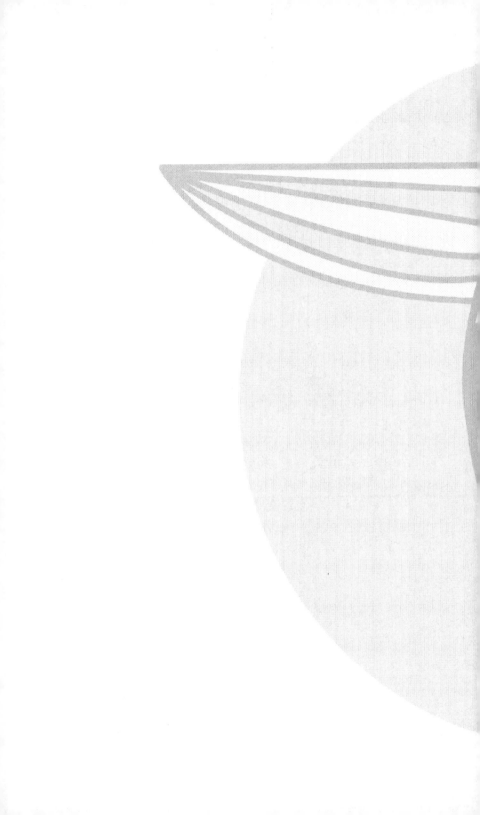

6

VIRTUOUS FREEDOM 2:
FREEDOM FOR

It is for freedom that Christ has set us free. Stand firm, then, and do not let yourselves be burdened again by a yoke of slavery.
Galatians 5:1

As discussed in the last chapter, if our foundational slavery is the compulsion of the Flesh, then our foundational liberation must be freedom from this compulsion and its consequences. We would need liberation from the control of our compulsions and pardon for the guilt of having obeyed them. This would be incomplete, however, without a new pattern to shape our lives. We are free from a specific slavery and free for a specific way of life. So what is that life, and how does it become a reality for us?

Most Christians know that, in Christ, we are justified—pardoned from guilt, counted righteous, and accepted by God. They know that, in Christ, we are also promised that the Holy Spirit will dwell in us, so we are not alone. In many churches today, we are attentive to the reality of our justification, but we neglect the other half of our salvation (which we call sanctification[1]). God's sanctification of us produces in us the virtues that direct what we are meant to do with our freedom. When

---

1   See the definition of "sanctify" in the glossary appendix.

we experience the freedom of Christ directed by true virtue, we start to look like Christ—the Perfectly Free and Virtuous One. This is why virtuous freedom is a critical indicator of substance.

Here is the point we speed past: growth is slow in our eyes. Painfully slow. We are the slowest maturing creature on earth, but the one with the most potential. Virtue and faith grow over decades. God is growing shoots to be planted in eternity. He is not in a rush like we are.[2] Virtue and freedom are worked out over a lifetime with fear and trembling. It may be discouraging to know you won't be done growing soon. But you will be amazed at what change you will see in a year or five years. As you grow, your vision will also grow, and you'll be able to see your transformation and appreciate its beauty, along with the good it does to others. Not only will you learn to see his spiritual life blossoming in you, but you'll learn to see it in others. You'll begin to see it everywhere.

THE LIBERATING POWER OF GOSPEL CONVICTIONS

The alternative to *coercion* and *compulsion* is faith directed by gospel *conviction*. God created us in his own image so that we would live in a way that expresses him and his dominion over creation through us. He created us to be embedded in his creation while thinking and acting like him. That has always been our purpose, but it is not normally the prevailing preference of our hearts.[3] That unity between our created purpose and our heart's preferences is part of what was broken by sin. The free-

---

2   See Psalm 90:4 and 2 Peter 3, especially verses 8-9.

3   The phrase "prevailing preference of the heart" comes from Jonathan Edwards' *Freedom of the Will*. He argued that the heart may be full of many motivations, but in each choice of the will, one preference will prevail, since to prefer nothing is indifference. Indifference may be free, but it is freedom with paralysis, which isn't of any use at all. So all free choices are determined by our strongest or prevailing preference —whatever we want the most. Whichever preference prevails, that is the object of our allegiance, and it is our god.

dom for which Christ has set us free includes those two being put back together.

The proper order of things is for something to depend on and serve that which is greater than it. We were meant to depend on and serve only what is greater than us—our Creator God, in whose image we were made.

By putting our faith in Christ, we depend on the Creator and Savior of creation rather than on our fellow creatures. We set our hearts, minds, and wills on his character and love it for all its loveliness.[4] Faith in Christ then forms our sense of what is good through the mind of Christ and reforms our character through virtue by these right Christ-centered convictions. These convictions form our character and recalibrate our conscience. Once faith has nourished Christ-like virtue in our character, our conscience will direct our freedom with faithfulness, godliness, and justice. We will increasingly experience the stabilizing maturity of virtuous freedom. We will live less and less in the compulsion of the Flesh. Rather, more and more, our prevailing preference of heart will be motivated by Christ-centered convictions. This is true freedom, and it is one of the great marks of spiritual substance.

The second freedom

It would have been great enough if Christ had come to set us free only from the compulsion of the Flesh and coercion of our idols. Hebrews 2:14-15 says Jesus came to "break the power of him who holds the power of death—that is, the devil—and free those who all their lives were held in slavery by their fear of death." We all need that. But Jesus was not

---

4 It's important to understand that we love God because he is the right object of love. He is deserving of love; he is lovely. Even an unloving lover can love what is lovely enough, but God loves us in spite of our unloveliness because of the strength of his love. He loves us in spite of our lack of deserving his love; we love God because we come to see a tiny glimpse of his real loveliness, which we have been suppressing all our lives.

content with this. He wanted more freedom for us. In fact, Galatians 5:1 isn't mainly about being free from sin and the Flesh. The passage is about being free from God's Law. If you really understand this, it is an incredibly freeing and focusing realization.

The Old Testament has a lot of laws in it—613 by traditional count. These laws governed most of life, telling people how to behave in myriad life situations. God used them to restrain sin and teach people about his character. While the Law was perfect, it was still just a set of laws. This means it had at least three problems.

First, all laws are expressions of universal truths applied specifically to particular situations, times, and cultures. No set of laws for humans can be timeless, because it will always have a context. Laws are always partly universal and partly bound to a specific situation and time. For example, the Law tells us what to do with oxen, but not cars.

Second, the Law was a time bomb. The Bible says that with sinful humans, laws simultaneously restrain sin and provoke it. Paul talks about this in Romans 7. He says he wouldn't have known what coveting was without a command that said, "Don't covet," but once he heard that law, his Flesh seized the opportunity and filled his heart with covetous temptations and desires. It was like the law just gave his Flesh ideas.

So while law *constrains sin* by forbidding it, it also *provokes the Flesh* like gasoline on a fire. Without something that deals with the Flesh, a law is just a time bomb, containing sin until the pressure builds to the point of exploding. To diffuse the bomb, people will either let some pressure out by sinning and then apologizing for it, or they'll reject the law altogether, so they never feel the pressure.

But if these were the only problems with the Law that Jesus wanted to fix, why couldn't he keep a revised Law *and* the gospel? If the Flesh can be killed in Christ and overcome in the Spirit, then it should be possible for the Law to constrain us without the Flesh using it to inflame us, right? Why couldn't Jesus have saved us from our sins, delivered us from the Flesh, and still preserved the Law? In other words, couldn't he have made us into people who are free to obey the Law because our Flesh doesn't get in our way anymore? In fact, this was the biggest confusion in the early Church. Most Jewish believers rightly had incredible respect for the divinely-given Law, so they assumed God would keep it as the basis of life in Christ. But he didn't. This suggests that God's end goal is more than just people who obey the Law. That's the Law's third limitation: as good as it is, it can't produce anything more than law-abiding people.

Galatians 5:1 says that Christ freed us so that we would actually be free *from* the Law. That is why the next verse tells Christians not to submit to the covenant of circumcision, because doing so would indicate that we're seeking to be justified by obeying the Law. For that to work we would have to obey the whole Law perfectly—to be "under" it (Galatians 5:18)—in order to be saved. To do so would be to return to a slavery from which we have already been freed.

Jesus freed us from the Law for two reasons. First, so we would not look to be made right with God by obeying the Law—moralism. Jesus, as the Christ, freely gives us forgiveness and righteousness through faith alone, the only justification we require.[5] He fulfilled the requirements of the Law perfectly for us, and that perfect fulfillment is credited to us when we are united with him through faith. The Bible simply calls this being "in Christ."[6] We are made right with God through faith apart from the Law (Romans 3:21) in a way that creates both gratitude and humility (Romans 3:27). This is the freedom of

---

5   See Philippians 3.

6   The phrase "in Christ" is used dozens of times in the New Testament. See especially 2 Corinthians 2:17; Galatians 2:17; Ephesians 1:3.

justification.

The second reason Christ freed us from the Law is just as important. It is the freedom of sanctification. He freed us from the Law in order to allow us to be maximally good. Paul reveals this in the following verses:

> You who are trying to be justified by the law have been alienated from Christ; you have fallen away from grace. For through the Spirit we eagerly await by faith the righteousness for which we hope. For in Christ Jesus neither circumcision nor uncircumcision has any value. The only thing that counts is faith expressing itself through love.
>
> **Galatians 5:4-6**

Faith in Christ is the means of our righteous standing—justification. It is also the means of the righteousness—godliness and holiness—"for which we hope." We are seeking a righteousness in practice "through the Spirit" that is shown not by obeying the laws of the Torah, but by "faith expressing itself through love." Law is good for what it can do, and the Torah was a perfect law for its purpose, but it cannot maximize good through changed people. Only the Spirit and faith can do that.

By law's very nature of imposing order to restrain evil, it also prevents good by limiting people's freedom. Zoning and building code laws make buildings safer and neighborhoods well organized, but they make housing more expensive and put safer housing further out of the reach of the poor. Assault laws keep people from attacking you, but they protect people who deserve it from getting a good punch in the mouth. Corporate policies standardize practices throughout the company, ensuring quality and organization, but they also keep workers from exercising good judgment in important circumstances to please customers. Even good laws limit some goods. Laws can't help having this drawback.

However, when virtuous people possess freedom, they are able to do good and exercise creativity where the Law cannot. Sin, like a gas, has no substance of good in it. Law, like rock, is substantive but unadaptable. Only virtue, like a liquid, can fill every crack and crevice in life's opportunities for good without

> When Christ forms this virtue through faith within, we need no law without. We can be trusted with the freedom to be creators.

losing itself; it has both fluidity and gravity. It is the perfect companion to freedom. When Christ forms this virtue through faith within, we need no law without. We can be trusted with the freedom to be creators.

Back to creation...again

There is a very important connection here to the creation story. God never repented of the purpose for which he made us. Salvation redeems creation and brings us back to our original purpose as God's stewards. God is taking us back to our beginning, and he's doing so to equip us for our eternal future. We've discussed this already:[7] when we were created, we were made to be God's stewards of creation. There are examples of this all through the Bible. All of them point to the fact that we are all God's stewards in his creation. In the account of creation, we see:

> God blessed them and said to them, "Be fruitful and increase in number; fill the earth and subdue it. Rule over the fish in the sea and the birds in the sky and over every living creature that moves on the ground."
>
> **Genesis 1:28**

God didn't give us creation; he gave us a job in his creation.[8]

---

7   See chapter 2, footnote 10 for further detail on what it means to be a steward.

8   Chapters 4 and 5 of this book discuss this in detail as well.

That job is to rule over it by filling it, subduing it, and helping it to flourish. Genesis 1 tells about God creating and fashioning creation, then putting the rest of the work in the hands of humanity. We are called to do his work—to bear his image in his creation as his stewards. This was our work in a perfect creation, it is our work under the present curse, and it will be our work in the new heavens and the new earth. We own nothing, but govern everything. We will never be gods, but we will always have God's work of creating and cultivating.

Free and faithful stewards

There was an important difference between a slave and a steward in the culture in which the Bible was written. Both did the work of a servant. However, most slaves had no freedom to choose *how* to do their work. They had no authority, only a set of chores they had to do in a certain way. In contrast, a steward governed all the affairs of the house. While he acted as a servant (as in, worked for the good of the house's master), a steward could have been a slave, a paid worker, or even a son in the household.

Whatever his standing, a steward was free in his work—free to use his judgment to invest and govern the master's affairs, as long as it was for the master's goals and according to his ethics. A faithful steward served only the authority above him, never the naggings of the household or his own desires.

> Virtuous freedom, grown in faith by the Spirit, is guided not by the constrictions of a law but by the convictions of a redeemed conscience.

The best stewards were the ones the master could trust the most.[9] Virtuous stewards needed no laws from their master,

---

9   The best example of this is in the story of Joseph in the book of Genesis. Joseph was the greatest steward of the Old Testament, except perhaps Moses. It was said of Joseph's masters that when he was in charge his master "did not concern himself with anything except the food he ate" (Genesis 39:6) and "the warden paid no attention to anything under Joseph's care" (Genesis 39:23). We are to see him as the perfect

and so were not limited by them. In exchange for maximum freedom, a virtuous steward could do the most good, unhindered by unneeded restrictions.

God's vision for us is not only to be free from our own fleshly compulsion and the coercion of our idols, but also from the constriction of the Law. Virtuous freedom, grown in faith by the Spirit, is guided not by the *constrictions of a law* but by the *convictions of a redeemed conscience.* These convictions flow from understanding the mind of Christ. They show us how to express faith in love. They help us to keep in step with the Spirit. They forge the habits and disciplines of spiritual substance.

Once we know that we're stewards and what a steward is supposed to do, does it matter what kind of stewards we are? Are we slaves, servants, or sons and daughters? We might easily be eternally happy as the slave or servant of such a king as God. It would certainly be an honor for us. King David once said he would have been content with an even lower position. He'd have taken any servant's job:

---

steward whom God then makes steward of all Egypt. He is surpassed only by Moses (who was apparently managing a tougher group than prison inmates), and Moses only by Jesus, the perfect Steward (Hebrews 3:2-5).

Better is one day in your courts than a thousand elsewhere; I would rather be a doorkeeper in the house of my God than dwell in the tents of the wicked. For the LORD God is a sun and shield; the LORD bestows favor and honor; no good thing does he withhold from those whose walk is blameless. LORD Almighty, blessed is the one who trusts in you.

Psalm 84:10-12

Yet, this is not the kind of steward God has made us to be. Jesus demonstrated that a son could be a perfect steward by showing us how he served the Father. He submitted to the Father in everything, even though he was his Son. In the book of Hebrews, we are told that Jesus was greater than Moses, the greatest man in the Old Testament. Why? Was it because he was a greater prophet than Moses? A greater leader? He was, but that's not the reason we are given:

...fix your thoughts on *Jesus*, whom we acknowledge as our apostle and high priest. *He was faithful* to the one who appointed him, just as Moses was *faithful in all God's house*. Jesus has been found worthy of greater honor than Moses, just as the builder of a house has greater honor than the house itself. For every house is built by someone, but God is the builder of everything. "Moses was faithful as a servant in all God's house," bearing witness to what would be spoken by God in the future. *But Christ is faithful as the Son over God's house. And we are his house...*

Hebrews 3:1b-6a

Jesus was greater than Moses as a perfectly faithful steward who was also a Son. Moses was appointed as the person in charge of all of God's wandering people—his whole house. The distinguishing mark of his life was that he was a faithful steward over that house. Jesus was an even more faithful steward over God's house; plus, he was the Maker and Heir of the house.

It is within this context that we hear Jesus tell his disciples that he no longer calls them servants, but friends. He says, "You are my friends if you do what I command. I no longer call you servants, because a servant does not know his master's business. Instead, I have called you friends, for everything that I learned from my Father I have made known to you" (John 15:14-15). Jesus doesn't give up his authority as the steward of salvation and creation. We are still under his authority, but we are also his friends, because he has revealed himself and his will to us. He has brought us into the inner circle of his purposes. He wants his stewards to be guided by his character and purposes, not by a rigid and limiting set of rules.

It is also within this context that we can understand again what it means when God calls us his children—his sons and daughters. Romans 8:17 says, "Now if we are children, then we are heirs—heirs of God and co-heirs with Christ, if indeed we share in his sufferings in order that we may also share in his glory." Different people connect with this truth in different ways. Being a son or daughter has many implications including acceptance, belonging, identity, assured rescue, as well as redemption, riches, and glory.

When we understand ourselves as stewards who are sons and daughters, it should do something to our perspective of our lives' work. We are not helpless children with no responsibility. We are steward-heirs of our Father's creation. We are part of the family business. The way we govern reflects on our Father— his creation, enterprise, and reputation. We are investing on

> He wants us to mature into faithful stewards who need no formal set of regulations and, as heirs, are no longer focused on winning the approval he has already given.

his behalf, in his name, and according to his ethics. We are not slaves restricted only to following commands. We are not servants doing insignificant chores. He wants us to mature into faithful stewards who need no formal set of regulations and, as heirs, are no longer focused on winning the approval he has already given. He wants to free us to strive in grace, through the Spirit, toward the righteousness for which we hope, by expressing our faith through love. He wants his children to be unleashed in virtuous freedom. He wants us to see that it is when we give ourselves to him fully that we become fully ourselves in the truest possible liberation until glory. It was, after all, *for freedom* that Christ set us free.

Virtue is verdant; it is lush with life and has the capacity to sustain other things. God is a god of life, of healthy expansion. Rebellion against God never produces anything new or life-giving. Devils would never have connected sex with procreation. They wouldn't even have connected it with love. But God connected pleasure, love, companionship, and new life in the same uniting act. Virtue is the same. It unites many goods in one garden of deepening roots, spiraling shoots, opening flowers, and branches bowing with fruit. We were freed from sin so we could live as people who are fully alive in Christ, which means living as virtuous people compelled in every way by the truth of the gospel and the love we give and receive. And with that freedom, we were called to take our place as stewards in the house of our Father.

SUGGESTED BIBLE MEMORIZATION

It is for freedom that Christ has set us free. Stand firm, then, and do not let yourselves be burdened again by a yoke of slavery.

Galatians 5:1

REFLECT AND RESPOND

1. How would you define sanctification in your own words?

2. How would you describe why Christ died to free us from the Law? Why couldn't he forgive us and keep the Law in place? Wouldn't that have made a better world?

3. How should our role as stewards change how we see our "what" and "why" in the world? How should seeing our role given at creation change our understanding of our lives in the age of redemption (after Christ's death and resurrection)?

4. How does God forge virtuous freedom in us through faith?

7

IN STEP WITH THE SPIRIT

Therefore, there is now no condemnation for those who are in Christ Jesus, because through Christ Jesus the law of the Spirit who gives life has set you free from the law of sin and death. For what the law was powerless to do because it was weakened by the flesh, God did by sending his own Son in the likeness of sinful flesh to be a sin offering. And so he condemned sin in the flesh, in order that the righteous requirement of the law might be fully met in us, who do not live according to the flesh but according to the Spirit.
Romans 8:1-4

Those who belong to Christ Jesus have crucified the flesh with its passions and desires. Since we live by the Spirit, let us keep in step with the Spirit. Let us not become conceited, provoking and envying each other.
Galatians 5:24-26

We've looked so far at three marks of spiritual substance. The first, sacrificial love, is the queen of the marks of substance. The second, the mind of Christ, gives us clarity on what holy love really is. Third, living free of the Flesh's compulsion and the Law's limiting coercion is the only way to live in real love, and for that, we need virtuous freedom forged by gospel convictions. All of this is still lacking one critical element. None of this makes any reference to God's empowering presence with us. How does God animate and empower the mind of Christ in us? How do we navigate the journey of daily improvising in a world full of change, ambiguity, and uncertainty? The answer is that God has not left us alone, but has given himself to be with us in the person of the Holy Spirit (John 14:17).

In fact, God's Spirit is the immediate agent in both our coming to faith and our growth in spiritual substance. Once you have eyes to see the work of the Holy Spirit, you will see him everywhere in the Bible and in your own life.

Much of what the Spirit does precedes our conversion. The Spirit is the one who first opens our mind and heart to Christ by awakening us, illuminating the truth of the gospel, and convicting us of the reality of sin and our need of God and his Christ. The Holy Spirit does the miracle of regeneration that creates new spiritual life in place of our spiritual deadness. He assures us that, in faith, we have been accepted and are united with Christ. Jesus sent the Holy Spirit not just to remind us about him or even to be *with* us, but to be *in* us. Through the work of Christ, God's Spirit is in us, uniting us spiritually with Christ, in whom the Father gives us all things.

So what about after our conversion? Does the Spirit just speak up when we're doing something wrong? Does he just drop a little moral guilt into our conscience so we feel conviction? No. The Bible says that we are to *live by* the Spirit. Romans 8:4 says that we "do not live according to the flesh but according to the Spirit." Just as the compulsions of the Flesh drove our lives before our conversion (Ephesians 2:3), now the leading of the Spirit fills our minds and drives our desires. Romans 8 continues:

> ...those who live in accordance with the Spirit have their minds set on what the Spirit desires. The mind governed by the flesh is death, but the mind governed by the Spirit is life and peace...

You, however, are not in the realm of the flesh but are in the realm of the Spirit, if indeed the Spirit of God lives in you. And if anyone does not have the Spirit of Christ, they do not belong to Christ.

Romans 8:5b-6, 9

The Father demonstrates holy, self-sacrificial love by preparing salvation, giving his Christ, and pouring out his Spirit. In Christ's life, teaching, death, and resurrection, he gives the mind of Christ to all who will believe in him. All who receive Christ and are renewed in God's self-sacrificial love are filled with and led by the Spirit. Those who belong to Christ have the Spirit of Christ. Those who have the mind of Christ have their minds set on what Christ's Spirit desires. If you only want a little of God, all this comprehensiveness will be off-putting and overwhelming.[1] But if you long for spiritual substance—to receive everything God has for you and can do in you—then the comprehensiveness of his salvation brings overwhelming joy.

THE NATURE OF CONTROL

Humans typically seek happiness in two ways. One is by following the compulsion of the Flesh. This is the life of libertines seeking gratification and pleasure.[2] The second is by living for approval, seeking to be justified in the eyes of others. These people live under the coercion of laws. If they are religious, they believe that if they obey God, then he will love

---

1   People sometimes say they don't want to be "too religious." But that's not a sign of being sensible. It's a sign of idolatry. The person might mean that he doesn't want to imitate the legalism of false religion. If that's the case, that's understandable. But if that stance means limiting how much of our life welcomes God's complete rule, then we are merely using God to manage part of our lives. We are trying to put God in the service of our idols. That doesn't work...at all.

2   If we strive for self-gratification, sensuality will lead to compulsiveness, addictive tendencies, deviance because of diminishing returns, relational isolation, stunted friendships, shallow character that is capable of enjoying only shallow pleasures, greed, and many other rocks on which our life can shipwreck.

them. If they are irreligious, they believe that if they obey others, others will love them, and they will love themselves. These are the lives of self-gratification and self-justification, respectively, which are both forms of self-glorification. Some people focus on gratification, and others focus mainly on justification. But most of us want the benefits of both. We don't just want the pleasure of sensual gratification; we also want the gratification of moral justification. We act as though doing what we want is a virtue, and we push this as far as we think other people will let us go before they call our bluff.[3]

These two ways of operating lead to slavery and destruction. When we strive for self-justification, we will fall short of even the small and meager set of laws we establish for ourselves. This will lead to pride, hypocrisy, or self-hatred. Since we will necessarily fail, we must either blind ourselves or elevate ourselves by judging others more harshly, which is self-glorification. Otherwise, we would have to admit that we have failed even the smallest moral tests that we have concocted for ourselves.

It has always been Jesus' intention to lead us away from self-justification, self-gratification, and self-glorification, and he offers in himself a new way to true justification, gratification, and glorification. All human lifestyles and philosophies have tried to satisfy all three of these human longings. This quest is not special to religion. Yet only Christ has the power to deliver them, if we will trust him.

---

3   It is through this dynamic that God uses the selfishness of men to force people to live under some basic morality. Jonathan Edwards called this "common virtue." By this, he means virtue that is focused on situation or benefit. This is in contrast to what he calls "true virtue," which is motivated by Christ and focused on being. Humans will limit their self-gratification out of a desire to be accepted by others and not punished by them. This natural law of exclusion and desire for justification keeps the Flesh restrained, though not redeemed. By ordering the world this way, God can hold the world back from chaos, keep questions of virtue before the eyes of sinful men and women, and maintain a distinction between common and true virtue. For further reading, see Edwards' essay, "The Nature of True Virtue."

Denying the Flesh, obeying the Law, loving our neighbor, and embracing our freedom

We have looked closely at Galatians 5, because it brings together so much of what spiritual substance looks like. Galatians 1-4 reclarifies the gospel: only through faith in Christ can we be justified and receive the freedom for which Christ set us free. Chapter 5 begins with, "It is for freedom that Christ has set us free." Then, in verses 13-17a, Paul says,

> You, my brothers and sisters, were called to be free. But do not use your freedom to indulge the flesh; rather, serve one another humbly in love. For the entire law is fulfilled in keeping this one command: "Love your neighbor as yourself." If you bite and devour each other, watch out or you will be destroyed by each other. So I say, walk by the Spirit, and you will not gratify the desires of the flesh. For the flesh desires what is contrary to the Spirit, and the Spirit what is contrary to the flesh.

Through the gospel, Christ is calling us to deny the Flesh, know and obey the spirit of the Law, love our neighbor as ourselves, and embrace the freedom for which Christ has set us free. How in the world are we supposed to do all of this? Is there some uniting principle to all of this? Yes, and it's fairly simple.

Paul is telling us the single principle by which we can do all the things Christ is calling us to do: to walk, to live by the Spirit. If you live by the Spirit, you won't live by the Flesh. If you live by the Spirit, you will love your neighbor and so fulfill all of the Law. If you live by the Spirit, you can have real fellowship and unity with other Christians. All Christian spirituality is by the Spirit. In Christ, that's really the definition of spirituality. Something spiritual is that which is done by the grace of God through his Spirit.[4] And this is why Paul uses the rest of chapter 5 to explain to us how to do this.

---

4   For more on this topic, hear my sermon, "What Do We Mean by Spirituality?" from January 8th, 2017 by visiting highpointchurch.org/sermons.

KEEPING IN STEP WITH THE SPIRIT

The earliest Christians didn't have a whole Bible. In fact, Galatians 5 may have been the only instruction on life in the Spirit that the Galatian Christians had in writing, so Paul gave them very clear ways to live by the Spirit. By setting our minds on the Spirit in this way every day, we will do what he calls "[keeping] in step with the Spirit" (Galatians 5:25). In order to live our entire lives by the Spirit, we have to intentionally stay in step with him in every minute of every day.

I remember running behind my brother in the deep snow of New York winters. I was younger than he and his friends, and I would tire out right away running through deep snow. The only way I could keep up with him was by putting my boots in the holes he made in the snow right in front of me. If I kept in step with where he stepped, I could move faster, farther, and more freely than I ever could on my own. The same is true with following someone while hiking or running. If you focus on matching them step for step, even placing your foot where they placed theirs, you will stay right with them. More than that, focusing on matching their stride will energize your pace, guide you to secure footing, and focus your mind. This strategy breaks even a long hike down into one step after another, and when you focus on the step right in front of you, you reach the summit before you know it.

If we are going to live in the Spirit, the only way to reach our goal is to walk with him all the time. If we live in the Spirit, let us keep in step with the Spirit.

Elements of keeping in step with the Spirit

Paul gives us five basic elements of living by the Spirit in Galatians 5. There is much more to learn about the work of the Spirit, but these are the most important things to remember daily in order to keep in step with him.

1. Hope for real righteousness

For through the Spirit we eagerly await by faith the righteousness for which we hope.

Galatians 5:5

Our longings are one of the most revealing things about us. What is your greatest longing? Pause and think seriously about that before you read any more. God has a goal for us in salvation, something for which he has redeemed us. He has redeemed us by Christ and given us the righteousness of Christ as a sheer gift. But this gift is also a seed. The completed righteousness of Christ that saves and justifies us is the same seed that grows a new righteousness in us. If we have been awakened in Christ to the glory and beauty of Christ's righteousness, and if we realize that we have been called to it, we will long for the righteous character of Christ to be formed in us.

This is not a new moralism, and it cannot lead to self-justification or bragging of any kind. By faith, we eagerly await this transformation. It comes to us through the Spirit, and it is something for which we hope. We will not be able to take credit for this future righteousness. Our ultimate righteousness of character will be as much a gift of grace as the righteousness that is credited to us the moment we believe in Christ. The fact that we will not have earned it should not make us long for it any less. It should make our hope burn all the brighter as we wait with bated breath for all we can receive through the Spirit. If we are following in the footsteps of the Spirit, he will lead us to this eager anticipation, this longing to be made like Christ. When we see the truth, beauty, nobility, and incredible value of the righteousness for which we were created, we will burn with longing for it through the Spirit. Far from making us self-righteous, this longing will make us humble, teachable, thankful, and joyful.

2. Express faith through love

For in Christ Jesus *neither circumcision [which is a law] nor uncircumcision* has any value. The only thing that counts is *faith expressing itself through love.*

Galatians 5:6

We talked about sacrificial love in chapter three. Holy love is at the heart of God's activity, and holy love will always be headed in the same direction as the Spirit. If you want to know the general direction the Spirit will be going today, you can bet on love. If you are going to walk with him, he will be walking toward love, service, forgiveness, and everything else that fits the character and mind of Christ. If you keep this in mind, you won't be surprised when he takes you in the direction of service and sacrifice. You'll see it coming. Not only will you react less strongly against it, but eventually you will actually desire it. If that happens, you will find yourself receiving some of the "righteousness for which we hope" (Galatians 5:5). Be prepared to be filled with thankfulness and joy.

3. Follow the Spirit's desires, not your Flesh's

So I say, walk by the Spirit, and you will not gratify the desires of the flesh. For the flesh desires what is contrary to the Spirit, and the Spirit what is contrary to the flesh. They are in conflict with each other, so that you are not to do whatever you want. But if you are led by the Spirit, you are not under law.

Galatians 5:16-18

It's kind of an odd saying: "…so that you are not to do whatever you want." It's easy to think that it means the Flesh will want to do one thing, and the Spirit will want to do another, and you'll always be full of some constant bickering disagreement between the Spirit and the Flesh. That's not what it means. The Spirit doesn't compete with the Flesh like that.

In these verses, "you" and "the Flesh" are the same thing. Paul says it this way to emphasize how rooted the Flesh is in your experience of yourself. Many of our desires are rooted in our bodily experiences. Our body is a good invention of God, but when it is disordered by sin, it works against us. And it is loud. It's like the Spirit is on audio, and the Flesh is on video. The Flesh throws a screaming tantrum, using all of our disordered bodily systems in its service. It uses our instincts, hormones, drives, brain structure, and reflexes to overload our minds and wills, directing us toward their most expedient gratification.

Yet, the voice of the Spirit is there. It isn't loud. It doesn't huff and puff. But it is clear and steady, speaking through the microphone of the conscience. In 1 Kings 19, God taught a prophet named Elijah about his voice. He did it at a time when Elijah's Flesh was screaming at God, because he felt like everyone was trying to kill him. This is how God responded:

> Then the LORD said, "Go out and stand on the mountain in the presence of the LORD, for the LORD is about to pass by." Then a great and powerful wind tore the mountains apart and shattered the rocks before the LORD, but the LORD was not in the wind. After the wind there was an earthquake, but the LORD was not in the earthquake. After the earthquake came a fire, but the LORD was not in the fire. And after the fire came a gentle whisper.
>
> **1 Kings 19:11-12**

This is where we get the idea of the "still, small voice of God," and this is what the voice of the Spirit sounds like most of the time. The Flesh will rage like a whirlwind, shake you like an earthquake, or burn through you like a forest fire, but the Spirit doesn't talk like that. He just simply, quietly, but absolutely clearly says, "That's not what I want. I want this." You will find that it conflicts with the tantrum of compulsion that rages inside you. It will humiliate your pride and seem unconcerned with your fears. His voice will seem like a gentle whisper, but it will be clear and almost self-evidently true. It expresses the Spirit's desires and always challenges us to trust God in some way. Finally, when you accept it, a deep peace will set in below the tremor of your fears.

If you respond to his desires, you will find yourself experiencing the opposite of what the Flesh warned would happen, because the Flesh is always exaggerating and bluffing. You'll find that the Spirit's desires lead to life, peace, and joy. You'll come to see your pride as disposable and destructive, and you'll recognize that your fears were controlling and shrinking you. You'll find the tantrums of the Flesh getting weaker and your own conscience getting firmer. Before long, you'll find that more and more, the "you" of the Flesh is weakening before the growing influence of a "you" that is increasingly in step with the Spirit. This is the growth of spiritual substance—real godliness. This is true spirituality.

This transformation follows obedience, which begins with responding to the Spirit's desires. You'll stumble at times, but God has revealed himself in Christ and the Bible and created the fellowship of the church in order to help you figure it out. He is a patient and longsuffering teacher. As time goes on, you'll find it gets easier and more rewarding to respond to the Spirit's desires, but not safer. It will always seem like dying, and it has always been the way to life.

4. Admit what you know by the Spirit

We need to admit to ourselves what we really do know about God that the Flesh wants to deny. It may seem like walking in the Spirit is where our list should end. What could we need to do beyond that? Being mature in Christ requires more than just yielding to the Spirit's promptings as situations arise. We need his overall education in God's word and in Christ.

Responding to the Spirit's desires is an internal and improvisational discipline connected to our conscience. Admitting what we already know in Christ is also an act of faith and conscience. However, it has less to do with responding to the moment's convictions and more to do with acknowledging what we are taught in Christ—what we have always actually known but didn't want to acknowledge.

When it comes to living as followers of Jesus, it's not a matter of reading the sheet music and performing every note perfectly. Walking in step with the Spirit is more like performing in a jazz ensemble. The notes aren't all written out for us. God wants to transform our minds to make us musicians who not only have mastered the needed technical skills, but are also able to improvise and adapt in the moment alongside companions who are contributing their own improvisations. We need to know not just the notes on the page, but also the feel of the music, the personalities and skills of our fellow musicians, and where we collectively are aiming to go. And all of that knowledge needs not just to be retrievable data in our heads, but known in our fingertips to the degree that we can react in real time to make something fluid, expressive, and exquisite.

Beyond giving momentary convictions, the Spirit teaches

us over time what is good, true, noble, excellent, beautiful, honorable, right, pure, lovely, admirable, and praiseworthy (Philippians 4:8). It is this knowledge of God and his truth that allows us to navigate the situations of our lives wisely and beautifully. But this is not just a process of acquiring information. It requires cooperation on our part. We have to admit that God's word is true, that it's good, and that we know it, even though our Flesh doesn't want to know it. Fear and pride can thrive only in the state of moral and spiritual denial.

It is important to remember that the Flesh doesn't capitalize only on our disordered lower drives and instincts. Sin has disordered every part of us. This includes our mind and patterns of thought.[5] The Flesh doesn't want to know what God plainly reveals, especially in his word and in his Christ. That is why the next verses say:

> The acts of the flesh are obvious: sexual immorality, impurity and debauchery; idolatry and witchcraft; hatred, discord, jealousy, fits of rage, selfish ambition, dissensions, factions and envy; drunkenness, orgies, and the like. I warn you, as I did before, that those who live like this will not inherit the kingdom of God. But the fruit of the Spirit is love, joy, peace, forbearance, kindness, goodness, faithfulness, gentleness and self-control. Against such things there is no law.
>
> **Galatians 5:19-23**

Don't miss that first line: "The acts of the flesh *are obvious...*" Our minds are constantly obsessed with making sin more complicated or less vile than it is. Self-justification and self-decep-

---

5   Theologians call this the "noetic effects of the fall"—the effects of depravity on our thinking. The sinful mind is full of all kinds of self-deception and self-justification. Because we bear God's image, there are some things we can't forget—things we can't not know. However, our sinful hearts conceal things, and the first person we lie to is ourselves. Lying to ourselves is fertile ground for pride, hypocrisy, self-justification, and unrestrained self-gratification. It is the only defense against the clear and natural moral demands to love, to worship God, and to respect the bond we have with our neighbor.

tion are our only hope of maintaining self-gratification, so we typically pretend that obvious injustice and wickedness are excusable and negligible. Every action, no matter how vile, has some extenuating consideration or enlightened explanation. If we cannot make evil sound good, then we can at least cover it in a fog of confusion, or we can accuse others of judging us and claim that they are guilty of the greater offense. Or we can act philosophical by questioning the foundations of reality and like Pilate, ask, "What is truth?" (John 18:38)

God's Spirit burns away this obscuring fog of the mind and confronts us with what we have always really known but didn't want to admit. Our failure to see is not an understandable limitation; it's a moral deficiency. It's a vigorous rebellion against reality. This is why Jesus says the work of the Spirit is to "prove the world to be in the wrong about sin and righteousness and judgment" (John 16:8). The word translated as "prove" here is also translated as "convict," which means to contradict and condemn our self-deception in a way that makes our rebellion and guilt obvious.

This is one of the Spirit's main roles, and he is unyielding in it. If we have the Spirit, he will continually press on us what we know but don't want to. He knows that we desperately need this moral and spiritual clarity. It is the only thing that can restore our conscience and reorder our loves. It is the only thing that can allow us to see the meaning and depth of his word and the glory of Christ. The Spirit loves the truth and knows both its value and our need of it. His divine love compels him to long to give you this gift of sight that comes from faith. He knows that clarifying moral truth through deep conviction is a necessary step toward growing holy love in us. God's truth and real self-knowledge are necessary components to the mind of Christ and indispensable to virtue. So, as the Spirit leads us to what God has spoken and shown about himself, we need to admit that we know it.

5. Kill the Flesh

Those who belong to Christ Jesus have crucified the flesh with its passions and desires.

Galatians 5:24

When we respond to the Spirit's conviction and education, we will increasingly learn to identify the presence and work of the Flesh. We will be more aware of lust and pride. We will recognize controlling fears, unforgiveness, envy, bitterness, rage, laziness, gluttony, and excessive indulgence for what they are. We will see not just outright wickedness, but also how good things are controlling us in ways they shouldn't.[6] This will help us see our need to escape diversion and embrace spiritual discipline, which we'll talk about in chapters nine and ten.

For our purpose here, we need to see a simple and difficult truth. Living in the Spirit means becoming an executioner of the Flesh. Godliness is not only a positive pursuit; it is also a negative and ferocious one. We tend to read over the word "crucified" because we have heard it so many times without ever having seen an actual crucifixion. We typically think of it like children think of shooting a person when they've seen ten thousand people killed on screen. It is a much more terrifying and brutal thing than we can imagine. I remember a combat instructor telling me, "If you shoot someone at any less than fifteen feet, you are going to be covered in their blood. You need to be mentally prepared for that." It makes one want to

---

6   See Paul's discussion of this in 1 Corinthians 6:12-20; 10:23-33. The idea that "I have the right to do anything" means that we are not under the Law, and nothing in the world is by definition forbidden. But Paul says this is only right if we walk by the Spirit and the gospel. This means three things. First, that nothing masters us. Second, that the logic of how and why we use something fits the gospel. (For example, going to prostitutes doesn't work, since we are the temple of the Holy Spirit, and sex is a union of body and spirit. If we are God's temple and in union with Christ, can we unite Christ or the temple with a prostitute? Um, no. That doesn't fit the gospel.) Third, that it is beneficial to our true good. In other words, does it lead to gospel ends of love and godliness?

throw up. I'm sure that is something like what Roman soldiers told new recruits about crucifixion.

Can you even imagine crucifying someone? Actually nailing someone to a tree to execute them? Now imagine the person looks exactly like you and is screaming, "You can't live without me! You don't even know who you are, you helpless freak! I don't deserve this! You're going to be miserable your whole life trying to repress me! I'll never die! Do you hear me? I'll NEVER die!"

The Flesh needs to die. Indwelling sin isn't a part of the real you. It's a thief, an infection, and a deformity—a perversion of you as you were made to be. It offers no symbiotic benefits. Listening to its voice isn't an act of authenticity. It is the counterfeit you. Though it promises life, it is leading you down to death. You have to kill it before it kills you. The Spirit will help you, but you have to find the ferocity, resolve, and even godly anger to participate in the work.

> Listening to [the Flesh's] voice isn't an act of authenticity. It is the counterfeit you. Though it promises life, it is leading you down to death. You have to kill it before it kills you.

At this point, we have to recognize one critical thing: *No one is saved who is unwilling to do this.* To have any honesty in trusting the crucified Christ means we *have crucified* (past tense) the Flesh. It's not something we have to do in order to be accepted in Christ, but it is part of what it means for Christ to save us. Part of the promise of what it means to be saved is to be saved from the slavery of indwelling sin—the slavery of the Flesh. Salvation isn't a buffet where you just take what you like. You can't say, "I'll take some forgiveness, the feeling of being divinely loved, and the encouraging presence of God, but I'm going to pass on freedom from sin. That doesn't appeal to me."

Sin is the object of God's wrath, and it is the very thing from which he delivers us, including both its hold on our hearts and the guilt it holds over us. We cannot trust him to save us from the guilt of our sins while simultaneously attempting to hold onto our sins and sinfulness. Yet that is what we do whenever we hide, protect, and nurture indwelling sin by not crucifying the Flesh. When we do this, we are trying to accept and reject Christ at the same time. We have two opposing allegiances.

Therefore, everyone who is in Christ has put and continues to put the Flesh to death. It is this ferocious but gracious striving that clears the ground for all the fruit of the Spirit—love, joy, peace, and a hundred other virtues of beauty. The Flesh seeks to spoil all of it.

We must come to three important realizations in chasing after Christ and understanding what real faith looks like. The first realization is that we have to follow him. The second is that we have to die with him: "Take up [your] cross and follow me."[7] Most think it stops there. But the third realization is that taking up our cross means not only that we must accept execution, but that we must also be executioners. It is not a call to

---

7   Matthew 16:24; Mark 8:34; Luke 9:23. In each Gospel, Jesus works this out over time. He calls people to follow him first. Then he tells them they will have to lay down their lives for him—like voluntarily picking up a cross and following him to the place of crucifixion, full of screams, blood, and rotting bodies.

violence against any human person, just against the fake persona of the Flesh. We are called to love our human enemies[8] but to be executioners of the Flesh. The Spirit is handing you a blade.

TRACKING HIS STEPS

Since we live by the Spirit, let us keep in step with the Spirit. Let us not become conceited, provoking and envying each other.

Galatians 5:25-26

In order to live in the freedom for which Christ has set us free, we have to live in the Spirit. To live in the Spirit, we have to keep in step with him. The key words in the verse above are "by" and "with." If it is by God's Holy Spirit that we live in Christ's freedom, then faith looks like keeping in step with him.

Older Puritan writers talked about the "frame" of our hearts and the way our souls are "tuned." John Owen said this about why it is so important to put the Flesh to death:

> [Sin] untunes and unframes the heart itself, by entangling its affections. It diverts the heart from the spiritual frame that is required for vigorous communion with God; it lays hold on the affections, rendering its object beloved and desirable, so expelling the love of the Father ... so that the soul cannot say uprightly and truly to God, "Thou art my portion," having something else that it loves.[9]

By keeping in step with the Spirit, we allow him to re-tune and re-frame our hearts so we can recognize the astonishing beauty of God, making him rightly attractive to our hearts and minds. However, this process must be in keeping with the freedom given in Christ (Galatians 5:1). We must willingly keep in step

---

8   Romans 12:19-21; Matthew 5:43-44.

9   John Owen, "The Mortification of the Flesh," *The Works of John Owen*, vol. 6, ed. William H. Goold (Pennsylvania: The Banner of Truth Trust, 2004), 22.

with him; he will not drag us along.

Owen says the Holy Spirit works in us and upon us as we are willing to be worked on. That is, he leads us in a way that preserves our liberty and free obedience to Christ. Obedience must be by faith, even if directed and empowered by God's Spirit. For the Spirit does not seek to lead us in a way that undermines his own work of forging in us virtue. The Spirit works to frame and tune our understandings, wills, conscience, and passions in a way that is in keeping with their integrity and freedom. He works *"in us and with us not against us or without us."*[10] Owen says this is in order that the Spirit's work can be an encouragement, facilitating our transformation, but cannot be a reason for us to neglect the work of **gracious striving** toward spiritual substance.

This work of the Spirit happens best when we are consistently seeking to be in step with him throughout our day and throughout our lives. When we seek to keep in step with the Spirit, we starve the idleness of soul in which the Flesh flourishes. The best way to keep weeds from growing in your garden is to position other plants and mulch around them. That is, the best way to combat weeds isn't to spend all your time plucking them out, but to do all the other things a gardener is supposed to do. Similarly, the more we attend to having the mind of Christ, growing in virtuous freedom, and keeping in step with the Spirit daily, the less opportunity indwelling sin has to tempt and confuse us. The result will be humble, self-sacrificial love. Or, to paraphrase Galatians 5:26, we will no longer be conceited. We will no longer provoke and envy each other. All four marks of substance—self-sacrificial love, the mind of Christ, virtuous freedom, and being in step with the Spirit—will take root in us and grow us into oaks of righteousness.[11]

---

10   Owen, "The Mortification of the Flesh," 20.

11   See Isaiah 61:3.

WHAT MAKES ALL THE DIFFERENCE

The more securely our hearts and minds are framed and tuned to the beauty of the gospel through the Spirit, the happier we will be in Christ. It turns out that a heart of joyful and thankful worship is the best guardian against all the temptations of devils, worldliness, and indwelling sin.

Yet when I said, "through the Spirit" in the line above, I didn't mean that as a throwaway line. There is a difficult reality here. The work of the Spirit is usually completely intangible yet utterly indispensable. You can come to believe there is a God who is morally serious. You may come to know that there is a moral law that you are supposed to conform to but don't. You may decide to try very hard

> The work of the Spirit is usually completely intangible yet utterly indispensable.

and even do very religious things to try to get better. John Owen called this the "foolish labor of poor souls."[12] Once our conscience has been awakened by the Law, we cannot stand against the power of our convictions, so we commit ourselves to all kinds of attempts to keep sin down and be good people. But if we are "strangers to the Spirit of God," all our striving is in vain.[13]

Owen says that even the most conscientious person seeking to be the best person they can possibly be is still powerless:

They combat without victory, have war without peace, and are in slavery all their days. They spend their strength for that which is not bread, and their labour for that which profiteth not. This is the saddest warfare that any poor creature can be engaged in. A soul under the power of conviction from the law is pressed to fight against sin, but hath no strength for the combat. They cannot but fight, and they can never conquer; they are like men

---

12   Owen, "The Mortification of the Flesh," 20.

13   Owen, "The Mortification of the Flesh," 20.

thrust on the swords of enemies on purpose to be slain. The law drives them on, and sin beats them back. Sometimes they think, indeed, that they have foiled sin, when they have only raised a dust that they see it not; that is, they distemper their natural affections of fear, sorrow, and anguish, which makes them believe that sin is conquered when it is not touched. By that time ... they must battle it again; and the lust they thought to be slain appears to have had no wound at all.[14]

Some people don't make any effort at all to be moral, but most people want to be good in some way. Owen gives us a chillingly realistic picture of those who have been awakened to moral law without the aid of the Spirit. It is especially true of those who have heard the Law of God, but do not turn in faith to the Spirit for real spiritual substance and the power to overcome the Flesh.

We cannot become good people on our own, especially not when we see with the mind of Christ what real goodness is. This is why everything in Christian faith is by faith through the Spirit of God. All is gift. Creation. Forgiveness. Existence. Everything, including the transformation we so desperately require. All of salvation is by faith—faith to long for real righteousness, because we trust it is real truth and beauty; faith to respond to the Spirit's desires when he makes them known to us; faith to accept and admit that we don't want to know the truth and accept his conviction in his word and in Christ; faith to crucify the Flesh with ferocity in order to be free; faith to seek to live every hour in step with the Spirit. This doesn't mean that we will literally hear sentences from him every minute, but we can follow his interests and desires. We don't feel our way along. We believe our way along.

Keep in step with the truth of the gospel, be sensitive to God's will in your conscience and spirit, and you will be in

---

14 Owen, "The Mortification of the Flesh," 20.

step with him more than you might think. "Since we live by the Spirit, let us keep in step with the Spirit" (Galatians 5:25).

SUGGESTED BIBLE MEMORIZATION

Those who belong to Christ Jesus have crucified the flesh with its passions and desires. Since we live by the Spirit, let us keep in step with the Spirit. Let us not become conceited, provoking and envying each other.

Galatians 5:24-26

REFLECT AND RESPOND

1. What is the most important concept you took from this chapter?

2. Review the five basic elements of walking with the Spirit.

   - Hope for real righteousness
   - Express faith through love
   - Follow the Spirit's desires, not your Flesh's
   - Admit what you know by the Spirit
   - Kill the Flesh

   Which needs more of your attention?

3. Explain, in as practical and concrete terms as you can, what it means to "keep in step with the Spirit" (Galatians 5:25).

4. The Bible says the "acts of the [F]lesh are obvious" (Galatians 5:19). What works of the Flesh did you not want to admit were obvious until God's conviction brought the truth home to you with force? Share some experience of Spiritual conviction and how it led to faith.

PART III

THE PURSUIT OF SUBSTANCE

8

WELCOME
TO THE ORDINARY

But perhaps God is strong enough to exult in monotony. It is possible that God says every morning, "Do it again" to the sun; and every evening, "Do it again" to the moon. It may not be automatic necessity that makes all daisies alike; it may be that God makes every daisy separately, but has never got tired of making them. It may be that He has the eternal appetite of infancy; for we have sinned and grown old, and our Father is younger than we.

G.K. Chesterton, Orthodoxy

I have seen the burden God has laid on the human race. He has made everything beautiful in its time. He has also set eternity in the human heart; yet no one can fathom what God has done from beginning to end. I know that there is nothing better for people than to be happy and to do good while they live. That each of them may eat and drink, and find satisfaction in all their toil—this is the gift of God. I know that everything God does will endure forever; nothing can be added to it and nothing taken from it. God does it so that people will fear [revere] him.

Ecclesiastes 3:10-14

...the growing good of the world is partly dependent on unhistoric acts; and that things are not so ill with you and me as they might have been, is half owing to the number who lived faithfully a hidden life, and rest in unvisited tombs.

George Eliot, Middlemarch

FEARING ORDINARY

An observer of our culture might guess that we believe nothing is worse than being ordinary. They would look at the way we worship youth and photoshop our models. They would see our avoidance of and aversion to long-term responsibility. They would see our celebration of leisure and luxury, our promotion of delicacies, and our obsession with celebrity. They might even notice a common undercurrent in our desire for "meaningful" work.[1] Everybody wants a vocation that is extraordinary, special, significant, and perpetually satisfying. They want life to be amazing. Although this may seem like wanting to "suck out all the marrow of life..."[2] (YOLO[3] and all that), it turns out that living this way will suck the marrow out of you.

I increasingly encounter people plagued by a constant fear of missing out (also known as FOMO). They fear that somewhere, something extraordinary is passing them by. In our time, the worldly heart is often driven by fear of being trapped in an ordinary, monotonous life. Roles and responsibilities seem like traps; like cages that threaten to keep us from opportunities

---

1 See the sidebar titled "A Double Error" for an example of how this plays out.

2 Today we use this quote from Henry David Thoreau to mean the opposite of what he meant. He went to the woods to get away from the busy worldliness he saw around him and focus on life's essentials, because he did not wish "when [he] came to die, discover that [he] had not lived. [He] did not wish to live what was not life, living is so dear...." Thoreau's solution was not Christ's, but he realized the typical human attraction to worldliness was empty. Later in the chapter, we will find King Solomon as a more reliable guide to a solution to the problem Thoreau saw.

3 An abbreviation for "You only live once."

for pleasure, recognition, or anything extraordinary. They will bind us to duties like monogamy, marriage, and children, and virtues like thrift and contentment.

A DOUBLE ERROR

The 2013 Millennial Impact Research Report sponsored by the Case Foundation reported that seventy-two percent of millennials want to work for non-profit organizations. I believe this comes partly from a misunderstanding of what people do in non-profits and what that means. All morally legitimate enterprises offer something of value and serve to enrich (not only in the monetary sense) the lives of communities. Providing groceries for people willing and able to pay for them isn't morally inferior to providing groceries for those unable to pay for them. All people need to eat. All teaching is a good, whether one's students are wealthy or poor.

The non-profit myth is built on practical and theological mistakes. Its practical mistake is assuming that the nature of a particular kind of work is dictated by whether or not people are willing to pay for it. In fact, it may be more likely that you are offering something worthwhile if those receiving the benefit are willing to pay for it. Much great work is done for profit, and much harmful work is done by non-profit enterprises. The theological error is thinking non-profit work is morally superior or inherently produces more good. This error actually ends in classism, because most poor people spend their days doing for-profit jobs. Does that make their lives less noble or their work less valuable? What work is more necessary than that of a sanitation worker or cook? What about a gardener or a nanny? Many of the jobs supported by free exchange of payment enrich society the most. Therefore, when a large swath of a group prefers non-profit work, I suspect they have not been taught a good theology of work.

The fact is, our desires for leisure, delicacy, excitement, variety, drama, and really anything worthy of social media don't match up with anything real about human life. Real human life is ordinary. It is primarily made up of roles, rhythms, responsibilities, and repetitions (what I call the Four Rs). Everything we do today has been done before, and we will do it again tomorrow. We will sleep, wake, shower, eat, work, dress...although probably not in that order. In the end, it is these ordinary things done competently, faithfully, and joyfully that make up a life worth celebrating. And it is these things that we must embrace in such a way that we find in them a life worth living. Real spiritual substance has to learn to embrace the ordinary—to welcome it.[4]

There is no escape from the ordinary

This is true even for the hedonist who goes out and follows his visceral desires for pleasure. Sensual pleasures don't last.[5] They can't fill even a day, because they are decreasingly satisfied by repetition. They require time to recharge their intensity.[6] It doesn't feel good to eat right after you've eaten. It doesn't feel good for someone to stroke your arm...for two hours. The ancient Greeks called this the hedonist paradox. Yet the sensual or visceral pleasures are the only pleasures the Flesh knows, and they're increasingly becoming some of the only pleasures known to modern man. The difference is that now we can also broadcast them on social media and get additional pleasure and recognition from how extraordinary we appear. But plea-

---

4   For further study on a theology of work, I recommend the following resources: (1) *Every Good Endeavor* by Tim Keller (2) The Oikonomia blog at www.patheos.com/ blogs/oikonomia (3) *The Oikonomia Series* books published by Christian's Library Press, starting with *Economic Shalom* by John Bolt (4) Episode 3 in the *For the Life of the World: Letters to the Exiles* video series produced by Acton Media (5) *Work: The Meaning of Your Life* by Lester DeKoster. Christians have never had more access to great theological thinking on work and economics than we do today. And since economics and psychology make up most of the secular religion, we need to redeem these areas of knowledge in Christ to reach people through their most noble desires to live a life of meaning and to make the world a better place.

5   I use "sensual" to describe anything related to our five physical senses: taste, touch, smell, sight, and sound.

6   This is very evident for fishermen: The most satisfying fish is the one you catch after a long time not catching anything. If you catch fifty of the same kind of fish in the same day, you aren't nearly as excited by the fiftieth—or even the fifteenth—as by the first.

sures of drink, food, sex, shopping, naps, power tools, hobbies, and so on diminish us when we treat them like more than they're meant to be, and they end up making our lives smaller, burning up much of our potential.

It turns out our worldly desire for the mythical extraordinary life (as seen on Snap-tweet-gram-book[7]) has turned our picture of reality upside down.[8] It has confused our understanding of what makes up a life of substance, and it has twisted our understanding about how humans find happiness. In fact, all this chasing after the extraordinary and pleasurable through worldly means is making us nothing but typical and miserable. The very things we avoid—God, family, work, celebration, tradition, church, service, worship, covenantal friendship, etc.—are the labors of love that bring the fulfillment for which we were created.

DON'T TAKE MY WORD FOR IT

Did you know that one how-to-be-happy book has outsold all others every year for the past fifty years? What if I told you it had done this for the last thousand years? What about three thousand? Since the Bible is the best-selling book of all time (and in virtually every individual year), and since one of its books is a happiness manual, that book is the best-selling happiness manual of all time.

Ironically, even most Christians think it is the most *depressing* book in the Bible. (Well, besides Lamentations. The title should give that one away.) The book is Ecclesiastes, and so

---

7   For those of us less active on today's (2017) social media platforms, this is a combination of Snapchat, Twitter, Instagram, and Facebook.

8   This is another example of how discernment can straighten out things that worldliness flips (see chapter two). In God's creation, the extraordinary life is found by embracing the ordinary with extraordinary character. Seeking the extraordinary life usually makes us small and typical—ordinary in the worst sense. God often uses the repetitive acts of faithfulness to forge the character of people he wants to lift up to larger things, like David becoming a man of music, prayer, and fighting skill while watching the sheep day, after day, after day.

far in this chapter, I'm just copying its author. In most modern English translations, the first two words of Ecclesiastes are, "meaningless, meaningless," but in older versions, that word was translated "vanity," and the more literal Hebrew rendering would be something like "vapor" or "mist." So the book opens with, "'Vapor, vapor, everything is vaporous,' says the teacher." See the connection? What about vapor are we supposed to relate to everything else? Mist is gaseous. It's not solid. It's insubstantial, and it disappears in the blink of an eye. It's the opposite of substance.

The author spends a large portion of the book making this argument: If you misunderstand God's purposes, you will miss happiness. Happiness is not found in achievement, vanity, sensuality, celebrity, intellectualism, getting drunk or high, or anything we use to grasp at pleasure or meaning. In fact, God has intentionally designed the world in such a way as to frustrate worldly attempts to grasp happiness and meaning. God wants us to receive happiness as a sheer gift from him as we go about ordinary lives of substance. He doesn't want us to forsake our lives chasing happiness, ending up with nothing but fistfuls of mist in the end. The best summary of this that I know is found in these verses:

> I have seen the burden God has laid on the human race. He has made everything beautiful in its time. He has also set eternity in the human heart; yet no one can fathom what God has done from beginning to end. I know that there is nothing better for people than to be happy and to do good while they live. That each of them may eat and drink, and find satisfaction in all their toil—this is the gift of God. I know that everything God does will endure forever; nothing can be added to it and nothing taken from it. God does it so that people will fear [revere] him.
> **Ecclesiastes 3:10-14[9]**

---

9   See also Ecclesiastes 5:18-20.

God has made any idolatrous attempt at happiness turn out to be a disappointing vapor. Solomon says God does it so that men will revere *him*. God has laid this on men like a "burden." We know that the universe has an eternity to it, and we cannot fathom its complete meaning. We see that everything is beautiful in its time—that our pleasures are abundant but cannot last. We can't hold onto pleasure or youth, and we can't get at the eternal foundations of meaning, at least not apart from God.

Solomon says that accepting these limitations is the key to human meaning and happiness. This "burden" will either crush or liberate each of us. In Ecclesiastes 2 and 3, Solomon reveals his own journey. He recalls that when he was seeking all the vapors of meaning and pleasure, it resulted in hatred. When he saw that it was all a mist, he said,

> So I hated life, because the work that is done under the sun was grievous to me. All of it is meaningless [a mist], a chasing after the wind. I hated all the things I had toiled for under the sun, because I must leave them to the one who comes after me. And who knows whether that person will be wise or foolish?... So my heart began to despair over all my toilsome labor under the sun.
> **Ecclesiastes 2:17-19a, 20**

Chasing the extraordinary and pleasurable led him to misery and meaninglessness. Pretty ironic. He hated it. Note what it led him to hate: life itself and all the things in his life he had worked for. In the midst of his anger, he also said, "my heart began to despair." Rage and despair. Nice. Is that what you're shooting for in life?

Then, he starts to see the connection between God, happiness, and work itself:

> A person can do nothing better than to eat and drink and find satisfaction in their own toil. This too, I see, is from the hand

of God, for without him, who can eat or find enjoyment? To the person who pleases him, God gives wisdom, knowledge and happiness, but to the sinner he gives the task of gathering and storing up wealth to hand it over to the one who pleases God.

Ecclesiastes 2:24-26a

In Ecclesiastes 2:10, he had already realized that "my heart took delight in all my labor, and this was the reward for all my toil." It wasn't the *accomplishment*, but the *labor* that he enjoyed so much. While he was doing the work his heart was full of delight, but when he surveyed the meaning of his work he saw it was a vapor, and it filled him with hatred and despair.

Does that remind anyone of doing the dishes over and over? You can be perfectly happy washing them and making them clean, but what have you accomplished? They are just going to get dirty again in a few hours. You've accomplished nothing in the eternal meaning of the universe. The result has no endurance, and by that measure, no significance. If you think about it long enough, it may make you a little angry. If you have sensitive emotional taste buds, and you consider the same thing being true of a more demanding task, you may even feel a little tinge of despair with your resentment.

> It is all mist and vapor, a chasing after the wind. It just leads to misery, hatred, resentment, and despair. You have to let it go. But how? The answer is to trust God by taking pleasure in what is wholesome and ordinary.

This is the "burden God has laid on the human race." Beauty and pleasure will fade; you can't hold onto them. There is a time for everything (Ecclesiastes 3:1-8), and nothing in our lives lasts like we want it to—nothing that isn't rooted in God. There is no toil, no labor for accomplishment or pleasure, that will satisfy the fact that God has "set eternity in the human heart; yet no one can fathom what God has done from beginning to end" (3:11b).

But what he also sees is that this burden isn't meant to be a curse; it is meant to help us give up trying to seek happiness through worldliness and idolatry. It is all mist and vapor, a chasing after the wind. It just leads to misery, hatred, resentment, and despair. You have to let it go. But how?

The answer is to trust God by taking pleasure in what is wholesome and ordinary. It's to show our faith by trusting God in the fading beauty and the temporariness of our accomplishments, taking pleasure in everything included in our "toil" (an intentionally negative word). Happiness is found by trusting God in the ordinary, "[eating] and [drinking] and [finding] satisfaction in all [our] toil." Solomon says, "This too, I see, is from the hand of God"[10] (2:24) and, "This is the gift of God" (3:13b).

In fact, Solomon pushed it even further. Not only does God give happiness to those who trust him, but he also grants the other thing we so obsessively seek: meaning. Solomon was

---

10 What does "too" refer to? What other thing did he reference earlier that is from the hand of God? We find the answer if we read the whole of the first two chapters: his misery and despair. He reveals in chapter 3 why he thinks this, saying this burden was put on men so that we would believe, leave the mist of worldliness, and find substance through trusting God in the ordinary.

seeking wisdom—real wisdom. He was working overtime for it. In all his toil, he was seeking to wring drops of wisdom from all the experiments of his life. But only after he hit the dead end of anger and despair and looked to God did he see the real path of meaning: "To the person who pleases him, God gives wisdom, knowledge and happiness" (Ecclesiastes 2:26a). Do you see it? God didn't just give him happiness and pleasure in his toil. He also gave him wisdom and knowledge, the ability to discern real meaning. This principle is found all throughout the Bible. The thing God intentionally frustrates in our independence and self-will he freely gives as a blessing when we trust and revere him, and he does it in the most unlikely way. Solomon accepted his limitedness and turned to God. When he did, he didn't just find himself happy. He found the knowledge and wisdom he was seeking all along.

WISDOM AND KNOWLEDGE

The book of Ecclesiastes is full of the wisdom and knowledge we need in order to find joy and satisfaction in the ordinary. It starts with accepting the burden God has put on humans, accepting that he is God and we are not, and letting go of seeking happiness in our worldliness and idolatry. We humans have no access to ultimate meaning outside of the Ultimate One.

However, God does not leave us there. He knows how hard it is for us to trust him in embracing the ordinary. He knows we are atheists at heart, fearing that we really do only live once, and that our lives will soon be spent. He knows our fear of missing out. So he instructs us more deeply in the knowledge and wisdom of embracing the ordinary. The more we understand ourselves and how God works, the more we can see that his way is not only just, but good, pleasureable, and meaningful. Remember, God is not against pleasure and meaning. He invented them. But he will not allow us to become apple

THE SUBSIDIARITY
PRINCIPLE AND SOCIAL JUSTICE

Only God can be responsible to love all of the universe equally at the same time. We are called to love God and our neighbor. For limited humans like us, love functions through concentric circles of responsibility, or what is sometimes called the "subsidiarity principle." That is, we are most responsible for what is closest to us—our families, neighbors, and brothers and sisters in the local church. We are called first to love those who are within our immediate roles and responsibilities. No one else is responsible for these people, and since love between people requires relationship, our love has to happen locally.

But that doesn't mean I have no responsibility to love anyone outside that circle. My responsibility doesn't end there; it just doesn't extend to the same extent to all people in all places. It diminishes as opportunity for love grows more distant. Love is also characterized by responsibilities we may have to the larger world, even if it is in relation to a much larger context. One example of this would be fighting to defend your country in a necessary defensive war. Another one for us would be the responsibility to vote.

Giving others what they deserve from us is justice, and when these actions are owed in the social arena, it is called "social justice." Therefore, social justice rightly understood is not a particular set of policies or a societal goal. It is the action we justly owe to those in our widest concentric circle of love.

So this doesn't mean we shouldn't care about poor people outside our own neighborhood or people who haven't heard the gospel in distant lands. It simply means you don't have to believe you are equally responsible to love every single one of the billions of humans on planet Earth at this exact second. You don't have to, and you don't have to feel terrible about it. The great danger is that we would look past the real people right in front of us, focused on some abstraction of humanity which has caught our imagination.

thieves when he has made us to grow orchards.

So what does it look like to embrace the ordinary? I suggest five essential practices below as a taste of the attitudes and practices involved. There are many more, but these will provide hours of reflection, and if you embrace them, they can change your life radically for the better. They will also provide ways to exercise faith consciously in every moment of your life. These practices and attitudes show how to trust God practically within even the worst crises of your life while simultaneously preparing you for them. You cannot grow in spiritual substance without them.

PRACTICES FOR EMBRACING THE ORDINARY

1. Embrace ordinary while rejecting typical

Most of the confusions of worldliness are rooted in something true. In this case, it's easy to confuse quality with position. Some positions are extraordinary in that only a few can occupy them, and they get more attention. An army can't have ten thousand generals and one soldier. There have to be more students than teachers and more voters than representatives. These distinctions are based on station and position. Stations and positions, by definition, cannot be evenly distributed, making some positions more ordinary than others.[11]

However, if happiness depends on having an extraordi-

---

11   I can't cover here many of the problems specific to dramatic specialization. One example, though, is jobs that take over lives in all-consuming ways and can't be otherwise. This mainly includes high-level executives and research and development scholars. In some ways, their lives are just as ordinary as others—sometimes even more given to repetition. These jobs seem to resist healthy balance, however. Christians should see such vocations as painful, sacrificial callings, similar to how we see military service. We should see such lifestyles as important for the general wellbeing, but as sacrifices that would be inhuman in an un-cursed world. Though we should treat such people with respect and maybe sometimes as heroes, we should never treat them as celebrities. We should also recognize that such callings are lonely trials that are often subject to intense temptations that grow with power, isolation, and other dynamics built into that vocation. Any Christian who is in or is considering such a vocation should seek out intense

nary position, then most of humanity must be unhappy, because there will always be more plumbers and teachers than senators, and there will only ever be one God. Position cannot be the measure for the extraordinary life that we all seek.[12] In spite of these facts, our deepest longing not to be ordinary is a good longing from God. The good way he wants us to be more than ordinary is in the quality of our character. He wants us to embrace the ordinary in our roles and responsibilities (the ordinary of position) while rejecting it passionately in our character (the ordinary of quality). He wants us to be ordinary people with an extraordinary quality of character—people of spiritual substance. Ordinary, but not typical.

> Whatever you're doing, you can do it with the quality and character of Jesus.

By this definition, becoming extraordinary isn't a competition; it actually grows best in cooperation. We can't have ten thousand generals and one soldier, but we can have ten thousand *excellent* soldiers and one great general, which makes for a fiercely capable army. There is no limit on how many women could be great wives, friends, or mothers, even if there is a limit on how many can become CEOs or professional singers. Seen in this light, pursuing spiritual substance is the only way to fulfill the longing God has put in our hearts to be something more. There is nothing more extraordinary than being like Jesus in the midst of an ordinary life.

The practical application of this is always immediate. Start

---

pastoral help and community with other Christians who can help them stay humble and grounded in their calling.

12 This is related to the fallacy that the life of a person in a non-ordinary position is not ordinary. The lives of "special" people in high positions are often more bounded by repetition and ordinary actions than the lives of others. They may have more power, they may benefit from special treatment, and their ordinary tasks may affect a lot of people, but they still cannot escape from roles, rhythms, and responsibilities, and their lives are often even more regimented and repetitious than the lives of those in many "ordinary" positions.

by asking yourself, "With what attitude and quality am I inhabiting this moment right now?" Love happens (or doesn't) in real, ordinary contexts. Every role, responsibility, rhythm, and repetition of family, friendship, work, and rest is an opportunity and avenue for love. Whatever you're doing, you can do it with the quality and character of Jesus. Every day at work, every trip to the grocery store, every conversation with a child, every time we stay up late with a roommate is a situation for ordinary, non-typical love, which is a genuinely extraordinary thing.[13] The ordinary life is full of drama and meaning, because virtually every moment is an opportunity for love or its denial. The first step into this bounty is expressing faith in Jesus by embracing the ordinary nature of life as a gift.

2. Accept limits in your personal rhythms

We've talked about how ordinary life is made up of repetitions in our roles and responsibilities, but God didn't leave it there. A slave has roles, responsibilities, and repetitions. What separates God's gift of the ordinary from oppression? The answer is a rich rhythm of work, rest, worship, and celebration. You can find all of this in the first five books of the Bible. God designed each week to be the standard rhythm of life: one day of rest for every worker—even the lowest slave and livestock[14]—and the responsibility to work productively for six days each week for everyone, even the bosses and owners. Then God sprinkled in celebrations and worship festivals throughout the year, giving rhythm to each full year. He even made every seventh year a year of rest, and every fiftieth year a double year of rest (since you would have just rested in the forty-ninth year).

---

13   It is tempting to believe that love breaks forth the most in exceptional moments, but that is a romantic fallacy. It confuses the experience of emotional bonding with the opportunity to love. The truth is the opposite. Virtually every moment is an opportunity for love or its denial.

14   See Deuteronomy 5:14.

God is a worker, and he made us to work. He is creative and productive, and he made us to be creative and productive. But he is no slave driver. He has not only given us the gift of rhythm, but he has commanded that we embrace his rhythm in our roles and responsibilities so that we do not oppress ourselves out of idolatry or out of a desire to please him.

Living in God's rhythms isn't easy. Rest is ultimately an act of faith, and we should practice it as such. How can a medical student or a restaurant owner afford to take a full day off? His competitors will slaughter him. How can you say no to your kids when their team plays on Sundays during church? In ceasing from our labor, we prove that we mean it when we say we trust that God has wisely ordered the world, that his commandments lead to our good, and that he is a good Father who provides for his children, even if it seems like the world will gobble up everything we need while we're sitting on our hands.

In our world, saying no to things that unravel God's rhythms for us is painfully difficult, but God has never apologized for asking us to live differently than our neighbors. He wants to show our neighbors something through that difference and to show us something about him. We are supposed to see that God is in charge of our lives. My friend Adam, who is a pastor, said this after he faced

> "I had trusted God to run the world, but I had not trusted him to run *my* world."

God's demand that he find a rhythm of rest in his life: "I had trusted God to run the world, but I had not trusted him to run *my* world." By demanding generosity, called a tithe, God handicaps our money, and by demanding rest, he handicaps our labor to force us to trust that God can make it enough. In the ultra-competitive world of sinful ambition, he holds us back. We have to trust him to rest not just from our work, but also from our anxiety and ambition. The kind of people we are matters too much. People who celebrate, rest, and worship become the kind of people he is pleased to bless. And in fact, they are already blessed by the very things he commands—blessed with rest, celebration, and worship. Accepting limits from God and living in his rhythms will make you more productive and more rested. It will focus and relax your mind and allow your heart to hold aspirations[15] without forfeiting contentment.

We are meant to be productive people but not busy people. The noble wife in Proverbs 31 was often up before dawn and went to bed after dark. She is remembered for her entrepreneurship and her arm muscles, among other things (and not her tweezed eyebrows). But godly productivity has boundaries. God is a father, not a tyrant, and he wants to give his children real rest—rest from both toil and anxiety. Remember this promise all your days:

> In vain you rise early and stay up late, toiling for food to eat—for he grants sleep to those he loves.
>
> **Psalm 127:2**

The faithful work of the Four Rs (roles, rhythms, responsibilities, and repetitions) does not exclude a fifth R: rest. The Sabbath commands in Exodus and Deuteronomy teach us that the Sabbath is about creation and redemption. It frees us from slavery to false gods that demand our work, and it opens the way to creativity.

Without rest, we cannot be obedient, and we cannot be free. God is not glorified by presiding over miserable slaves—over a factory of workers who get no break. Our productivity in six parts is meant to match with rest in the seventh part. God has given life a rhythm.

---

15 There is a difference between ambition and aspiration.

3. Honor producing and serving over consuming and receiving

I have not coveted anyone's silver or gold or clothing. You yourselves know that these hands of mine have supplied my own
needs and the needs of my companions. In everything I did,
I showed you that by this kind of hard work we must help the
weak, remembering the words the Lord Jesus himself said: "It is
more blessed to give than to receive."

Acts 20:33-35

It may seem like rest is more neglected than any of the
Four Rs, but if that was true at one point in our cultural history, I'm not sure it is anymore. Overwork is a form of pride and
greed, but underwork manifests both sloth (laziness) and envy
(wanting the fruit of other's work for yourself). Pride, greed,
sloth, and envy are included among the seven deadly sins for a
reason: they are common and deadly.[16]

The Bible's view of work is just as profound and foreign to
our culture as its view of rest. It's fair to say that most people
don't love to work. A few people have what they consider their
dream job, but they are the exception, not the rule. Some are
genetically industrious and can hardly stand still. A few more
have learned to find pleasure
and pride in their work. But
since the Fall, humans have gen-
erally found Solomon's words
about work to be true: it is toil.

> The Bible's view of work
> is just as profound and
> foreign to our culture as its
> view of rest.

If we had our way, we would prefer not to work so long as the
money came from somewhere. In fact, most people want to re-
tire as soon as financially possible to enjoy a life of leisure. Regardless of our financial position, that's the human condition.

---

16   One of the ways this list of sins helps us (beyond warning us of deadly threats) is
by reminding us that they are universal and predictable. We are all predisposed to all
of them in varying degrees. Knowing them well is helpful, because it gives us a target
for vigilance and a name for our specific enemies. Knowing and studying the seven
deadly sins is something everyone should do. It is especially helpful to do with children.

The passage quoted above from Acts 20 is part of a farewell address that Paul gave to the elders of the church in the city of Ephesus. In these few lines, he says a lot about work. He emphasizes that he was free of envy and didn't claim any kind of entitlement. He didn't covet anything anyone else had worked for, and he worked hard to provide for himself and anyone working with him. While he clearly taught that ministers should be paid by the ones they serve, he never wanted new believers to think his ministry was for money, and he expected his fellow ministers to work too.[17]

Instead of receiving pay he deserved for ministry, he showed them that by hard work, "we must help the weak," because as Jesus said, "It is more blessed to give than to receive" (Acts 20:35). Think about that line again:

It is more blessed to give than to receive.

That verse is about more than generosity. It is mainly about productivity. Paul says it is "by this kind of hard work" that we help the weak. Productivity is a blessed thing, therefore work is a blessing, and unemployment is a curse. When people are

---

17 Paul was not confused on this point (whether a minister should be paid by the church or earn their way). In his missionary practice, he was teaching the culture of Christ to those from a Hellenist culture. These cultures had very different values about manual work and the place of educated teachers. So Paul knew Greeks would be cynical about teachers asking for money (thinking them greedy), but would look down on them if they didn't (thinking they weren't good enough to command a fee). He also knew that Greeks looked down on working with one's hands. Such work was considered the work of the uneducated poor and slaves (following Plato and Aristotle). Important, educated Greeks with Paul's level of education would not spend their days sewing tents. Paul was seeking to completely change within the church the Greco-Roman understanding of work, entitlement, and dignity in relation to work. Later, after the church was well planted, Paul insisted that when someone gives their full time to your spiritual good, that person should receive from your material possessions. He likens not honoring such a person with provisions to God's command forbidding the Israelites from "[muzzling] an ox while it is treading out the grain" (Deuteronomy 25:4). How unthankful is it to deny a few mouthfuls of grain to the animal by whose power you plow your field? He makes this argument twice in the Bible, first in 1 Corinthians 9:9, and then in 1 Timothy 5:18. In both cases he is talking about people who give their full time to teaching and leading the church with godliness. In the first instance, he is talking about himself and other traveling missionaries. In the second, he is talking about stationary elders in the local church.

unproductive, they are almost always unhappy. Consider, for example, how people often feel like a burden in their final years if they are too frail to make recognizable contributions.[18]

Arthur C. Brooks, president of the American Enterprise Institute, has done an enormous amount of research on happiness.[19] As part of this work, he surveyed more than twenty-five hundred research articles on what makes people happy. He found that happiness is highly predictable. In addition to genetics and the kind of circumstances that we can't control, but which don't have long-term effects on our happiness, it turns out four things within our control have a significant effect on our happiness:

1. **Faith** (worldview): Do you have a philosophical or theological framework that makes sense of suffering and explains your existence in time and space?

2. **Family**: Do you have people who love you and share your life with you?

3. **Community**: Do you have two to three authentic friends

---

18   "Recognizable" is an important word here. The frail elderly have roles that we often neglect and are hard for them to see. This includes their role as keepers of wisdom and memory. History is no substitute for memory. It includes their role in advising and approving of younger generations. Though they are slow to embrace change, they are often quick to see worthless fads or imbalances for what they are. They are also important partners in forming our character toward loving, sacrificial service and humility. If this were embraced in our culture (both in young generations seeking and honoring the contributions of the elderly, and in the elderly embracing their unique responsibility), the lack of employment and physical capacity that comes with old age wouldn't carry as crippling of a blow. In fact, we might see that the greatest wealth of human capital we have is in our elderly mothers and fathers, and if we included them fully in our lives, that wealth would enrich us all in ways we cannot now predict. Think about this command from Leviticus 19:32: "Stand up in the presence of the aged, show respect for the elderly and revere your God. I am the LORD." Do you think this command was done away with in Christ (like animal sacrifices) or increased and internalized in the gospel (like Jesus saying looking at a woman lustfully is adultery, or that hating a person is like murder)? I think it's the latter.

19   See www.thepursuitofhappiness.com for Brooks' writing and speaking on this, along with his book Gross Domestic Happiness (2008). His talk The Secret to Happiness, featured on the website, is a great intro to the material and is only about twenty minutes long.

and have a real relationship of commitment and charity toward others in your community?

4. **Work**: Are your energies employed in some vocation or calling that benefits other people? Do you think what you do matters?[20]

It turns out that productivity and service make life better. They fulfill us and support happiness. They keep us strong so we can help the weak. They promote love by allowing us to enrich each other's lives through production and exchange of things we all want and need. This is why work is love, and also why love is work. It's also why you don't need to work for a non-profit organization to do meaningful work. God has given all people the gift of access to meaningful work. Maids, cooks, mothers and fathers, scholars, CEOs, farmers, golf caddies,

ON UNEMPLOYMENT AND INDOLENCE

Christians should always distinguish between unemployment and indolence. Indolence is when someone will not work and does not long to be productive. For this person the Bible gives the rule: "The one who is unwilling to work shall not eat" (2 Thessalonians 3:10; see also Ephesians 4:28). Someone who does not long to be productive has no right to the productivity of others. They love no one, not even themselves. But unemployment is when the desire to work cannot find the opportunity for work that will pay. A man may wish to work and be a conscientious worker, but there may not be a job. This is part of what the Bible calls poverty. It is a misfortune, and such a person deserves compassion. That compassion should lead us to share with him not only food and shelter, but also the opportunity to work and be productive, so he can earn his own bread and have some to share with others. Work is not just a means to the good of wealth; it is its own good, allowing human dignity to be expressed through our created purpose.

---

20 Arthur C. Brooks, "Formula for Happiness" (14 Dec. 2013), The New York Times, http://www.nytimes.com/2013/12/15/opinion/sunday/a-formula-for-happiness. html (accessed 19 June 2017).

sewage workers, city arborists, friends, grandparents, amusement park portrait takers, and sculptors all produce things that enrich the lives of others. Even salesmen, who don't actually make anything, enrich the lives of both producers and receivers by connecting the two.

We need to understand one more important distinction in this arena: There is a difference between work and employment. Employment is productivity traded for a wage, but there are many more ways than employment to work productively. Home maintenance, cooking meals, cleaning bathrooms, raising or watching children, volunteering, gardening, helping people who are having difficulties, mentoring and discipling people, and many other means of productivity are real work. Work is judged first not by its wage, but by whether or not it is productive—whether it provides for people's needs, enriches the lives of others, or prepares you or others to do so.

When God's people value being productive and serving others more than receiving and consuming, our work instantly becomes more meaningful, and Monday through Friday are given the dignity they deserve. Furthermore, seeing work in light of Christ will preserve the dignity of people who cannot be employed but find ways to be productive, and it will teach us not to resent helping the weak. Rather than wishing someone else would do our work for us, we will become people who are actively looking for ways to serve others. It is a blessed state.

> When God's people value being productive and serving others more than receiving and consuming, our work instantly becomes more meaningful, and Monday through Friday are given the dignity they deserve.

However, we can never forget that believing "it is more blessed to give than to receive" is an act of faith. It cannot be rooted in worldliness and the service of Mammon. The goodness of work, even under the curse of toil (Genesis 3), is a distinctly Judeo-Christian idea. It has been partially adopted in many places, but until recently in America it was actually called the Protestant work ethic. It wasn't called this because Protestants are the only people who work, but because Christians worked out of and preached the belief that work is an act of faith, and productivity is part of human dignity. We believe sloth, envy, greed, and pride are deadly and dividing. We believe our own labor should supply the work of our hands, and that we should produce enough extra to help the weak. We believe it is a blessing to serve others and produce, and that it is more blessed to be productive and generous than to receive and consume.

4. Cultivate an attitude of thankfulness

Shout for joy to the LORD, all the earth. Worship the LORD with gladness; come before him with joyful songs. Know that the LORD is God. It is he who made us, and we are his; we are his people, the sheep of his pasture. Enter his gates with thanksgiving and his courts with praise; give thanks to him and praise his name. For the LORD is good and his love endures forever; his faithfulness continues through all generations.

Psalm 100:1-5

Now when Daniel learned that the decree[21] had been published, he went home to his upstairs room where the windows opened toward Jerusalem. Three times a day he got down on his knees and prayed, giving thanks to his God, just as he had done before.

Daniel 6:10

And whatever you do, whether in word or deed, do it all in the name of the Lord Jesus, giving thanks to God the Father through him.

Colossians 3:17

---

21 For context, this decree declared that "anyone who prays to any god or human being during the next thirty days, except to [the king of Babylon], shall be thrown into the lions' den," (Daniel 6:7) and it was specifically designed to kill Daniel.

Thankfulness has always been a secret to happiness and a demand of grace. Think about Daniel, one of the greatest heroes of the Bible. The Bible is not bashful about including its heroes' flaws, but it says *nothing* bad about Daniel.[22] He was a Jewish nobleman enslaved as a young man, probably genitally mutilated to be made a eunuch,[23] and forced to live as a slave in a foreign land until his death. Daniel 6 records the king of Babylon issuing an edict that anyone who prayed to anyone but himself for thirty days would be thrown in a den of lions to suffer a horrific death. Daniel responded by praying three times a day to give God *thanks.* To clarify, Daniel had been abused and enslaved, prayer was only temporarily banned, and the penalty was death—a bad death. Faced with this reality, Daniel prayed in order to thank God not once, but three times every day.

The apostle Paul tells us that we should give thanks *in everything,*[24] and Psalm 100 says that gratitude is rooted in knowing that the Lord is God, and that we are his.[25] As with love, every moment is a call for thankfulness, because responding to God's loving goodness is part of every moment.[26] God deserves our

---

22　Other than Jesus, Daniel is probably the only person in the Bible about whom this can be said whose story is more than just a few lines. Joseph is the other possible candidate, but Joseph was impetuous as a youth, and it contributed to his family's problems. At the end of his life, his economic policies strengthened the ownership and authority of the Pharaoh in Egypt, arguably making the Egyptians slaves of the pharaoh, and perhaps contributing to the slavery of the Jews. Joseph is a great hero, but this should show us how unique Daniel is.

23　The Bible doesn't explicitly say Daniel and his friends were genitally mutilated by the Babylonians. But we are told he was put under the care of the chief of the eunuchs and that the Babylonians were not shy about such things. Also, God promised Hezekiah in Isaiah 39:7, "And some of your descendants, your own flesh and blood who will be born to you, will be taken away, and they will become eunichs in the palace of the king of Babylon." So God promised that part of the pain of the exile would be that many of the best of the royalty of Israel would be emasculated in this way.

24　1 Thessalonians 5:18.

25　Psalm 100:3.

26　The most basic disposition of thankfulness is humility—self-forgetfulness that does not covet attention and credit.

thanks, but we also need to experience thankfulness.

Look again at the list of four things that support happiness. Did you notice that consumption didn't make the list? Why? Consumption by itself is a visceral pleasure, so it is by nature momentary. Such momentary things cannot be stable supports for a state of being like happiness. The same is true of receiving. Receiving and consumption by themselves are pleasures that lead not to happiness, but to more craving. This is one of the reasons why the wrong kinds of charity and parenting can hurt the people who receive them and create envious entitlement—the opposite of thankfulness.[27]

Consumption and receiving can only support happiness through thankfulness. Thankfulness takes our pleasure in receiving something beyond the gratification of the object to something greater. This pleasure registers in our minds and hearts as we delight in our relationship with the giver, their favor toward us, and their sacrifice in providing the gift. It delights in the goodness of the giver, creator, or producer of what we enjoy. It leads us to enjoy the gift in a way that honors them and increases the creator's rightful reputation while rejecting the impulse to hoard credit for ourselves.

In this, thankfulness can make all pleasures transcend our bare physical senses, combining them with the pleasures of truth, goodness, beauty, dignity, and God's glory. In doing so, thankfulness takes what would typically lead to craving and entitlement and raises it to joy and peace. Only thankfulness can easily combine physical pleasures with the higher abstract pleasures like goodness, truth, and beauty. This doesn't diminish physical pleasure or consumption, but transfigures it into something deeper and more complete. In this way, even physical pleasures can increase our substance and forge character

---

27 Entitlement is, by definition, the idea that I deserve more than I have received. Thankfulness is the idea that I have been the recipient of grace and have received more than I deserve.

when united with higher realities through thankfulness. That is why the discipline of thankfulness is not only right, but necessary.

Thankfulness, like a plant, has to be cultivated through practice and ritual. If you don't already, thank God every day when you pray. Be specific. Like Daniel, maybe you should do it three or more times a day. Confront feelings of craving and entitlement with thankfulness. Thank other people for every little grace. Praise God for very simple things. Strive in God's grace to fill your heart continually with an attitude of thankfulness toward God and others.

Many happiness consultants and psychologists talk about the benefits of thankfulness. They will tell you it's good for you, and it is. But it is self-defeating to pursue thankfulness for the sake of enhanced gratification. Thankfulness will not bless you if misused as an idol. It will not draw your soul up to greater enjoyment if you try to drag it down to be consumed. Like all things that produce blessings, you have to do it for the right reason.

Start with worship: God deserves your thanks in everything. You are not a thankful person compared with all that God has done for you. Continue with faith: Trust God, believe in his great goodness toward you, and give him the appreciation he deserves in everything. Go on and on, in every tiny facet of your life, until you really start to feel thankful—like God really has been good to you. This might take a while. It may take weeks, but you'll usually feel a strong change in a few days. The whole Bible teaches that when we do the right thing for the right reasons, God freely gives us the blessings he has hidden in righteousness. Thankfulness not only opens us to this blessing, but it gives us eyes to see God's glory and goodness in it, multiplying our pleasure in proportion to our faith.

5. Approach the world with fascination, not snobbery

Has a kid ever said to you, "I'm bored," as though it's your job to entertain him? The reply in our house is, "Boring people get bored." This is the negative version of William Dean Howells' saying, "The secret of a man who is universally interesting is that he is universally interested."[28] I have found this to be true again and again.

Worldliness has many unexpected negative effects, and one is that it makes us boring and snobbish. We don't devote any attention to a thing unless it interests us, and very few things capture our interest. A bored snob is one of the most tedious things in creation. This deformity comes from believing that snobbery is a sign of higher knowledge and refinement of taste. We think we're snobs because we're cultured. In fact, our snobbery destroys real culture.[29]

> We think we're snobs because we're cultured. In fact, our snobbery destroys real culture.

John Piper once said that theology is interesting because it explores how God relates to everything in the universe and how everything relates to God. That's a pretty wide swath of interest. And that is the point. Everything in the universe is full of wonder. Everything deserves our fascination. When an atheist says, "Science is interesting," he is not being too broad, but too narrow. He is quoting the God who has made everything worthy of interest, because he has made everything worthy of wonder.

Psychologists sometimes say people with attention deficit

---

28 William Dean Howells, "Oliver Wendell Holmes," *Literary Friends and Acquaintances* (Urbana, Illinois: Project Gutenberg), http://archive.org/stream/oliverwendellhol03395gut/old/whowh10.txt (accessed 27 May, 2017).

29 For a great discussion on how cultural sophistication destroys real human culture, see Letter 13 in C.S. Lewis' *The Screwtape Letters*. In this letter, the demon Screwtape instructs another demon on tempting humans, "You should always try to make the patient abandon the people or food or books he really likes in favor of the 'best' people, the 'right' food, the 'important' books."

disorder (ADD) struggle not with focusing on one thing, but with not paying attention to everything. It's a wonder we don't all suffer from this. Concentration isn't the result of a lack of interesting things. It is either the nearly supernatural ability to block out a flood of heartbreaking wonder, or it is a mark of extreme dullness. Proper concentration has within it the realization that we can't possibly be as fascinated as the world is fascinating. We can't spend all our time wondering about all the wonders of the world.

Thankfulness leads us to appreciate God's many wonders, and the fascination and wonder that attention yields will create in us a geyser of thankfulness and joyful laughter.

In order for us to enjoy the world as we were meant to, rather than being consumed by our own drive to consume and control, we must enter the structure of a new ordinary.

THE FULL CIRCLE

Did you notice that we started with ordinary but ended with the joy of wondrous fascination with the whole universe? Embracing ordinary allows us to embrace the rhythms of work, rest, worship, and celebration. It makes us see our productivity and creativity as rooted in God's creation and production. Like God, we can produce, create, and serve, blessing others with life and provision. This leads to thankfulness to the God who provides for us and made us like him. As this thankfulness grows in us, it will lead us to look more widely at the world. The more we see, the more wonder we will find, and the more fascinated we will become with everything. We will "geek out" in both the learning and the doing. Everything will be interesting, and our ability to take pleasure in things will expand infinitely.

This isn't just about happiness. It's also about the substance that can only come through real wisdom and knowledge. As Solomon said: to those willing to believe God and please him, he freely gives wisdom and knowledge.[30] And it's a very special kind of knowledge. It's the kind of knowledge that makes us godly as it makes us fascinated, thankful, and joyful. Consider how many secrets of truth, joy, wisdom, and knowledge God has hidden in embracing the ordinary. Ordinary life is the "burden" (Ecclesiastes God has laid upon us. Yet this "burden" is God's way of leading us into rest, reality, dignity, productivity, love, thankfulness, deepened and constant pleasure, stable happiness, fascination at everything, and wonder toward God. This is the dynamic of blessing, and it starts with trusting the God who is willing to burden you in order to bless and forge you.

In the last three chapters, we'll take a deeper look at three other elements of becoming people who have the mind of Christ, keep in step with the Spirit, flourish in a life of virtuous freedom, and overflow with self-sacrificial love.

---

30   See Proverbs 2.

SUGGESTED BIBLE MEMORIZATION

And whatever you do, whether in word or deed, do it all in the name of the Lord Jesus, giving thanks to God the Father through him.

Colossians 3:17

In everything I did, I showed you that by this kind of hard work we must help the weak, remembering the words the Lord Jesus himself said: "It is more blessed to give than to receive."

Acts 20:35

In vain you rise early and stay up late, toiling for food to eat—for he grants sleep to those he loves.

Psalm 127:2

I have seen the burden God has laid on the human race. He has made everything beautiful in its time. He has also set eternity in the human heart; yet no one can fathom what God has done from beginning to end. I know that there is nothing better for people than to be happy and to do good while they live. That each of them may eat and drink, and find satisfaction in all their toil—this is the gift of God. I know that everything God does will endure forever; nothing can be added to it and nothing taken from it. God does it so that people will fear [revere] him.

Ecclesiastes 3:10-14

REFLECT AND RESPOND

1. What are your Four Rs (roles, responsibilities, repetitions, and rhythms)? List them and include the simplest, most ordinary things like taking a shower and locking the doors before bed.

2. Which of the Four Rs are the hardest to do (a) for their own sake? (b) as productivity? (c) with thankfulness? or (d) in a state of wonder?

3. In what situation or area of life do you need to exercise faith by trusting God in the ordinary?

9

ESCAPING DIVERSION

The only thing which consoles us for our miseries is diversion, and yet this is the greatest of our miseries. For it is this which principally hinders us from reflecting upon ourselves and which makes us thoughtlessly ruin ourselves. Without [diversion] we should be in a state of weariness, and this weariness would spur us to seek a more solid means of escaping from it. But diversion amuses us, and leads us unconsciously to death.[1]

Blaise Pascal

Therefore, my beloved brothers, be steadfast, immovable, always abounding in the work of the Lord, knowing that in the Lord your labor is not in vain.

1 Corinthians 15:58, ESV

FINDING THE SPY

Professor Jim Stigler did an experiment with American kids to test their focus and grit. He gave them an impossible math problem to test how long they would work on it. How long do you think it was before the average American kid gave up?

---

1   Peter Kreeft, *Christianity for Modern Pagans: Pascal's Penseés Edited, Outlined, and Explained* (San Francisco: Ignatius, 1993), 171.

Answer: less than thirty seconds. When Stigler did the same experiment with Japanese kids, he had to cut the kids off after an hour. Oh, and these were first graders.[2] This difference between the two nationalities isn't a genetic difference. It's a difference in character fostered by different cultural values and environments. For many of us, diversion and ease have taken over the primary place of our God-given capacity for grit and focus. The evidence of our culture's ensnarement in diversion is all around us.

It's no secret that our attention spans and tolerances for sustained mental exertion or uncomfortable topics have taken a serious hit.[3] We've already touched on this idea. In chapter one, we considered the crippling and shallowing effects of technologies that cater to our cravings. In chapters five and six, we talked about how our quest to satisfy those desires ensnares us in profound slavery. So why do we accept a slavery that has no literal chains? Why don't we rouse ourselves to freedom? Enter diversion. The really sinister effect of diversion is that it numbs and blinds us to our slavery. All it needs to do is draw our attention and energy toward useless things; then we won't

---

2   Alix Spiegel, "Struggle for Smarts? How Eastern and Western Cultures Tackle Learning," NPR, http://www.npr.org/sections/health-shots/2012/11/12/164793058/struggle-for-smarts-how-eastern-and-western-cultures-tackle-learning (accessed 14 June 2017).

3   Examples of these attention-diminishing effects include: The Facebook effect (paying attention to what and whom we like); the Twitter effect (demeaning reasoned argument by limiting thoughts to one hundred forty characters); the Instagram effect (favoring pictures over words); the bailout and welfare effect (someone will catch us if we fall, so we don't need to be vigilant); the news cycle effect (constant movement with no sense of relative importance or proportion, confirming our biases and feeding our fear and pride); the entertainment effect (displacing active leisure with passive amusement); the video game effect (replacing real experiences—farming, city planning, romancing, etc.—with virtual ones); the socialistic effect (we are part of a story we can't control, and success and failure is about privilege, not grit); the technological effect (it takes less physical effort to do things, and we do fewer things for ourselves); the notification effect (our portable devices are programmed to interrupt us at any moment with trivialities, diverting us from full engagement in the present, local moment); and the FOMO effect (fear that we're missing out on something, somewhere, which distracts us from what we are doing).

face the Flesh, see our idols, or think about our real purpose. From there, our Flesh takes care of the rest. In the end, there is no path to spiritual freedom and substance without the conviction that we must escape diversion.

Though the situation may be dire in the U.S. right now, diversion certainly wasn't invented here. The 17th century French scientist and mathematician Blaise Pascal saw diversion as the greatest of human miseries, because it keeps us from facing what perpetuates all of our other miseries. It's a universal human temptation, but it's almost universally ignored, or at least only half-heartedly resisted. Diversions aren't overpowering, but because they seem innocent, most people don't focus urgently on escaping them.

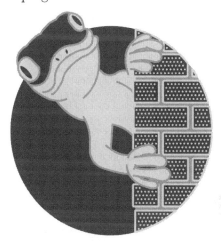

One of the Proverbs warns that "a lizard can be caught with the hand, yet it is found in kings' palaces" (Proverbs 30:28). Some things are simple enough to handle, but they still slip past us. Distraction is like that. It takes its toll steadily, but almost imperceptibly.[4] It charms us with a thousand winsome diversions while infiltrating and weakening our heart, mind, and body. Any particular diversion may be innocent on its own terms, but by definition, every diversion diverts us from some-

---

4   See C.S. Lewis' *The Screwtape Letters*, Letter 12.

thing that requires our attention.[5] It's easy enough to catch lizards, but, still, there they are.

Diversion is a particularly sneaky adversary. It's sort of like a spy sent out from the army of sins. It's an expert in being unnoticed, seeming harmless, and slipping past defenses. A good spy uses its enemy's own people and resources against them. Combating diversion is more like counterespionage than open battle.[6] Our problem is that we are easily persuaded to join the spy in his destruction, because the alternative is to expose him, and we've come to love him too much. Diversion is not only a subtle idol; it might be our favorite. Of all our idols, we may rely on this one the most. Marx called religion the opiate of the masses, anesthesia to help them not feel the pain of life.[7] He was wrong. The opiate of choice for humans has always been diversion. Pascal described our condition in this way: "Being unable to cure death, wretchedness, and ignorance, men have decided, in order to be happy, not to think about such things."[8] Diversion doesn't stalk us; we invite it in, eager for some stimulation, gratification, or escape.

RUNNING AWAY

It's amazing how much modern people crave constant stimulation. A 2014 study offered startling insight into our need for stimuli and our discomfort with stillness.[9] The study placed participants in a quiet, empty room for fifteen minutes.

---

5   This is the difference between diversion and leisure. Leisure is what we do when we have no duty to be doing something else. Diversion takes our attention away from where it's supposed to be.

6   Counterespionage is the practice of combating espionage—finding and dealing with spies in our midst.

7   Karl Marx, *Critique of Hegel's 'Philosophy of Right'*, ed. Annette Jolin and Joseph O'Malley (Cambridge: Cambridge University Press, 1982), 131.

8   Kreeft, *Christianity for Modern Pagans*, 170.

9   Susan Cosier, "Afraid of Solitude," *Scientific American Mind*, http://www.nature.com/scientificamericanmind/journal/v25/n6/full/sci (accessed 14 November 2016).

There was nothing for them to do, but they were left with a button that would deliver an electric shock to their ankles. In the course of the fifteen minutes, sixty-seven percent of the men and twenty-five percent of the women, rather than sit in a room by themselves doing nothing for a quarter of an hour, chose to inflict on themselves a shock that they earlier said they would pay to avoid.

The study's seemingly absurd result begs the question: What's our problem? Why do so many of us prefer something we know is painful over a short span of quiet? It suggests that, somehow, sitting with ourselves in silence without diversion creates a boredom or anxiety that is more painful than physical pain. How can this be? Pascal called this "misery." His words from the 17th century have lost none of their relevance:

> The only thing which consoles us for our miseries is diversion, and yet this is the greatest of our miseries.[10] For it is this which principally hinders us from reflecting upon ourselves and which makes us thoughtlessly ruin ourselves. Without [diversion] we should be in a state of weariness, and this weariness would spur us to seek a more solid means of escaping from it. But diversion amuses us, and leads us unconsciously to death.[11]

Peter Kreeft doesn't pull any punches in his commentary on these words. The reality is that,

> We *want* to complexify our lives. We don't *have* to, we *want* to. We want to be harried and hassled and busy. Unconsciously, we want the very thing we complain about. For if we had [rest], we would look at ourselves and listen to our hearts and see the great gaping hole in our hearts and be terrified, because that hole is so

---

10 In quotes like this, Pascal is addressing the normal, typical person in the normal human state. His more precise diagnosis would have been that Christ is the only true consolation for our misery.

11 Kreeft, *Christianity for Modern Pagans*, 171.

big that nothing but God can fill it.[12]

When we are left alone with our thoughts, we must acknowledge and reckon with our discomfort. We have no escape from unpleasant realities, and our hearts violently recoil from the prospect of that exposure. One of our church staff members described her experience with this phenomenon:

> Some time ago, I felt convicted to fast from online media for a month. The itchiness was intensely uncomfortable. After days of feeling my cravings throbbing inside of me, days of sitting in prayer and marveling at what was going on in my head and heart, I began to wonder, "What is it about funny YouTube videos that I crave so much?" As I prayerfully pondered it, I came to a bitter realization. I was lonely. Really lonely. I realized that most of my close friends either lived out of town or were busy with their married lives. Watching people have fun together on YouTube gave me the pleasant rush of companionship, but in reality, it left me alone in my room day after day, numbing my misery while keeping me from the very things (and the One) that would cure it. With the added perspective of hindsight, I can also see that I was harboring the seeds of bitterness; seeds that were sprouting from the fertile soil of a belief that God (and maybe other people as well) was withholding something good from me.
>
> Before the fast, I genuinely had no idea that I was lonely, so I never felt the heaviness of it. And I couldn't see that I was allowing the thorns of worldliness to gain ground, thorns with the potential to choke out my faith. I suddenly felt the weight of sadness on my chest and the tightening grip of worldliness around my neck. There in the silence, with nowhere to run but to God, I began to taste the real healing that he had been holding out to me all along.

---

12   Kreeft, *Christianity for Modern Pagans*, 168.

I had been so afraid of facing the pain, that I numbed myself into thinking I didn't need a cure. I had also come to love my diversions so intensely, that I tried to guard them from God's view for fear that he would pry them from my hands, leaving me desolate.

In the end, my seemingly innocent diversions were masking a deadly disease of the Flesh. And the real-time effects of this slavery were that I would stay up too late, robbing the next day of focus and energy to serve God as a steward. When others needed my best, I was too distracted and undisciplined to be of much use. When I tried to exercise discipline to improve, my undisciplined will gave out prematurely. I couldn't carry my own weight, and my constant craving meant I couldn't even enjoy God's gifts. I couldn't steward, I couldn't grow, I couldn't be satisfied, and I couldn't take steps to correct my course.

With this revelation, the Spirit began his work of renewing my mind to be like that of Christ, and I took specific actions to co-operate with him in that work. In the end, it took five months of cutting myself off from the internet at home and some highly regimented spiritual disciplines to get back on track. Getting to bed on time allowed me to feel and think again, and it strengthened my will. Over time, I was able to let go of the bitterness I was feeling toward God, and I rediscovered the sweetness and satisfaction of his companionship. This soothed my ache while also giving me the energy and attention to pursue the relationships that were available to me. The craving hasn't gone away completely, but I come to him with it now rather than hiding from him to satisfy it.

The deadly secret of escapist diversion is that we aren't evading anything except that which would make us well.

WHERE IS IT? YOU'RE SWIMMING IN IT.

Our attraction to diversion needs more focused attention than ever, because our lives are increasingly saturated by powerful and beneficial new tools. Most of these new tools have screens, but now we even have voice-activated digital companions at our command. My four-year-old loves ordering ours around. These tools open numerous and constant portals for diversion, leaving no moment of our day when we don't have the option to distract ourselves immediately in precisely the way we prefer. Diversion isn't just more immediate, it's much more captivating, too. These technological changes, which are highly physiologically addictive to our brains, make newer generations of diversions more intensely engrossing than ever before.[13] Consequently, we need never face uncomfortable thoughts or strain ourselves.

Diversions are a quadruple threat:

1. They are always present, even in our pockets.
2. They offer immediate service.
3. They offer nearly infinite variety in likes, games, news, etc.
4. They engross our senses, blocking out less noisy rivals.

The very instruments that could enable us as stewards to achieve new heights of creativity and productivity are, in many cases, actually distracting us from both. Technology offers real and incredible benefits, but if we don't learn to master it, it will master us.

---

13 For example, our brains hyper-focus on video in an incredibly engrossing way. Our brains release pleasure chemicals when we get notifications and when we do small tasks like watch short videos or play short games. The combination of technology being able to access our senses and the response of our body chemistry to that stimulation makes the temptation to indulge in them nearly overwhelming. And when you add to this that they are in your pocket or on your desk, accessible every waking moment, this is a recipe for being mastered. It would be like living in your favorite restaurant with free food and never not feeling hungry.

GRABBING THE SALMON

Diversion is hard to recognize, mainly because we think of it as something else: leisure, relaxation, fun, sustenance, hobbies, and so on. It comes in small, quick ways, and it's often pulling us toward things that are fun or harmless in themselves. After all, diversion isn't demanding our allegiance; it just wants our attention for a few minutes. And what's wrong with that? Aren't these things perfectly permissible? Yes, most of them. However, this is precisely the mentality in which diversion thrives.

Discerning when good things like relaxation, leisure, and fun have become diversions can be a little like trying to grab a salmon without killing it. How do we reject the idol of diversion without replacing it with the idol of legalism, like taking hold of the salmon by sticking a harpoon through it? The Bible teaches us how to think this through in 1 Corinthians 6:12-20 and 10:23-11:1. In both cases, the Christians in Corinth have argued, "but isn't it permissible to do _____?" Paul's answer isn't a simple "yes" or "no." Instead, he offers four gospel categories to reveal if we are making excuses for being diverted from our real purpose. He implicitly asks and answers these questions:

1. Is it beneficial (for your true good)?
2. Is it constructive (for the true good of others)?
3. Will it master you?
4. Does it align with who you are in Christ?

In 1 Corinthians 6, the issue is, strangely enough, whether going to prostitutes is permissible leisure if you are a Christian. In Greek cities, brothels were public, legal, and used frequently by men of all ages. It was a normal male diversion, even for married men. They said, "food for the stomach and the stomach for food" as a euphemism for their sex drive, arguing that we shouldn't deny our natural cravings (1 Corinthians 6:13). What's wrong with a little diversion? Paul's response is direct: This fails all four tests. It isn't beneficial. It isn't constructive. It will master you. And if you are the temple of the Holy Spirit and part of Christ's body, how can you unite yourself with a prostitute? That's insanity (1 Corinthians 6:15, 19-20).

The issue in 1 Corinthians 10 is whether a Christian could eat meat from animals that were sacrificed in dedication to pagan gods, which was pretty much all the meat in the market in some cities. For this one, the tests lead to a different answer. Since "the earth is the Lord's and everything in it," the meat belongs to God, not to Zeus or Poseidon. So, it's fine to eat it. Question four checks out, and the others aren't relevant. But if you're eating it in a temple festival in honor of the false god, you can't eat it, because you're participating in worshiping pagan gods. Test four doesn't check out in that situation—nor do one and two. If you're in a home and someone says, "This was offered to an idol," or "This meat is in honor of Zeus"—that is, if your host makes an issue of it—then don't eat it. Eating it in that situation isn't beneficial or constructive for anyone's faith. Questions one and two don't check out. For something to be permissible, all four questions must check out. If it's not permissible, then—in the best-case scenario—it's a diversion. It's diverting you from your purpose, identity, virtue, and love. It is confusing your ability to have the mind of Christ and is not in step with the Spirit.

Let's bring it into our times. Some leisures are plainly sins, in that they can't be squared with question four. Using pornography, for example, doesn't pass the fourth test. Nor does women reading relationally pornographic novels. Gossiping about people would fail the fourth test. So would shoplifting or beating people up for fun. Such things can't be wholesome leisure, even in moderation. But what about eating? Entertainment? Sports? How do we know if we are falling into a diversion mentality? The answer is found in the first three questions: Is it beneficial to your true good or contributing to your growth in spiritual substance? Is it constructive for the true good of others? Is it likely that what you are using will start using you? These questions require us to be discerning. The answer isn't always obvious. However, with a little honesty, humility, and community, we can get pretty good at catching when something permissible is becoming a diversion. The minute you see it diverting you, it is no longer an innocent enjoyment; it is espionage. A spy is in the gates.

DIVERSION DOING DOUBLE DUTY

Discerning diversion has one major complicating dynamic. Diversion not only edges in before we engage the focus necessary for discernment, but it weakens our ability to focus at all. We can see this in the testimony earlier in this chapter. Focus is like a muscle. It can get in shape and fall out of shape. Disciplines like studying the Bible pay a double dividend. We learn about God, and we also strengthen our minds and our passions. Diversion also charges a double cost. The gratification-distraction effect of diversion doesn't just keep our attention off of Christ, it deadens our passion for him while our focus atrophies like an unexercised muscle. By deadening our passions and weakening our focus, diversion essentially sucks the oxygen away from the flame of our faith. All the right ingredients for spiritual fire may be there, but without the oxygen of attention and time, nothing will burn in us. There won't be any passion. This is why the Bible bids us in Romans 12:11, "Never be lacking in zeal, but keep your spiritual fervor, serving the Lord."[14] This verse demands that we do something to keep up our passion for and devotion to God. We can't have a passive attitude about loving Jesus. He's not a TV show. We have to actively give God the time, focus, and attention to keep the fire burning. We have to intentionally flex the muscles of attention, focus, and concentration instead of accepting the weakening allurement of diversion.

Yet, we need to go one step deeper to see the thing that keeps the typical person spinning in a gratification-distraction cycle until his fire for Christ burns softly or is extinguished entirely. We have talked about the fact that our attention spans and grit have weakened. We have talked about how technology has made diversions more intense and gripping. We have even talked about how diversion slips past our discernment like a spy. But why do we get tricked by this spy so often? Is it just how our brains work? Is it just the reality of chemistry? Why don't we seem to want to be led by the Spirit? Why can't we keep this lizard out of our lives?

Scripture gives us two more images that are helpful for understanding this idea. One is a very short story told by Jesus:

> Again, the kingdom of heaven is like a merchant looking for fine pearls. When he found one of great value, he went away and sold everything he had and bought it.
>
> **Matthew 13:45-46**

---

14   The assumption in the verse is, "Don't let anything stop you from having zeal—a passionate heat for God and the gospel. If you keep a fire burning, you keep giving it what it needs to burn."

The other is from the story of the Israelites after they had been liberated from their slavery in Egypt:

> The rabble with them began to crave other food, and again the Israelites started wailing and said, "If only we had meat to eat! We remember the fish we ate in Egypt at no cost—also the cucumbers, melons, leeks, onions and garlic. But now we have lost our appetite; we never see anything but this manna!"
>
> **Numbers 11:4-6**

These stories are similar, yet they couldn't be more different. In both stories, people long for something they see as valuable. But in the first story, the merchant does something hard to get what's truly valuable. In the second, the Israelites longed for different food, because they were tired of their discomfort. Even more importantly, in the first story the merchant sees real value, and in his passion for the prize, he focuses all his resources to get it. In the second story, the Israelites want to escape their hardships. They wish they were somewhere else, and they become delusional about how good they had it in Egypt, the land of their slavery and genocide. They daydream about the foods they ate. They even say they ate "at no cost." Of course they didn't pay for it! They were never paid for any of their work, because they were slaves. Diversion had served up what it always does in the end: delusion.

THE VERY GOOD NEWS

For all the slipperiness of the spy-lizard of diversion, its remedy isn't that complicated. In Jesus' story above, the merchant saw something valuable and believed it was worth whatever it cost to have it. The same is true for us. In and through Jesus, God has given us everything we need for divine life in Christ and the spiritual substance of godliness.

> His divine power has given us everything we need for life and godliness through our knowledge of him who called us by his own glory and goodness. Through these he has given us his very great and precious promises, so that through them you may participate in the divine nature and escape the corruption in the world caused by evil desires.
>
> **2 Peter 1:3-4, NIV 1984**

God is able not only to give us the liberation of life and godliness, he is able to help us sustain our focus and passion for the truth. He can keep us from the delusion that we were better off when we were slaves by unmasking our diversions for what they are. In 2 Peter, this immediately follows the encouragement to believe in Christ:

> For this very reason, *make every effort* to add to your faith goodness; and to goodness, knowledge; and to knowledge, self-control; and to self-control, perseverance; and to perseverance, godliness; and to godliness, brotherly kindness; and to brotherly kindness, love. For if you possess these qualities in increasing measure, they will keep you from being ineffective and unproductive in your knowledge of our Lord Jesus Christ. But if anyone does not have them, he is nearsighted and blind, and has forgotten that he has been cleansed from his past sins.
>
> **2 Peter 1:5-9, NIV 1984**

The faith that escapes diversion is the faith that believes making "every effort" to grow in godliness is part of the prize. It is the faith that believes that God gives us something of infinite value on the road of gracious striving and discipline (like the merchant selling "everything he had"). This faith, and it alone, can see diversion for the thief it is and can embrace the discipline that leads to substance.

IN OUR JOY

One of the best examples of a life changed by escaping diversion is the life of William Wilberforce. He is remembered as a courageous and unstoppable force in the campaign to abolish slavery in Great Britain. He, perhaps, could be a poster boy for being "steadfast, immovable, always abounding in the work of the Lord, knowing that in the Lord your labor is not in vain" (1 Corinthians 15:58, ESV). He dedicated his life to a war in which, in the face of intense resistance, he persevered twenty years before his first victory and forty-six years to finally reach his goal. One person said of him, "It is necessary to watch him as he is blessed with a very sufficient quantity of that Enthusiastic spirit, which [is] so far from yielding that it grows more vigorous from blows."[15] That's 18th century British talk for, "Punch the guy over and over, and you only make him stronger." But he wasn't always like that.

In his early years, Wilberforce freely indulged in all the privileges and comforts of his fortunate birth, having a taste for gambling, fine food, and engaging company. Even his position in Parliament was more in service to his own reputation and gratification than to the good of the British Commonwealth. Reflecting on that time, Wilberforce regretted, "The first years I was in Parliament I did nothing—nothing that is to any purpose.

> "[Wilberforce] knew only a marathon mentality, rather than a sprinter mentality, would prevail in this cause."

My own distinction was my darling object." Following his conversion to Christianity, Wilberforce "bemoan[ed] the 'shapeless idleness' of his past. He was thinking particularly of his time in college at Cambridge—'the most valuable years of life wasted, and opportunities lost, which can never be recovered.'"[16]

---

15 John Pollock, *Wilberforce* (London: Constable and Company, 1977), 223.

16 John Piper, *The Roots of Endurance: Invincible Perseverance in the Lives of John*

This realization compelled Wilberforce to waste no more hours, to lose no more years. Wilberforce wrote in a letter, "I daily become more sensible that my work must be affected by *constant and regular exertions* rather than by *sudden and violent ones.*"[17] John Piper calls this the difference between "cardiac Christians" (constant and regular like a beating heart) and "adrenaline Christians" (sudden and intense, then quickly fading). Piper comments on this: "In other words, with 15 years to go in the first phase of the battle [Wilberforce] *knew only a marathon mentality, rather than a sprinter mentality, would prevail* in this cause."[18] He filled his days with voluminous study of the Bible and of ideas he had never been diligent enough to master in his younger days. He called these and other disciplines "trifling sacrifices" when compared to the "frivolous pleasures of dissipation, or the coarse gratifications of sensuality."[19] His discipline was not sustained by simple force of will or guiltiness of conscience. He was enraptured by a greater glory—one that eclipsed his other desires. Like the man in the parable who found the pearl of value, Wilberforce had found a treasure for which he would joyfully give up everything else he had.

THE INVITATION

Escaping diversion takes sweat. It is a form of gracious striving. But it is not mainly an accomplishment of effort. It is a question of faith. Do you think that growing in godliness is part of the great treasure of Christ? Are Jesus and his work so beautiful to you that becoming like him is as valuable as

---

Newton, *Charles Simeon, and William Wilberforce* (Wheaton: Crossway, 2002), 126.

17   Pollock, *Wilberforce*, 116.

18   John Piper, "Peculiar Doctrines, Public Morals, and the Political Welfare: Reflections on the Life and Labor of William Wilberforce, 2002 Bethlehem Conference for Pastors," *Sermons*, Desiring God, http://www.desiringgod.org/messages/peculiar-doctrines-public-morals-and-the-political-welfare (accessed 14 June 2017).

19   John Piper, *Amazing Grace in the Life of William Wilberforce* (Wheaton: Crossway, 006) 66.

escaping hell or gaining heaven? Do you see the character of God as right, good, noble, beautiful, and honorable? This is all part of the "knowledge of him who called us" and part of his "very great and precious promises." The goal of these promises is that we would "participate in the divine nature and escape the corruption in the world." But "[making] every effort" to add virtue to our faith requires first that we have faith in the value of Christ's virtue—his kindness, self-control, perseverance, holiness, and love.[20]

In the end, the best reason to be turned by faith resolutely against diversion and toward discipline is that Jesus did so to save us: "As the time approached for him to be taken up to heaven, Jesus *resolutely* set out for Jerusalem" (Luke 9:51). A more literal translation would be "he firmly set his face to proceed to Jerusalem." Jesus knew exactly what awaited him there. Even in his day, a thousand diversions were available to him which would have seemed infinitely more pleasant. There were pretty girls everywhere. There were feasts to enjoy and beautiful places to explore. There was respect to be gained. But if Jesus had been distracted from his misery, we would still bear all of ours without a remedy.

You have to see that. You have to focus on it and give it your attention. You have to let it percolate in your passions. Don't let your attention flutter. Every day, look on his work; look on every episode, every act, every benefit, every implication. Be astonished. Let it lead you with "constant and regular exertions rather than [with] sudden and violent ones."[21] Learn to see the disciplines of substance as trifling sacrifices. See that your spiritual substance is both part of what motivated Jesus' resoluteness and what his work was done to accomplish. Focus on this and let it stoke your passion and zeal for God.

---

20 See 2 Peter 1:3-9.

21 Pollock, *Wilberforce*, 116.

SUGGESTED BIBLE MEMORIZATION

His divine power has given us everything we need for life and godliness through our knowledge of him who called us by his own glory and goodness. Through these he has given us his very great and precious promises, so that through them you may participate in the divine nature and escape the corruption in the world caused by evil desires.

2 Peter 1:3-4, NIV 1984

REFLECT AND RESPOND

1. Describe the effects of distraction and diversion on your life.

2. Review the four tests for what is permissible:

    a. Is it beneficial (for your true good)?
    b. Is it constructive (for the true good of others)?
    c. Will it master you?
    d. Does it align with who you are in Christ?

    How do these relate to discovering if something is a diversion? Think of a few examples in your life that might be diversions or sins, and run them through these tests. Try doing this with other people.

3. Based on your experiences, what do you think about the following statements?

    -   "Focus is like a muscle. It can get in shape and fall out of shape."
    -   "....diversion doesn't just keep our attention off of Christ, it deadens our passion..."

4. How are we supposed to "keep [our] spiritual fervor, serving the Lord"?

5. What kinds of diversion are you most prone to?

6. What diversions do you need to escape right now?

7. What are you being diverted from? What is the thing God wants you to face? Him? Your character? Pursuing a mark of substance? The state of your family? (You may have to pray and focus on this for awhile—maybe discuss it with a mentor or mature Christian friend.)

10

EMBRACING DISCIPLINE

Keep watch over yourselves and all the flock of which the Holy Spirit has made you overseers. Be shepherds of the church of God, which he bought with his own blood. I know that after I leave, savage wolves will come in among you and will not spare the flock. Even from your own number men will arise and distort the truth in order to draw away disciples after them. So be on your guard! Remember that for three years I never stopped warning each of you night and day with tears.

Acts 20:28-31

THE OVERLOOKED EVERYTHING

We've all seen training montages in movies. You know what I'm talking about. We're shown a bunch of short scenes between when the hero decides that he or she has to do something and the climax when he does it. Whether it's in *Mulan*, *Rocky III* and *IV*, *Pumping Iron*, *Batman Begins*, *G.I. Jane*, the *Karate Kid*, *Kung Fu Panda*, or *Wonder Woman*, we're always shown a sequence of training clips set to dramatic music so we know our hero has worked really hard to prepare for their great conflict. (And yes, I'm listening to "I'll Make a Man Out of You" while writing this.)

As dramatic as it is, though, that sequence usually doesn't

last more than ninety seconds, if that. That's because the most decisive part of the story is also the most boring. The part of the story that takes the longest in real life gets the least screen time. This can give us the impression that such transformations are either fairly simple to achieve or impossible for normal mortals. But neither is true.

It is true that humans are weak, especially if we expect to be. We, of all creatures on earth, take the longest to develop. We have no weapons or shields built into our bodies. We can't fly or regenerate limbs. But we do have three advantages that make us utterly unlike Earth's other creatures. The first two are pretty commonly recognized: opposable thumbs and the capacity for higher thought. While the third advantage is lesser known, it is at least as important. We have a greater capacity for disciplined mastery. Other animals may practice things and develop rudimentary skills, but not like humans—not in the same developmental way that produces terrific mastery over one's body and environment. If you compare two lions or ostriches, their abilities will be almost identical. But compare the average Joe with a Navy Seal, a concert pianist, a professional mathematician, a master woodworker, or anyone who has mastered something, and you will see a great difference.

We human beings, while maybe seeming like little more than mostly hairless bipeds, have the God-given ability to shape ourselves with will and discipline in a way that most of us can't imagine. We who have been coddled by secular modernity and technological marvels have incredibly low opinions of human capability. Think of how we sometimes talk about the poor, as though they are irrational livestock that are incapable of choice, self-control, commitment, moral rectitude, and rationality. People didn't used to talk this way; this is a prejudice of modernity. Consider also how easily we let ourselves off the hook morally. I can't tell you how many men have told me it's impossible to look at an attractive woman without lusting after her, much less to thrive in celibacy. Think of how quickly we excuse ourselves for overindulging in anything or for gossiping. I've heard women excuse themselves for adultery as if it was as necessary as defecation. This is nothing new. Shakespeare mocks our excuses in *King Lear:*

> This is the excellent foppery of the world, that, when we are sick in fortune, often the surfeit of our own behaviour, we make guilty of our disasters the sun, the moon, and the stars; as if we were villains of necessity; fools by heavenly compulsion; knaves, thieves, and treachers by spherical pre-dominance; drunkards, liars, and adulterers by an enforc'd obedience of planetary influence; and all that we are evil in, by a divine thrusting on. An admirable evasion of whore-master man, to lay his goatish disposition to the charge of a star!
>
> **King Lear, Act 1, Scene 2**

In the 1600s, people blamed the alignment of the stars for their moral weakness, and in 2017 we blame our genetics and brain chemistry. But it is an evasion, and we know it. For though we excuse ourselves of our own weaknesses, we rage in anger at those who offend and damage us in their weakness. We know full well they should have exercised more mastery of themselves.

Ninety-nine percent of people who start marathons finish them, though most hit a wall at mile sixteen. Freedivers spearfish in seventy feet of water just holding their breath, with the record freedive being seven hundred and two feet.[1] It's fairly normal for people in diving sports to be able to hold their breath for four minutes, and the record is over twenty-four minutes.[2] Saracen archers were expected to be able to shoot

---

1   "World Records," *AIDA International,* https://web.archive.org/web/20070426072434/http://www.aida-international.org (accessed 7 July 2017).

2   "Longest time held breath voluntarily (male)," *World Records,* Guinness World

arrows fast enough that the third arrow was fired before the first arrow hit its target at seventy yards, and they had to do it *on horseback* just to be considered ready for battle. Forty-day fasts are completely doable. Monks often go without sexual intimacy or even talking for decades, and, contrary to Freudian myth, they don't go crazy. It's not even all that hard once you build up the necessary disciplines.

A former Navy SEAL named David Goggins has made popular the training rule of thumb called the forty percent rule. This rule says when your mind tells you that you are totally out of gas and you can't go any further, you've only used up forty percent of your real capacity. You have sixty percent left.[3] He also happens to have set a world record for the most pullups in twenty-four hours (4,025).[4] Oh, and until he underwent treatment in 2009, he also suffered from an undetected atrial septal defect (a hole in his heart) that limited his heart to about seventy-five percent of its normal capacity. That means that when he took third place in the one hundred and thirty-five-mile race across Death Valley in 2007, it was harder for him than it would have been for you with equal training.

With that in mind, for how many minutes can you read in one sitting? How long would you work on a math problem before giving up? How long do you normally stick with a resolution to exercise? Do you hold to the amount of television you predetermined you would watch for the week? How is not eating after 8pm going? What about not talking to your wife, husband, parent, or roommate that way?

My point is not to shame you (along with myself). I'm trying to give a realistic picture of what's possible and show what a liability our lack of discipline is. I'm not just talking about

---

Records, http://www.guinnessworldrecords.com/world-records/longest-time-breath-held-voluntarily-(male) (accessed 7 July 2017).

3   Jesse Itzler, *Living with a SEAL*, (New York: Center Street, 2015), 53.

4   "Achievements," David Goggins, http://davidgoggins.com/athletic-achievements (accessed 7 July 2017).

physical or mental discipline. Morality and spirituality have their own disciplines—even more important ones. But it's critical to remember that, even as Jesus calls us to exertion, he does so by grace. We're called to discipline so that we can survive and thrive; so we can accomplish things we never thought possible; so we can experience the unleashing not just of our

> **If we change our mentality about spiritual discipline, we will do whatever spiritual disciplines we require.**

mental and physical capacities, but also of moral and spiritual potential we didn't even know existed. We don't need to kill ourselves any more than we need to let ourselves comfortably off the hook. What we need is the gospel-driven discipline to work and rest in gracious striving.

DISCIPLINE AND DISCIPLINES

When Christian leaders teach about spiritual discipline, they usually focus on spiritual discipline*s*. That refers to a set of practices that help us grow spiritually. It includes things like Bible reading, fasting, prayer, fellowship, listening to preaching, participating in worship, and so on.

Spiritual practices are great, but they're not what I'm going to focus on here. Rather than starting with spiritual *disciplines,* I want to start with spiritual *discipline.* If we change our mentality about spiritual discipline, we will do whatever spiritual disciplines we require.

By **spiritual discipline**, I mean the internal training of the heart, mind, and will to do what it takes to be and become a substantive disciple of Jesus. In the next few pages I want to focus on four kinds of discipline that we don't often talk about. I'm calling them martial (or military) disciplines. We don't think much about these disciplines, because modern, bureaucratic cultures are built for predictability and safety and therefore require submissive and docile citizens. To avoid disruption and violence, secular modernity does everything possible to extinguish the wild, virile, and brutal capacity of the human spirit.[5]

The problem is that our capacity for power and brutality is not the *result of sin* but is a God-given faculty that has been *corrupted by sin*. Extinguishing our capacity for power and strength makes us not only physically and mentally vulnerable to crime, abuse, and deception, but also utterly unprepared to fight the intense and brutal fight against sin, the Flesh, worldliness, and devils. The Christian's spiritual and moral battle is a constant, vicious, and brutal conflict. The gospel answer is not that our capacity for strength and brutality should be simplistically and rebelliously unleashed; rather, it should be developed and disciplined for proper and necessary action.

Before you read on, I need to ask you to have an open mind as you read the next few paragraphs. Some readers, especially those who have been victims or witnesses of violence, may feel a very negative emotional reaction to these ideas. What I say here will feel wrong to some. But if you read carefully, consider the biblical passages I reference, and pay attention to the argument I'm making, I think you'll find there is a lot of truth here—truth that we actually desperately need. I believe that if we don't reckon with this truth, we will be left to be continually victimized our entire lives.

THE MARTIAL DISCIPLINES

Vigilance: Knowledge and awareness of your enemy with constant attention to its advance, especially in your most vulnerable places

Brutality: The ability and ferocity to deliver the full killing blow against the proper adversary without hesitation

---

5   Examples of modern structures that make it possible for us to be tame and docile include safety technology, lawsuits, and insurance.

or reserve

Training: Constant, structured preparation for tomorrow's unknown conflict by diligently developing greater capacity and capability today

Cooperation: Enhancing our potential in all situations through cultivated teamwork

Let's look at each of these disciplines up close.

Vigilance

Vigilance is a constant theme of the Bible, starting no later than Genesis 4, when God confronts Cain about not being vigilant about his murderous heart. By allowing his hatred to grow for his brother, Cain's brutality was unleashed against the one he should love and protect rather than against the Flesh, which was poisoning his heart, mind, and soul. The cost of a lack of vigilance is on display throughout the Old Testament. The New Testament displays it with equal intensity and warns directly against it. In Acts 20:25-32, Paul gives his last words to the leaders of the church in Ephesus. In those eight verses, he gives six separate warnings to keep watch over themselves and over God's flock. Then he gives three more warnings about what's at stake, calling those who would distort the truth "savage wolves." Paul ends by saying, "So be on your guard! ... I never stopped warning each of you night and day with tears."

> You need to know your enemy. You need to know your defenses. You need to know your weaknesses. And you need to be constantly watching for attack.

Our first step in vigilance is to recognize that none of the advancements in physical safety produced by secular modernity provide for spiritual or moral safety. Spiritual vigilance is something you must develop. You need to know your enemy. You need to know your defenses. You need to know your weaknesses. And you need to be constantly watching for attack. To do this, we need to recapture a lost understanding of human nature, the nature of sin and temptation, and spiritual cooperation—the fourth martial discipline.

Second, concerning human nature, we need to understand the effect that our sinful condition has on us and others. The only way we can learn to understand our sinful condition is by recognizing that we are not special. We are subject to the same humanity as everyone else. We bear God's image as part of a great creation, but we are twisted in our depraved condition. The good news is that much of the raging of the Flesh is predictable. The standard human idols are approval, power, comfort, and control. Medieval Christians categorized the seven deadly sins as pride, greed, lust, envy, gluttony, wrath, and sloth, because these are the predictable patterns of our present condition. They're sin's most notorious and effective plan of attack. Knowing them allows us not only to be vigilant against them, but also to be diligent in building the fortifications of their corresponding opposite virtues: humility, charity, chastity, patience, temperance, kindness, and diligence.

Third, growing in the discipline of vigilance requires understanding our own self-deception. Theologians have called the effects of sin on our mind and reasoning the "noetic effects" of the fall. That is, the moral defects of spiritual depravity cloud and corrupt our thinking. Understanding the dynamics of our self-deception is one of the most critical areas of the discipline of vigilance; we must grow in it as fast as possible and never stop growing. Wherever self-deception goes unchallenged, it leaves a door wide open to the enemy. It's the glitch in our firewall. The only way to remedy this is to grow in the wisdom and knowledge of discernment and vigilance and to do so by God's grace with the help of others. Mentors, close and wise friends, elders, and even your enemies can alert you to self-deception you have missed. This is much easier to receive if you accept that because of sin's noetic effects, you are deceiving yourself about multiple things

> The outpost where you're not vigilant is the point where you will be conquered.

at this very moment. If you receive criticism with that assumption, your heart will burst with gratitude rather than resentment when one of these deceptions is exposed.

The outpost where you're not vigilant is the point where you will be conquered. The clamoring of the Flesh is never silent long, and like the devil leaving Jesus in the desert (Luke 4:13), it only leaves in order to wait for an opportune time to return.

Brutality

Spiritual brutality is having the guts and grit to do whatever it takes to break free from sin and overcome the Flesh. One doesn't need to read the words of Jesus long to know that he tells us to be ready to die in order to follow him. Luke 9:23-25 is a good example:

> Then he said to them all: "Whoever wants to be my disciple must deny themselves and take up their cross daily and follow me. For whoever wants to save their life will lose it, but whoever loses their life for me will save it. What good is it for someone to gain the whole world, and yet lose or forfeit their very self?"

Or consider John 6:54-56:

> Whoever eats my flesh and drinks my blood has eternal life, and I will raise them up at the last day. For my flesh is real food and my blood is real drink. Whoever eats my flesh and drinks my blood remains in me, and I in them.

How do you think that was supposed to make people feel? His original hearers were a mix of nauseated and livid. Why would Jesus intentionally offend people so terribly? While Jesus was clear in the preceding verses that it was a spiritual teaching, not a cannibalistic one, he did mean for the image to have a certain brutality. He *means* to offend our squeamishness. He's trying to awaken something in us that we're uncomfortable with, something we fear. But the very part of us that we fear—our intense capacity for ferocity[6]—is a divine gift empowered by the Spirit to give us the strength to fight the battle against indwelling sin.

It's hard enough to seriously release control of our life into the hands of Christ. It feels like, and sometimes literally is, the road to execution. Whether we become martyrs or disciples, we all must lose our life to save it. However, what if that's only half of it? Being willing to die to save our life in Christ is hard enough. But what if he demands that you must also be willing to kill to save it? Are you uncomfortable yet?

> Being willing to die to save our life in Christ is hard enough. But what if he demands that you must also be willing to kill to save it?

I'm not talking about murder—not in the physical sense against other humans. That is forbidden by God at every point in **revelation history**. But there is a ferocity that *is* absolutely demanded by him. In Christ and by the power of the Spirit, we are appointed as the executioners of our *Flesh*. We are commanded to use all the internal brutality necessary to free ourselves from its oppression—to kill the Flesh before it kills us. Coming to Christ brings peaceful clarity and forgiveness, but it

---

6   A much longer discussion is necessary to discuss the God-given human capacity for brutality and how the gospel provides for and redeems that capacity. In particular, we don't have space here to discuss our capacity for physical brutality and how that relates to our redemption. In this section, I focus on spiritual brutality. The Bible is explicit about the importance of spiritual brutality and says virtually nothing about physical brutality. In fact, one could be a pacifist concerning physical brutality yet still recognize the clear biblical teaching of our need for spiritual brutality.

also starts a war within the human chest.

Faith in Christ brings forgiveness through justification, new life, the presence of the Spirit, and the promise of freedom from sin's power to destroy us. But the very moment Christ gives us peace with God, his Spirit leads us into war against the enslaving tyranny of indwelling sin, rooted in the Flesh, inflamed by the devil, and reinforced by worldliness. The Spirit brings about a new life in us that leads us to the true virtue we call the "fruit of the Spirit" (Galatians 5:22-23)—virtues that bring great freedom and happiness. But the Spirit also empowers us for the brutal execution of the Flesh. Consider these Bible passages:

> *Put to death*, therefore, whatever belongs to your earthly nature: sexual immorality, impurity, lust, evil desires and greed, which is idolatry. Because of these, the wrath of God is coming.
> **Colossians 3:5-6**

> For if you live according to the flesh, you will die; but *if by the Spirit you put to death the misdeeds of the body, you will live.* For those who are led by the Spirit of God are children of God.
> **Romans 8:13-14**

> Those who belong to Christ Jesus *have crucified the flesh* with its passions and desires. Since we live by the Spirit, let us keep in step with the Spirit.
> **Galatians 5:24-25**

John Owen summarizes this idea in his warning to "be killing sin, or it will be killing you."[7] To further stress the brutality that is required, he continues: "Now, it being our duty to mortify, to be killing of sin whilst it is in us, we must be at work. He that is appointed to kill an enemy, if he leave striking before the other

---

7   John Owen, "The Mortification of the Flesh," *The Works of John Owen*, vol. 6, ed. William H. Gould (Pennsylvania: The Banner of Truth Trust, 2004), 9.

ceases living, doth but half his work."[8] Yuck. You can almost hear the hacking and gurgling. And that's the point. We read over these ideas so easily now, because we're so distanced from the reality of death. At the time when these commands were given, the vast majority of people knew what it was like to kill an animal with their own hands. Killing was an up-close, bloodstaining business.

Indwelling sin is our implacable and irredeemable enemy. Unlike human enemies who still bear the image of God, sin has no redemptive potential; it is nothing but an infection preventing our full redemption. We are called not only to kill it, but to crucify it—to kill and dispose of it in the most brutal, painful, and humiliating way possible. We are to give it no delay, no quarter, and no mercy, but to inflict upon it the blood-splattering and bone-crushing brutality it deserves.

Where sin lives, it infects, steals, kills, and destroys. It spoils potential, robs happiness, degrades creation, and defies God himself. It is the most heinous, hateful thing in all of creation, infecting and polluting the bearers of God's very image, wielding divine gifts for evil. If we saw sin for what it is, we would have no trouble mustering the spiritual ferocity necessary to put it to death. We would not fool with it. We would not treat an execution like a picnic.

Yet I fear the average American Christian does not hate or want to kill indwelling sin half as much as he might a Muslim extremist. But they, as with all human enemies, are included in Jesus' command to love your enemies, do good to those who hate you, and lend to those who steal from you without expecting to get paid back (Luke 6:27-30). The right object of hatred dwells within. Your greatest enemy is in bed with you; it's in your skin with you.

The irony here is that without brutality toward our indwelling sin, we can never really love others—especially our

---

8   Owen, "The Mortification of the Flesh," 11.

enemies. If we are not brutal with indwelling sin, sin will brutalize others through us. We will be selfish, conceited, angry, factional, bitter, fearful, and distrustful. Only brutality against the Flesh can lead to true and real tenderness toward others. Love can only come from a warrior's heart.

> Only brutality against the Flesh can lead to true and real tenderness toward others. Love can only come from a warrior's heart.

What are you prepared to do?

In Acts 19:17-19, the people of Ephesus burned the equivalent of more than four million dollars worth of magic and occult scrolls when they realized they were symbols of false salvation and affronts to the true Lord. They didn't sell them. They burned them. In Matthew 5:29-30, Jesus says,

> If your right eye causes you to stumble, gouge it out and throw it away. It is better for you to lose one part of your body than for your whole body to be thrown into hell. And if your right hand causes you to stumble, cut it off and throw it away. It is better for you to lose one part of your body than for your whole body to go into hell."

Apparently, this wasn't a slip of the tongue, since he's recorded saying it again in Matthew 18:9 and Mark 9:47.

Now, you might believe that Jesus is using hyperbole here, and he doesn't actually want you to gouge out your eye if you look at a man lustfully or envy someone's SUV. But if it's hyperbole, what is the key idea being overstated for effect? Why would Jesus say something that brings up an image as gruesome as a gouged-out eye and a severed hand? The point is simple: You have to be prepared to do whatever it takes.

What are you prepared to do? To get free of pornography, would you load accountability software on all your devices and have one copy of your accountability report sent to your mom or your spouse? Would you quit your job to get untangled from adulterous temptation at work? Would you get rid of your television if you knew you couldn't leave it off when you should be investing in your children or your friendships? Would you cut up your credit cards if you couldn't stick to your budget and limit your greed? Are you willing to apologize deeply, thoughtfully, and with real humiliation when you gossip, lose your temper, or use sarcasm to diminish others?

All of these things entail sacrifices of our pride, privacy, comfort, money, and approval from others. Do you see a common theme? *Worldliness.* Our unconscious second religion makes the actions necessary to secure our spiritual freedom seem unthinkable. A new Spirit-empowered ferocity is required to overcome the comfort, power, approval, and control of worldliness. It takes disciplined ferocity to unleash the brutality necessary to crucify the Flesh that stands against the crucified Christ.

SPIRITUAL BRUTALITY VERSUS ASCETICISM

In earlier periods of monastic life, some Christians used physical pain to punish themselves for the presence of indwelling sin and temptation. This is part of asceticism, and it does not produce mental, moral, and spiritual freedom. But one can see how early Christians could get that notion from this Bible passage:

Everyone who competes in the games goes into strict training. They do it to get a crown that will not last; but we do it to get a crown that will last forever. Therefore I do not run like someone running aimlessly; I do not fight like a boxer beating the air. No, I strike a blow to my body and make it my slave so that after I have preached to others, I myself will not be disqualified for the prize.
1 Corinthians 9:25-27

Here Paul is using training for a marathon to illustrate the spiritual discipline necessary to overcome and be vigilant against sin. Discipline is necessary to run the race, and vigilance is necessary so that he is not "disqualified for the prize."

The discipline of spiritual brutality is an internal mental, moral, and spiritual discipline that must be led by the Spirit as an application of faith. In Christ, we not only died to the worldliness of sensuality, but we died to the worldliness of legalism too. Although we may use external rules and systems to help us in vigilance, the work of spiritual brutality happens within the human heart and mind. It is the ferocious drive to attain the mind of Christ. It is the fight to truly live out of thankfulness and joy in Christ rather than fear and pride.

Paul's point in this passage is not that we must overcome the Flesh by physically abusing our bodies. To think so misunderstands what Paul says about the Flesh. The Flesh is partly rooted in our physical experience because of its connection with our instincts, desires, and nervous system. But the Flesh is not the body; it is our depraved and twisted instincts and desires. Our bodies existed before the Fall, and God declared them, with all their desires and instincts, "very good" (Genesis 1:31). It is their bent, twist, depravity, and corruption which comes from sin that creates the poisonous mixture called the Flesh. Therefore, asceticism, or being particularly aggressive toward our bodies, is not a wise approach to destroying the Flesh. Consider Paul's words in Colossians 2:20-23:

> Since you died with Christ to the elemental spiritual forces of this world, why, as though you still belonged to the world, do you still submit to its rules: "Do not handle! Do not taste! Do not touch!"? These rules, which have to do with things that are all destined to perish with use, are based on merely human commands and teachings. Such regulations indeed have an appearance of wisdom, with their self-imposed worship, their false humility and their harsh treatment of the body, but they lack any value in restraining sensual indulgence.

Paul says harsh treatment of the body and the legalism that comes with it are part of "the elemental spiritual forces of this world," meaning worldliness. It is essentially attacking worldliness with worldliness, trying to fight license with legalism. It is a "false humility"—unnecessarily harsh and utterly ineffective in restraining the Flesh.

Sin is not cute

We need brutality, as well, to carry us through another obstacle. We must be prepared to look into the face of the indwelling sin we are determined to kill and see not a menacing beast, but a cute little baby fox. Discipline prepares us for this moment by allowing us to remember the truth about what is in front of us. The Flesh affects our reason, will, and emotions as much as it affects our physical instincts. That means that when you look at the sins of your Flesh, you'll see fluffy baby foxes, not rabid wolves. Unless you're ready, you'll never be able to bring yourself to kill them.

Scripture addresses this in what may seem like an unlikely place. Song of Solomon is filled with romantic love. At one point, the two lovers have apparently gotten away from the city to have a romantic interlude in a rural vineyard. But amidst all their celebration of the health and fertility of their love, they sing, "Catch for us the foxes, the little foxes that ruin the vineyards, our vineyards that are in bloom" (Song of Solomon 2:15).

You see, foxes were common in Israel, and every spring they would have litters of kits. Before foxes become hunters, they need to cut their teeth by chewing on stuff. And in a vineyard, there is only one kind of large vegetation they can cut their teeth on: grape vines. So that's what they do. They frolic around the vineyard and chew the grapevines, ruining them just when they are in bloom.

For the newlyweds in the romantic poem, the line has two meanings. Most literally, you can have either foxes or wine, but you can't have both. So the cute little foxes need to be rounded up and destroyed if you want the vineyard to be fertile and produce wine. Metaphorically, the bride is calling on her lover to protect their love by destroying anything that could come between them. Doing so was a demonstration of the ferocity of his passion for her.

The things that will ruin our future and destroy the flowing wine of God's blessing will look like cute baby foxes when it's time to deal with them. You'd better get ready to kill something, spiritually speaking, that seems lovely and harmless if you want to have a future.

In a sermon once, I told the story of how I caught a rabbit in my garden and killed it with my bare hands first thing on a Sunday morning. People complained about that story. They wanted to hear that I was up early Sunday morning praying instead of killing fluffy animals. They were disturbed by the image of their spiritual leader smashing the head of a fuzzy bunny. But that story shouldn't be disturbing. It should be comforting.

I was vigilant over our garden that year, and in the summer and fall we had a great harvest— probably a hundred pounds of green beans alone grown in my tiny suburban plot, from which we blessed numerous people. This year, I got busy with church work and traveling, and I wasn't vigilant over my crop. The rabbits got through my fence and devoured everything. They ate the cabbage, kale, lettuce, and herbs. They bit off the pea plants and the bean plants as they sprouted, destroying the whole year's growth. I tried to be vigilant, but I wasn't vigilant enough to fight the rabbits. They multiplied, they got hungry, they found the weak points in my defenses, and they devoured the season's harvest.

> To become spiritually substantive, we don't just have to be ready to die. We have to be ready to kill.

To become spiritually substantive, we don't just have to be ready to die. We have to be ready to kill. We have to declare untempered and absolute war on indwelling sin. We cannot stop striking so long as it remains living. And the reality is that sin will never be fully extinguished on this side of heaven, so we can never take a vacation from killing it with the utmost brutality. Understanding and embracing the spiritual discipline of brutality, especially when put together with wisdom and vigilance, is one of the most definitive steps in becoming a person of spiritual substance.

> **Without spiritual brutality, spiritual substance is ultimately impossible.**

Without spiritual brutality, spiritual substance is ultimately impossible. If you are not killing sin, you are inviting it to kill you. It is cutting its teeth on your future right now. So give no quarter to its furry face. Catch the foxes, or there will be no wine.

Training

While we know not what tomorrow will bring and know all too well how far we have yet to go to look like Christ, the heart of spiritual discipline is always seeking to grow, progress, and be formed into the image and mind of Christ. This is why substantive disciples need a training mentality. This requires coming to at least three realizations, all of which can be found in Hebrews 12:1-11. I encourage every Christian to study this passage in depth, but I will highlight just a few key verses as we go through this section.

First, training requires a single-option mentality. That means that you only accept one option as a possible result. If quitting is an option, and the task is profoundly difficult, then you will take that option. People tend to persevere when they give themselves no other choice—when failure is unthinkable. Hebrews 12:1b says, "let us throw off everything that hinders and the sin that so easily entangles. And let us run with perseverance the race marked out for us…" The single-option mentality requires throwing off all other options, hindrances, and distractions. All discipline requires single-mindedness, and spiritual discipline is no exception.

The second realization is that God is our trainer. The job of a trainer is to put the right stresses on players to make them better. You can't see God as a trainer and think that his job is to make your life easy. The Father's providence works for our growth in the stresses we need in order to grow.[9] The Holy Spirit is our constant and present counselor—inspiring, instructing, illuminating, rebuking, convicting, and focusing us on the training we require next. Jesus is the concrete example on whom we fix our attention and from whom we learn about God's good character and will (Romans 12:1-2). The book of Hebrews continues:

> ...fixing our eyes on Jesus, the pioneer and perfecter of faith. For the joy set before him he endured the cross, scorning its shame, and sat down at the right hand of the throne of God. Consider him who endured such opposition from sinners, so that you will not grow weary and lose heart.
>
> **Hebrews 12:2-3**

By calling Jesus the "pioneer and perfecter of faith," the Bible is telling us that Jesus is the best and perfect example of the race we are called to run. His race did something we could never do, and in saving us, he did for us what we can't do for ourselves. His work was also the perfect example of a human life lived completely for God—throwing off every entanglement, hindrance, and distraction. Seeing his determination through opposition can prepare us for the hard road of training. If the road wasn't long and hard, he wouldn't have to prepare us to "not grow weary and lose heart." When we see the triune God training us, we can see purpose in difficulty, and we will no longer be trapped in the immature mentality that hardships are a sign that God doesn't care about us.

The third realization is that we must receive all hardship as discipline—as training. This is perhaps the hardest of the three

---

9   When Romans 8:28 says God works all things for good, it doesn't mean "for our liking." He works all things for the overall good and our true good—mainly our holiness and spiritual substance.

realizations. For this, we look at Hebrews 12:5-7:

> And have you completely forgotten this word of encouragement that addresses you as a father addresses his son? It says, "My son, do not make light of the Lord's discipline, and do not lose heart when he rebukes you, because the Lord disciplines the one he loves, and he chastens everyone he accepts as his son." Endure hardship as discipline; God is treating you as his children.

It is difficult for us to accept words like rebuke and chasten—words that seem to imply punishment—alongside the word "discipline." It's fairly understandable that people read this verse to mean that we should endure hardship as punishment. Because in modernity we have tried to remove rebukes and punishments from the process of training and development, it's natural for us to see discipline as meaning *either* training *or* punishment. But no original reader of this letter would have thought of it in those terms, especially if they had read the Old Testament. The part of the verse above in quotations is from Proverbs 3:11-12. Chapters 1-9 of Proverbs are a sustained exhortation to wisdom and discipline—to substantive life in God. Early readers of Proverbs and Hebrews would not have seen discipline as being within the category of punishment. They would have understood that rebuke and punishment were parts of the larger picture of disciplining a child to become an adult—painful aspects of a more holistic training, which are all included in the idea of discipline. Knowing the context of the Proverbs quotation helps us understand the meaning of these verses. The author of Hebrews is pointing his readers back to the Bible's longest teaching on disciplined wisdom; he is also pointing to Jesus, who was unjustly oppressed by sinful men.

Since the author of Hebrews includes Jesus in the category of those who suffered hardship, it's clear that accepting all hardship as discipline does not mean accepting discipline as punishment. Jesus was not being rebuked or punished by God. It might be better to say "accept all hardship as training." If we develop a training mentality, we'll learn to embrace hardships as training rather than being discouraged by them and continually asking God, "Why is this happening to me?" A *training mentality* drives us forward. A *questioning mentality* destroys our motivation and keeps hardships from having their best transformative effect.[10]

> Accepting all hardship as discipline does not mean accepting discipline as punishment.

This also means that we can turn most of our lives into training, because life is tough. With a training mentality, we won't grow only when we are doing spiritual practices. We'll find that almost every situation in our lives that could be an opportunity for faithless questioning is also an opportunity for training.

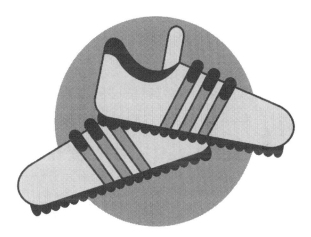

Cooperation

Substantive discipline realizes that we do best together. Jesus didn't leave behind a single successor; he left behind the Church. He put together a band of disciples with little obvious

---

10   For more on this topic, I recommend that you visit highpointchurch.org/sermons and find my sermon "Waste Nothing" from 6 March 2016.

hierarchy, but who loved each other and were clear on their mission. The Bible emphasizes the importance of fellowship. We are commanded to hold each other accountable, to bear each other's burdens, to encourage one another, and to spur one another on toward love and good deeds.[11] Unfortunately, many Christians who get a vision for substantive discipleship progressively become spiritual loners. It's complicated to be focused on discipline when others think you're being legalistic or uptight. The growing believer will often feel out of place or feel a sense of superiority growing in her heart. And at the end of the day, it's undeniably true that more people bring more complication to your life. But Jesus both gave us to each other and taught that sacrificial love is the queen of the spiritual marks. Community doesn't only bring complication; it can also bring strength.

Cooperation improves vigilance, since other people see your weaknesses much more easily than you. They can tell you're going off track before you notice, and more eyes make the vigilant safer. Ever try sneaking up on a flock of birds? It's basically impossible. You can't beat three hundred forty eyes. But some Native American tribes taught their children to play "touch the deer," because despite a deer's superior individual vigilance, it still only has two eyes.

Cooperation helps us master spiritual ferocity and brutality. Since we have so few good cultural role models of proper human ferocity, our practice of it requires the supervision of a community committed to its proper use. Left without proper focus, ferocity can become devoid of love. The Church gives us good role models for spiritual ferocity as well as accountability in its application.

Cooperation also helps us train. Everyone trains harder with someone else cheering them on. Just being around each other and being committed to the same goal pushes everyone

---

11   See Galatians 6:2; 1 Thessalonians 5:11; and Hebrews 10:24-25 for examples.

onward. When we're surrounded by people who are committed to spiritual training, we will find ourselves moving farther and doing so faster. Cooperation brings out the best of our competitiveness.

EMBRACING JESUS
IN EMBRACING DISCIPLINE

We've considered a lot in this chapter, but this last point may be the most important. We embrace discipline in order to embrace Jesus; we don't do it so that God will approve of us. God approves of Jesus and applies that approval to us through justification by faith. We don't do it so that we can control our lives. We must trust God's loving providence and know that we can never control our lives, and we shouldn't want to. We don't embrace discipline so that we can have power. We grow in discipline through the Spirit's empowerment, and what we freely receive we are called to freely give (Matthew 10:8). We don't do it for our comfort, because discipline will keep us on mission, and mission is always drawing us into discomfort.

We embrace discipline in order to embrace Jesus. Philippians 3:12-14 says it this way:

> Not that I have already obtained all this, or have already arrived at my goal, but *I press on to take hold of that for which Christ Jesus took hold of me.* Brothers and sisters, I do not consider myself yet to have taken hold of it. But one thing I do: Forgetting what is behind and straining toward what is ahead, I press on toward the goal to win the prize for which God has called me heavenward in Christ Jesus.

That is the only gospel-centered way to see the call to embrace discipline. Embracing discipline must be embracing Jesus. But wait—let's pause the Sunday school answer and get more specific. Look at the verse a little closer. It doesn't say, "I press on to take hold of Jesus." It says, "I press on to take hold of *that for which* Christ Jesus took hold of me." What is that? It is the purpose for which Jesus saved us—the end he has in mind. It is that those he saved would both become his and become like him. He took hold of us to be God's and godly. Or, to use the words of the preceding verses:

> What is more, I consider everything a loss because of the surpassing worth of knowing Christ Jesus my Lord, for whose sake I have lost all things. I consider them garbage, that I may gain Christ and be found in him, not having a righteousness of my own that comes from the law, but that which is through faith in Christ—the righteousness that comes from God on the basis of faith. I want to know Christ—yes to know the power of his resurrection and participation in his sufferings, becoming like him in his death, and so, somehow, attaining to the resurrection from the dead.
>
> **Philippians 3:8-11**

It's all there. Jesus took hold of us to give us his righteousness. He put the resurrection power of the Spirit in us and grows us in righteousness as we share in his sufferings; ultimately we become like him even in the kind of death we die: completely entrusted to the purposes of God the Father. That is what we are striving toward by embracing discipline. It is why we throw off everything that can hinder or entangle us by escaping diversion. That is what the "pioneer and perfecter of our faith" (Hebrews 12:2) is pioneering and perfecting in us through faith. It is spiritual substance.

This striving and unhindering of ourselves requires discipline, especially what I have called the martial disciplines. It means making war not against our human enemies but against indwelling sin. It means unleashing the ferocity necessary to put to death the Flesh and to utterly reject the constraints of worldliness in how we do it. It means becoming single-option mentality people who endure all hardship as training with the goal of substantive godliness.

When you see it this way, embracing discipline doesn't belong in the ninety-second training montage of our lives. It's so much more interesting than that. It is part of the great romance and drama of walking in the Spirit. It is the greater part of seeking out and knowing the good, pleasing, and perfect will of God in all the depths of his riches and knowledge. It is learning the wisdom of the only wise God. And like lovers in a vineyard, we must kill the little foxes in the spring so we can spend the long winter drinking the wine and enjoying each other.

SUGGESTED BIBLE MEMORIZATION

Not that I have already obtained all this, or have already arrived at my goal, but I press on to take hold of that for which Christ Jesus took hold of me. *Brothers and sisters, I do not consider myself yet to have taken hold of it. But one thing I do: Forgetting what is behind and straining toward what is ahead, I press on toward the goal to win the prize for which God has called me heavenward in Christ Jesus.*

Philippians 3:12-14

REFLECT AND RESPOND

1. What are your thoughts and feelings about spiritual discipline?

2. What teachings were new to you in this chapter?

3. What do you think of each of the martial disciplines?

   - Vigilance
   - Brutality
   - Training
   - Cooperation

4. Would you consider your life disciplined in a "gracious striving" kind of way?

5. Why do you think Jesus died and rose to take hold of you?

6. Which of the four martial disciplines are you most prone to dismiss? Which do you need the most?

7. How could embracing the martial disciplines help you grow in the marks of substance?

11

BELONGING TO THE FORMATIONAL COMMUNITY

Then Jesus came to them and said, "All authority in heaven and on earth has been given to me. Therefore go and make disciples of all nations, baptizing them in the name of the Father and of the Son and of the Holy Spirit, and teaching them to obey everything I have commanded you. And surely I am with you always, to the very end of the age."
Matthew 28:18-20

Therefore, as God's chosen people, holy and dearly loved, clothe yourselves with compassion, kindness, humility, gentleness and patience. Bear with each other and forgive one another if any of you has a grievance against someone. Forgive as the Lord forgave you. And over all these virtues put on love, which binds them all together in perfect unity.
Colossians 3:12-14

THE CULTURE THAT FORMS US

This book ends where it began, with how culture and community affect who we are. In the first chapter, we explored how secular modernity is a deformational community when it comes to spiritual substance. Modernity has brought many benefits that have greatly increased the quality of our lives. Much of it is consistent with the gospel, and modernity has been greatly influenced by Christianity for the good of all.[1] However, as we have explored, much of the present culture doesn't help us become people of substance—nor do the structures within the culture. They aren't designed to, and living in them has a deformational effect on all of us. In chapter two, we discussed how abandoning the world isn't our calling. Jesus said he came to make us holy and to send us into the world. Escape isn't an option.

In parts two and three, we discussed the marks of substance and many of the practices that help form in us the substance of godliness. But none of these can succeed on their own, and they are not intended to. God's solution for the deformational community is simple: He created his own formational community to exist in the midst of the worldly world. The only way to overcome the deformation that happens in our community, systems, and culture is for us to be immersed in a *formational* community, system, and culture. Jesus called this the church, and it is the most underrated institution in the universe. We have to clear this up, because our misunderstanding of the church leads us to underrate it.

> God's solution for the deformational community is simple: He created his own formational community to exist in the midst of the worldly world.

Secular modernity, problematic as it is, is not to blame for our lack of substance. The fault lies with our neglect of God's good design in his two formational institutions: the family and the local church.[2] In this chapter, we can only look at the latter,

---

1   See the reading recommendations at the end of this chapter for more on the topic of Christianity's positive influence on modernity.

2   You may have noticed throughout the book that there is variance in whether the word "church" is uppercase or lowercase. Though Scripture doesn't make a distinction in the way it writes the word for "church," it is common in English to capitalize "Church" when referring to the full, global Church and leave the word lowercase when referring to a specific local church or local churches in general. I have followed that guideline here, though in some ways it is an artificial distinction. Local congregations are the heart of the Church and are most often what the biblical authors had in mind. They are

but much of what could be said about the church is also true of the family. And in many formational categories, the family should be first. Yet the world is full of physical and spiritual orphans and people alienated from godly community through all kinds of relational carnage. God has made sure that at least one formational community is open to and includes everyone who belongs to Christ. It is a body, a family, a community, and an institution. It is one of the only physical and concrete gifts we have from God in this age, and embracing it is part of the path to substance. Of course, the church is much more than *just* a formational institution. However, despite our obsession with asking "why?"—"why do I need the local church?"—it is this formational dynamic that modern secular people tend to undervalue or misunderstand. Understanding the formational nature of the church answers part of the question: you need it to become a person of spiritual substance. That is what we'll explore in this chapter.

A COMPLETE ENVIRONMENT

The concrete local church is a formational community specifically designed by Christ to be an environment that forms people of substance. It is the place where the gospel can not only be heard, but also seen, experienced, and absorbed in a comprehensive community in which Christ is Lord. Nothing else in Christian faith or experience can do this. Only the concrete local church can be a comprehensive community in which the structures, assumptions, leadership, and culture can be built on the assumptions and truth of the gospel message. Only this environment can reframe a cultural climate around Christ and create a spiritual habitat in which gospel character

the context in which all of God's truths find their expression through the daily lives of his people. The global Church does not exist without local manifestations, and all that is true of one is also true of the other. Because of this, I have used "church" more often and reserved the capitalized "Church" for cases in which the broader nature of the Church is significant to the idea being conveyed.

can be absorbed in community.

The local church is the environmental hub of the wheel of Christian spirituality. It is itself Christ's expression of the culture of heaven in a worldly world. It is where we hear the gospel declared and remember through the Lord's Supper that the central event in history was the death and resurrection of Jesus. It is where we see the miracle of salvation happening in people through baptism. Through weddings, we celebrate the sacredness and wholesomeness of the ordinary roles and rhythms of creation. Through funerals, we celebrate lives lived, acknowledge the reality of death, and remember the gospel hope of resurrection. We express faith in God in worship and prayer. We seek to hear his word and know his will through reading Scripture, listening to preaching and instruction, and receiving education from one another. We see the first fruits of heaven in the expression of people's spiritual gifts (1 Corinthians 12) and the development of spiritual fruit (Galatians 5:22-23). In churches, we become members of an intergenerational, multiethnic, and even international family who see each other regularly and learn to put up with each other in love (Colossians 3:13).

The simplest way to consider this truth about the local church is to try to think about how people change. Most of us grew up in families. How much of what you learned there were you directly taught with words? There were some, but you learned an enormous amount every second from the environment—the structures and culture—of your family. You learned from how the rooms were laid out, when it was time for dinner, the tone of voice your father used in the morning, where you would sit around the table, and whether the dog was allowed inside the house. There were ten thousand things from my childhood home that I absorbed but cannot name. I was not explicitly taught many of them, but I learned them nonetheless. That is how people develop. They become like the people around them. They absorb the culture of the environment in which they find themselves. It would be great if every child could absorb the gospel in a Christian home, but the fuller vision of this is the local church.

INFLUENCE AND TIME

It's been said that we become like the people we eat with. That is, we don't absorb culture and influence equally in every context. We absorb more in some environments than others. Sharing a meal matters more than others because it is a more intimate, family-like form of community.[3] This means that Jesus' formational community doesn't have to take up your whole life. It doesn't have to be a commune, as long as we absorb his influence at a rate strong enough to make us substantive disciples and overcome the influence of worldliness.

People absorb culture more substantively if they experience the environment with immersion and intimacy. Time in the culture is less important than how deeply you are in it, what the bond is based on, and how close your relationships are in that community. For example, will eating with five people you love while talking about something you're passionate about for forty minutes impact you more or less than waiting in an office for four hours with fifty other people you don't know? If volume equals impact, the impact equations for these two scenarios would be:

IMPACT POINTS

BEING WITH FRIENDS : 5 people × 40 minutes = 200
WAITING IN THE OFFICE : 50 people × 240 minutes = 12,000

According to this math, the office visit is sixty times more im-

---

3   This is why in many cultures hospitality and serving food are at the center of their cultural lives. Meals have been the central event of family life for thousands of years, and to invite someone to the table is like inviting them into the family.

pactful. But I think we all know that's hogwash. *How much* time is not what matters. There does have to be significant time for immersion and intimacy, but it's not the volume of time that primarily makes the difference. What makes even more of a difference is who you are in community with, what the community is about, and how the community is interacting with each other about its passion.

The local church is Christ's specially designed formational community, crafted for immersion, intimacy, and bonding in a shared passion, truth, and identity. The church is gathered together around Christ, his gospel, and everything that relates to them. It is an immersive community of consistent relationships where people dive into significant, meaningful actions together. We sing together. We eat together. We pray together. We encourage, correct, and exhort each other. We baptize each other and eat the Lord's Supper together. We watch each other grow up and grow old. And we spend time in meaningful fellowship with each other. Sometimes we even have to confront and discipline one another.

Every Christian needs the local church both to be and to become a substantive disciple. We need a place where people can experience the culture of King Jesus; a place where we can simultaneously hear the gospel preached and see it lived.[4] We need a place where our connection with God frames our connections with others; where we can grow in our understanding of the gospel and knowledge of the Bible; where we are supported in embracing the ordinary rhythms and responsibilities of work and family. We need a place that helps us escape diversion and embrace discipline by embracing Christ and saying goodbye to worldliness. We all desperately need the local church for our spiritual formation, and that's exactly how Jesus designed it to be.

FOUR CRITICAL IMPLICATIONS

Four implications of these truths are important for us to consider. First, *we must be immersed in and intimately connected to the local church.* You don't have to be at the church every minute. The Bible doesn't specify how many hours per day one should be at church, how many times per week or month, or what one should be doing there. It assumes that you will worship, hear teaching, have real relationship with other believers, pray, serve others, use your spiritual gifts, and give. You have a lot of freedom in how exactly to live that out. At High Point, we encourage people to come to worship every Sunday, be in a small group, and then do whatever else they need for growth or whatever they can do to help other people receive what they

---

4   Experiencing the culture of Jesus requires that a community's character is substantive and concentrated enough to make it possible to recognize when you're inside of it. Only a healthy church or family can provide this. People need a place where Christ is King, a community in which his ways and his rule are respected and loved—a place where his teaching guides life and where people treat each other according to his care, service, and love. Families and churches are the only places that can offer this experience over long periods of time. This is one reason Communist and other collectivist movements have attacked the family and the church. They realized how powerful the effect of these formational institutions of God are. By God's grace, the family and the church have the power to form Christians according to a radically different way of seeing the world and to show visitors another way of living. If they are spiritually healthy, it is an overwhelmingly attractive alternative way of living.

need. But whatever we choose, we should ask ourselves: Is it intimate? Am I immersed? Am I connecting over our shared identity and passion for the glory of Jesus and the truth of the gospel? Is Christ's formation of spiritual substance in me outstripping what I'm absorbing in the deformational environment of the world?

Second, *we must not undermine the integrity of the gospel environment in the local church for the sake of relevance to the secular culture.* Bringing the gospel of the City of God to bear relevantly on the City of Man is part of our mission to make disciples. Bringing the truth and power of the gospel to bear on the real questions and experiences of the people around us is called **contextualization**; and it's one of High Point's core values. It can be very difficult to be "relevant" to the worldly-minded person while still placing a strong emphasis on the gospel, which they don't have a taste for yet. These two things will always be in tension with each other.

Yet we shouldn't confuse religious language and protective culture with pursuing gospel substance. As residents of the City of Man,[5] seeking Christ means we must constantly consider how Christ confronts, embraces, rejects, and redeems the realities of our secular city. That is true relevance. And while we have these conversations about Christ and the world, we will be relating to the world from a completely different set of assumptions; namely the mind of Christ. Our assumptions about the work and kingdom of King Jesus may feel completely irrelevant or even combative to our neighbors who have not believed the gospel. It will leave us with a difficult question: Is it possible to embody and proclaim the good strangeness of Christianity while also showing people that we're not as unlike

---

5   St. Augustine of Hippo made famous the ideas of the City of Man and the City of God, referring respectively to the world in which we live currently and the kingdom of God—the domain in which God's rightful rule is recognized and honored.

them as they think?[6]

However we try to negotiate our responsibility to meet our secular neighbors where they are, it can't be at the cost of the richness and substance of the gospel community in our local church. Displaying the truth, grace, and life-changing power of the gospel in the local church is our first priority. Only by doing so as a formational community can we seek to bring it to bear wisely on the questions, interests, and experiences of our non-believing neighbors.

Third, *we must vigilantly and courageously guard the spiritual health of our church*. Once we see that the church is not just a place of gospel declaration, but also of gospel absorption, we have to ask ourselves, "What are people absorbing here?" Attending to the real spiritual health of individuals and of the whole community is hard work that takes courage and nerve. Years ago, when I was studying to be a pastor, I worked as a security guard with a deeply Christian man who was doing a PhD in Old Testament at my seminary. One night at about 2am, I asked him if he had ever been or considered being a pastor. His whole demeanor changed. He said, "I was a pastor. That's why I'm here now doing a PhD, so I'll never have to be one again." Both sensing his pain and brimming with curiosity I asked, "Why do you say that?"

I had already done plenty of case studies on why pastors quit. Most get burned out or don't have the temperament for it. Sometimes people in the church attack the pastor's wife or

---

6   One key way we can make these two things come together (that we believe very different things from our neighbors, yet are not that different) is to use religious and spiritual words when talking about secular things and secular words when talking about religious and spiritual things. For example, I might refer to overwork as idolatry or to political extremism as fundamentalism, while using psychological or economic language to explain spiritual and religious truths. Once this is established, you can reintroduce religious language for spiritual things. Bridging the gap between these domains that secularism artificially separates can help to bring meaning back to words that have been lost to many. Once they have heard the words "salvation" or "idolatry" rightly related to things they're familiar with, they may understand again what these words really mean and be able to apply them again to spiritual and religious ideas.

children, or the church is so dysfunctional when the pastor gets there that he can't turn it around. I was becoming quite the little expert on pastoral case studies. But this man didn't say any of those things. He just said, "I quit when I realized that no one will fight for the church. Good people won't actually stand up to the bullies, deal with abuse, or face opposition. Church people are all cowards. You [as a pastor] can go ahead and stand up for her, but no one will stand up with you."

I know that sounds bitter. It sounded bitter to me that night, and I think it was. But I can't tell you how many times I've seen that in a church or heard it from someone about their experience in a church or as a pastor. It shows up in case after case, and I've seen it first-hand. The average church-goer is terrified of conflict and unwilling to fight for the spiritual health of the church. The vast majority of even the most devout Christians, when they see real spiritual dysfunction and decay in their church, just leave. They don't fight. That's wrong. Substantive Christians know that the environment of the church—its collective spiritual health—is what the people (especially kids) of that church will absorb, whether they are seekers or saints. When we realize that the atmosphere of the church is seeping into the hearts of everyone present, none of us can be complacent about the church's health, the beauty of its love, or its tenacity in the truth.

> If the spiritual substance, health, and beauty of our church cannot shine with the radiance of a city on a hill, we have no change worth offering the world.

So many Christians want to change the world into something great, and in pursuit of that dream, write off their local church as a lost cause. Jesus seemed to teach that any Christian who wants to change the world should start with their church and their neighbor.[7] If the spiritual substance, health, and beauty of our church cannot shine with the radiance of a city

---

7   1 Peter 4:17 (start with the church); James 2:8; Galatians 5:14; Romans 13:9;

on a hill, we have no change worth offering the world.

Fourth, *we must embrace and support the authority that Jesus has instituted within his church.* We live in a society that is deeply distrustful of authority. If power corrupts then so must authority. And if that authority assumes the right of spiritual judgment and discipline, our worldly absorptions shriek with terror. Yet, this is precisely what God designed, and he did so for the beauty, health, and purity of his formational counter-community. He has set up spiritual authority through elders and demanded that that authority bring discipline into the church when necessary for its health.

It is not the world that is to display his glory, carry the culture of heaven, or create a reputation for his name among men and women. The Bible says it this way in 1 Corinthians 5:9–13:

> I wrote to you in my letter not to associate with sexually immoral people—*not at all meaning the people of this world* who are immoral, or the greedy and swindlers, or idolaters. In that case you would have to leave this world. But now I am writing you that you must not associate with anyone who claims to be a brother or sister but is sexually immoral or greedy, an idolater or slanderer, a drunkard or swindler. Do not even eat with such people. What business is it of mine to judge those outside the church? *Are you not to judge those inside? God will judge those outside. "Expel the wicked person from among you."*[8]

What might be most surprising in this paragraph is that Paul tells them not to judge people who are really terribly wicked. As examples, he lists people who are sexually immoral, are obviously greedy, swindle and cheat others, and worship false gods. These people stink! All "good people" in the world,

---

Mark 12:31, etc. (start with your neighbor—your main responsibility to love).

8   This last line is an echo of commands God gave in the Torah. See Deuteronomy 13:5; 17:7; 19:19; 21:21; 22:21, 24; 24:7.

regardless of their religious or irreligious convictions, would judge and separate from them. And yet he's telling Christians not to separate from them. It's God's job to judge those outside the church, not ours.

But Paul also says that we can't turn a blind eye when people claim to be Christians and openly act like they aren't. Just like we aren't supposed to turn a blind eye to false teaching, we aren't supposed to turn a blind eye to openly false living. The first step is always kind and private correction.[9] But if a professing believer will not be corrected after multiple attempts at gracious correction, Paul teaches that we must "expel the wicked person," not only so their wickedness doesn't infect the whole church, but also so the disciplined person can feel himself outside the promise of salvation and be drawn to repentance and salvation (2 Corinthians 2:6-8) and then be joyfully reunited with the church. It is our God-given responsibility to uphold the integrity of the message and environment of the gospel in the local church.

That responsibility is entrusted to the whole congregation, but is normally led by the pastor and elders who have become its leaders. This means that if we understand how Jesus has set up the local church, we should expect and encourage the elders to lead in all matters of spiritual shepherding, including church discipline, even if they have to confront and correct us. Often, if elders are active in teaching, encouraging, exhorting, and correcting Christ's flock, there will be very few cases of church discipline. Most people will either be gently corrected before things go too far, or they will remove themselves, knowing the integrity and consistency of the elders.

Concerning the elders, a wise flock takes the office and work of elders very seriously and encourages the best and most godly men in the congregation to present themselves for the work. It selects them very carefully, not elevating anyone who

---

9   Matthew 18:15-18; see also 1 Peter 4:17.

isn't qualified by the biblical standards laid out in 1 Timothy 3 and Titus 1. Finally, it prays for them constantly, knowing the importance and difficulty of their work. It's hard work to fight for the church with tenderness—to fight with ferocity while loving people compassionately. Honor them for what they do.[10]

EMBRACING FORMATIONAL COMMUNITY

When we see the church for what it is, as Christ's formational counter-community, it will change how we participate in and support the local church. With our minds framed by this reality, we will:

- know that every Christian should be an immersed and intimate member of the local church.
- know that what can feel like difficult intimacies—corporate singing, asking people for prayer, etc.—are essential to our transformation.
- want our church's relevance to be achieved through substantively and explicitly displaying the truth, grace, and life-changing power of Christ.
- be willing to stand up and fight for the church and her health either as leaders in the church, or when leaders need our support (assuming they aren't the problem).
- make the spiritual health and godliness of our local church a top priority. We won't settle for it being a nice religious organization.
- strive to take hold of that for which Christ took hold of us (Philippians 3:12).
- embrace church authority in church discipline as a necessary function of church health.
- pray for and be careful in selecting people for church authority.

10   See Hebrews 13:17 and 1 Timothy 5:17.

There is only one way to help a person who has been deformed by the wrong kind of community: for him or her to be immersed in the right kind of community. Jesus has created the church to be this community for us—and for others through us. Such a community must have a certain structure, ethos, and environment. The only such community in the world that has this is the gospel-centered local church. It is the place where godliness is found, shared, and displayed in its most concentrated beauty.

Such churches are the best incubators for substantive believers with the mind of Christ living in step with the Spirit. As they increasingly obey "everything [Jesus] commanded" (Matthew 28:20), they will become increasingly intergenerational, multiethnic, and international.[11] As they expand into their purpose, they expand their capacity for love in the hard places. The church is the heavenly glory of the supernatural Christ and his salvation made seemingly ordinary. Embrace it, and substance, wisdom, and blessing will embrace you.[12]

CONCLUSION: DOING THE IMPOSSIBLE

As we come to the end of this study together, you may have a nagging question still in your mind: Is the vision of life laid out in this book actually possible? For us? For you? Here's what I know: It is definitely impossible if we are worldly people—shallow, vaporous, fragile, and looking to everything and everyone but Christ. But in Christ, God said:

> *His divine power has given us everything we need for life and godliness* through our knowledge of him who called us by his own glory and goodness. Through these he has given us his very great and precious promises, so that through them you may partici-

---

11 This happens to the degree that these characteristics are possible given a church's local demographics and relational opportunities outside its immediate neighborhood.

12 Proverbs 3:18; 4:8.

pate in the divine nature and escape the corruption in the world caused by evil desires. *For this very reason, make every effort* to add to your faith goodness; and to goodness, knowledge; and to knowledge, self-control; and to self-control, perseverance; and to perseverance, godliness; and to godliness, brotherly kindness; and to brotherly kindness, love. But if anyone does not have them, he is nearsighted and blind, and has forgotten that he has been cleansed from their past sins.

2 Peter 1:3-9, NIV 1984

Everything we need for life and godliness has been given as a gift to us in Christ because of God's own gloriousness and goodness. This should change our perspective on the impossible. If Jesus was generous enough to give us an impossible forgiveness, why should he not also give us everything we need to be formed in the godliness for which he created us?

But if we see this, we will also take seriously that he says we must "make every effort" to receive these gifts and grow and develop in their transforming power. Receiving substance is a sweaty business. Effortful receiving is the very essence of pursuing spiritual substance. It is what it means to live out saving faith in real life. This is the purpose for which Christ forgave us and a central part of his cosmic plan for the redemption of all things. It is the single great calling of your life, because it is the single great purpose of your creation and redemption. It is the road to your greatest purpose and happiness. It is the means by which God can be seen as glorious and good—for our joy and the good of all creation.

If this sounds overwhelming to you, my final exhortation to you is to meditate on the nature and promises of the One who has invited you to it. If you are in Christ, the very same power that raised Jesus from the dead and seated him at the right hand of God is alive in you (Romans 8:11). In the words of the apostle Paul:

I pray that the eyes of your heart may be enlightened in order that you may know the hope to which he has called you, the riches of his glorious inheritance in his holy people, and his incomparably great power for us who believe. That power is the same as the mighty strength he exerted when he raised Christ from the dead and seated him at his right hand in the heavenly realms, far above all rule and authority, power and dominion, and every name that is invoked, not only in the present age but also in the one to come.

Ephesians 1:18-21

The people of God have always fixed their hope not on their own ability, but on our Father's perfect strength and immeasurable compassion. In Christ, you are stronger than you've ever imagined, and you lack nothing—absolutely nothing.

The simple goal of this book is to help burn away the fog of worldliness with all its confusions and move us deeper into a seriousness about discipleship that will produce glorious spiritual substance in our lives. Growing in spiritual substance will make us deeper, more resilient, and stronger, as well as unshakable in hope and peace. It will help us pursue the virtues that can "keep [us] from being ineffective and unproductive in [our] knowledge of our Lord Jesus Christ" (2 Peter 1:8). In short, its goal is to help those of us who have received Christ to go on in becoming like him in real spiritual substance, no matter how worldly this world becomes.

As another pastor said before me:

Do everything without grumbling or arguing, so that you may become blameless and pure, "children of God without fault in a warped and crooked generation." Then you will shine among them like stars in the sky as you hold firmly to the word of life. And then I will be able to boast on the day of Christ that I did not run or labor in vain.

Philippians 2:14-16

Let us strive together in grace to be all that God has made us to be, and let's do it for the unspeakably great joy set before us (Hebrews 12:2).

SUGGESTED BIBLE MEMORIZATION

Therefore, as God's chosen people, holy and dearly loved, clothe your-selves with compassion, kindness, humility, gentleness and patience. Bear with each other and forgive one another if any of you has a grievance against someone. Forgive as the Lord forgave you. And over all these virtues put on love, which binds them all together in perfect unity.

Let the peace of Christ rule in your hearts, since as members of one body you were called to peace. And be thankful. Let the message of Christ dwell among you richly as you teach and admonish one another with all wisdom through psalms, hymns, and songs from the Spirit, singing to God with gratitude in your hearts. And whatever you do, whether in word or deed, do it all in the name of the Lord Jesus, giving thanks to God the Father through him.

Colossians 3:12-17

REFLECT AND RESPOND

1. Three components of being part of the formational community are immersion, intimacy, and shared passion. Do these characterize your experience in the local church?

2. Do you feel and think about the church the way Jesus says he does in the Scriptures? If not, what is stopping you?

3. Is the spiritual health of your church causing people in it to absorb spiritual substance or worldly dysfunction? If it's not healthy, how can you fight for its health in a constructive way that tends toward unity and demonstrated humility?

4. How do you feel and think about church discipline and spiritual authority? Are you fearful or cynical because of past experiences or things you've heard? Do you get involved in choosing the leaders of your church? Do you pray regularly for your leaders in the church and their families?

FOR FURTHER READING

Protestants: The Faith That Made the Modern World by Alec Ryrie

Books by Rodney Stark, especially *The Victory of Reason* and *How the West Was Won*

APPENDICES

GLOSSARY

This is a specialized glossary, in that it doesn't attempt to represent the full denotation of the given term but seeks instead to highlight and clarify a particular meaning which is closest to the way the term is used in this book. Many of these entries go beyond a straightforward glossary for the sake of fleshing out the meaning of unfamiliar terms.

Each definition ends with an indication of the chapter in which the term was introduced, though many were used throughout the book.

Brutality   (N) The ability and ferocity to lay the full killing blow against the proper adversary without hesitation or reserve. (Ch 10)

Common grace   (N) Blessings resulting from God's generosity to everyone regardless of whether or not they deserve it (which no one does) or have come to faith in the Savior. Rain and sun, governmental order, and being made in God's image all fall into the category of undeserved blessing. Common grace is also the result of all people possessing the image of God. Even when we are in rebellion against God, we still can't help but do things that image him in certain ways. Many of these things are beneficial to humans even if not done out of worship, love, and obedience to God. (Ch 1)

Contextualization (N) The work of communicating and practicing biblical truths in a way that is clearly recognizable and relatable within a specific culture without sacrificing the integrity of the message. When we contextualize any aspect of the gospel story, we must be students both of the gospel and of the target context, so we are able to bring the gospel to bear on the experiences and assumptions of a specific cultural time and space. (Ch 11)

Cooperation (N) Cultivated teamwork which enhances our individual potentials. (Ch 10)

Discernment (N) The ability to differentiate between what we should receive, what we should reject, and what we should redeem. (Ch 2)

Flesh (N) The seat of human desires that are not submitted to their divine purpose and are rooted in the lower, unregulated drives for bodily relief, self-protection, and self-assertion. It is a biblical category referring to the rebellious and self-gratifying passions of the sinful condition that are opposed to the Spirit and faithfulness. From the Greek *sarx*, meaning flesh. (Ch 1)

Gracious striving (N) Refers to working hard toward a goal, realizing that your work cannot achieve success on its own and that it does not entitle you to anything. In Christ, this refers to the fact that we labor and work for godliness, but that it is still something received as a gift from God, freely by his grace, and out of the riches of Christ—not our own effort or work. A good rule of thumb is this: if the way you are looking at this could lead to you bragging before people or feeling entitled toward God, then your striving is no longer gracious (See Romans 3:24-4:8, 1 Corinthians 1:28-31, Galatians 6:13-14, Ephesians 2:9). (Ch 7)

Holiness (N) The quality of being pure, other, and special after the pattern of God. (Ch 3)

Mammon (N) A term used in the Bible to describe loving the things of the world as things unto themselves—specifically, loving them for the pleasure, security, and self-importance we can extract from them. It is often personified as a wicked master or false god—a rival for our affections. From the Greek *mammonas*, meaning riches. (Ch 1)

Revelation history (N) The unfolding of God's revelation, primarily as recorded in Scripture from Genesis to Revelation. (Ch 10)

Sanctify (V) To set apart (make holy) for a specific purpose with a very specific identity. To be sanctified is to be made holy in practice in this life—to progressively become what we have been declared to be in Christ. This happens through the event of regeneration when we come to Christ, and the presence of the Holy Spirit, faith, and the habits of grace that God has given us to help us grow in the family of God called the Church. (Ch 2)

Spiritual discipline (N) The internal training of the heart, mind, and will to do what it takes to be and become a substantive disciple of Jesus. (Ch 10)

Steward (N) A servant who manages the affairs or property on behalf of another. One who owns nothing but governs everything. (Ch 2)

Training (N) Constant, structured preparation for tomorrow's unknown conflict by diligently developing greater capacity and capability today. (Ch 10)

Vigilance (N) Knowledge and awareness of your enemy with constant attention to its advance, especially in your most vulnerable places. (Ch 10)

Virtue (N) The state of one's character consisting of right belief and right desires and motivations made reliable in practice through habit. Virtue can be understood narrowly regarding individual virtues like love, humility, cheerfulness, and the like. In such cases, right conviction and right habit are in place in reference to this one individual virtue. However, a virtuous person must ultimately focus on the complete scope of virtue, namely how all the virtues rightly interrelate in a fully-formed character. The Bible refers to this holistic sense of virtue, when integrated fully with Christian truth, as godliness or holiness. Note that the concept of virtue is not only about right thought or belief (faith), but always carries the properties of habit and strength (obedience). From Latin root *vir*, which originally meant simply "man" but later came to carry the meaning of the moral excellence all men and women should possess to be fully formed humans. (Ch 3)

Visceral (ADJ) Deriving from a human drive that is neither the heart nor the mind and is rooted in physical urges and the selfish urges of instinct. It refers to the desires that come uncontrolled and unreasoned out of our desires, often related to our most bodily urges—wrapped up in pleasing our nervous system as efficiently as possible. These passions are embodied in the seven deadly sins: rage/wrath, gluttony, sloth, envy, pride, lust, greed. From the Latin *viscera*, meaning internal organs or guts. (Ch 1)

Worldliness (N) Derived from "world" (Greek *kosmos*), and used by New Testament authors (e.g. John 3:16) to refer to all of creation that does not stand consciously under God's rule as Creator, King, and Redeemer. Worldliness, then, refers to everything in human life that is not in line with the gospel and truth of God in Christ. Worldliness is what is of the world—that which is opposed to the kingdom of God. Worldliness is an antonym of something like "kingdomness" (in line with God and his kingdom)—the word most often used in the New Testament for this idea is "godliness." (Ch 1)

Worldly (ADJ) Characterized by behaviors and ways of thinking that are in rebellion against God. The Greek word is *kosmos*, from which we adopted the word cosmos, signifying everything in the material world. It is used in the New Testament not to describe something as worldly in the sense of being of the Earth or of created things. Rather, it describes behaviors and beliefs that affirm rebellion against God within his own creation. To be worldly is to see sin as normal and to conform to it, rejecting God as our Maker and rightful King. It is dedication to created things and what we can get for ourselves out of them rather than allegiance to our Creator. (Ch 1)

THE CAVALRY:
ON TRUMPETS AND HORSES

When I began this book almost two years ago, it was going to be called *Cavalry*. It was going to be a book about how a church can become what it was meant to be, why most churches don't reach their redemptive potential, and how we can.

The idea for the title came from a quote from Tim Keller that I can't find and only vaguely remember. He said something like, "Leaders in the church have all kinds of visions, but they don't have the cavalry to actually get those visions accomplished. They can blow the trumpet, but there are no horses to carry out the charge." There's a huge difference between having a vision and having an impact, just like there is a big difference between sounding a trumpet and actually unleashing a cavalry charge. It's one thing to have a trumpet; it's another thing to have five thousand horses trained for battle and ready to go. There is no shortage of visionary trumpet blasts. The shortage is in the horses.

When a church seems to be doing poorly, it's fairly common for people to assume that it's lacking "vision." People say, "What that church needs is a visionary leader!" This is what often passes for a sophisticated answer for church woes. In the last fifty years or so, our culture's demand for leadership books and success gurus has continually grown. Every Christian leader seems to know that they should be casting the vision; dreaming a big, hairy, audacious dream. I hear it everywhere. And yet so few of these visions or dreams become realities. So few redemptive ideas become redemptive stories. These days, people just seem to yawn at them.

I have become more and more convinced over the course of twenty years of ministry that the typical church's problem isn't really a lack of vision. I believe what we lack is character and conviction. We need courageous, humble, sacrificial godliness. I believe we are not short on trumpets. Churches are short on horses. Dreams are a dime a dozen and spring up overnight. Substantive, godly Christians are forged through years in the gracious striving of sanctification. This is what we lack, and when it is missing, we dream up crummy dreams— dim and worldly visions. If we want to live redemptive stories rather than just dream redemptive dreams, we need a renewal in character and conviction. If we want to lead a movement advancing the gospel in the world, we need people of spiritual substance. The trumpet needs a cavalry. We can only do this together.

I have tried to simplify and clarify the path to this spiritual substance in the preceding pages. Yet, for the church to be great, we require one additional and very specific conviction. It might even be called a vision, but it is not a vision *for* the church. It is a vision *of* the church. It is a conviction about the potency of the people of God, the power of our message, and the potential for redemption in our generation—even in our most difficult cities.

FINDING THE BAR

I've been told through all my years in ministry—through my whole life, really—what is and isn't possible in churches. Most of my church experiences have been unsatisfying and didn't seem to resemble at all the idea or experience of the church in the Bible. I have since studied the statistics on church decline and church growth. I've been told that if you can do what the "good churches" are doing, you're a success. Growing churches make up six percent or less of all churches, so it's easy to think that if you're in that group, you're doing great. This bar of success is not only intoxicating for pastors, but for all Christians. Everyone wants to be a success.

There is a subtle distinction here that can be very destructive if we miss it. Very soon in our desire for success, we move from looking for *inspiration* to looking for *validation.* The first can be life-giving and faith-building. The second is deadly. Looking for inspiration from churches where God is moving in great ways can be very motivating, especially if you have personal relationships with them. This is because you are not looking so much at the outcome statistics as at the fiery faith, sacrifice, and creativity of those doing the work. When we simply look at impersonal reports of what churches in America are doing numerically, we end up looking primarily for validation: checking how we measure up.

There are few things as deadly as this. We will tend either to fear our stagnant numbers or take pride in our growth (even if we find it through creative counting). Looking for validation instead of inspiration leads us away from faith and grace. We start to crave the validation of success and fear the shame of failure. We stop thinking about what we are doing and become fixated on outcomes we can't control. Why do we fall for this worldly obsession with validation? Why would we allow ourselves to look at some man-made bar of success to affirm our work in the gospel?

We like to think that it's because we want to be realists about how we're doing. Measuring is being honest. We are clear-minded people. Right? But what if I told you that's not the reason we look to "successful" church statistics to tell us what we should be? What if I said that it is a coping mechanism to deal with our disappointment with the church, the gospel, and God himself?

When we look at this sort of "success" a little closer, we see that very few of those churches are actually leading people to

Christ and making significant differences in their communities. Few are marked by godliness, high biblical literacy, or generosity in investing their resources in the kingdom of God. I have no interest in attacking these churches, but isn't it foolish to judge ourselves by them? So why do we do it?

Let me offer a rarely-stated reason we may be tempted to look at such churches as our standard: We don't really think anything more is possible. We fear that no matter how much we sacrifice for a redemptive vision, the cultural soil of our generation is simply too hard and barren. The time isn't right. We live in a moment in which the gospel is in decline.

The Bible tells us about a time when God's people felt this way, and he talked to them about it. In the beginning of Haggai, God asks them, "...is it time for you to build your really nice houses rather than build the house of God?" (1:4, paraphrase). God starts out tough and in their faces. In the verses that follow, he says that he will undermine the wealth they built for themselves if they continue to neglect his house, but he doesn't end with that motivating threat. God's deeper word for them is in chapter 2. Underneath their pride in their worldliness lurks their real issue: spiritual fear. The work of God that they were participating in "seem[ed] to [them] like nothing" (Haggai 2:3). It didn't seem to be going anywhere. It didn't seem historic. It didn't seem like something that would be revered and remembered forever, so they concluded it wasn't worth doing. That's why they had given up. That's why they had settled for something less. And God's message to them is, "Be strong...and work. For I am with you" (2:4b).

Jesus had a different perspective than the Israelites. His success was also minimal. At the end of his life, even after his resurrection, the disciples only numbered about one hundred twenty in the upper room, with possibly five hundred total. That probably didn't seem like all that big of a deal, but that didn't faze Jesus in the slightest. No builder builds because he sees the building. Faith has a sight all its own, and it is the only sight that can create.

KEEPING UP WITH THE FRUIT

Every builder builds out of faith.
Every warrior fights out of conviction.
Every mother nurtures in hope.
Every farmer plants in trust.

We may tell ourselves that this generation cannot believe and be shaped by the gospel, but that's a lie. That's our fear and atheism talking. Jesus taught and modeled the truth for us:

When he saw the crowds, he had compassion on them, because they were harassed and helpless, like sheep without a shepherd. Then he said to his disciples, "The harvest is plentiful but the workers are few. Ask the Lord of the harvest, therefore, to send out workers into his harvest field."

Matthew 9:36-38

After this the Lord appointed seventy-two others and sent them two by two ahead of him to every town and place where he was about to go. He told them, "The harvest is plentiful, but the workers are few. Ask the Lord of the harvest, therefore, to send out workers into his harvest field. Go! I am sending you out like lambs among wolves."

Luke 10:1-3

"My food," said Jesus, "is to do the will of him who sent me and to finish his work. Don't you have a saying, 'It's still four months until the harvest'? I tell you, open your eyes and look at the fields! They are ripe for harvest. Even now the one who reaps draws a wage and harvests a crop for eternal life, so that the sower and the reaper may be glad together. Thus the saying 'One sows and another reaps' is true. I sent you to reap what you have not worked for. Others have done the hard work, and you have reaped the benefits of their labor."

John 4:34-38

The harvest is not limited by the crops. In reality, the fruit is rotting on the vine before the harvesters can pick it. Frankly, the way Jesus sees the world is the opposite of how we see the world. We believe we are many harvesters harvesting barren trees twice picked over. We think we are going over corn fields already combined, searching for a kernel here and a broken cob there. This is how I feel more than I want to admit. I'd venture to say most of us feel the same, but we are wrong.

Our pride and fear tell us that the realization that we're wrong is bad news. We know that if the problem is not the crop, then the problem is us. That stings. It feels unreasonable. But in reality, it's great news. So what if it implies our failure? It means our pessimism is false. It means that there is a harvest to be brought in and that the gates of hell must fall against the charge of a true cavalry. It means that the gospel is the power of God for the salvation of everyone who believes (Romans 1:16), and there are many more who would believe than we thought. It means that God's election is not stingy, but generous. And it means that, like any harvester, the greatest thing that can happen happens in the midst of a normal, humdrum life. Normal—not typical. The sound of a charging cavalry might seem astounding and rare, but it is made up of a thousand perfectly typical sounds: the steady beat of a single horse's steps.

The church can be that cavalry. We can harvest this field. It is time to be strong and to do the work. Not because its success is obvious. Not because the vision is great. Not even because we will accomplish a great vision. The temple they finished in Haggai wasn't anywhere near as great as the temple of Solomon. They died without knowing that the Messiah would come to that temple. All they knew was that God had given them something to do, and they couldn't waste their lives and money on slightly better houses. They couldn't keep covering over their fear. Faith demanded something: strength, work, and trust. It is the same for us.

This is why this book ended up being about forging spiritual substance in each of us. If we become people of substance, and if we believe that Jesus created a church that would bring in a harvest, then whatever the vision, this is no time to sit on our hands in thinly veiled pessimism. It is no time to get caught up in the world, because we think nothing is going to happen in the kingdom.

Jesus is working to take in a harvest, and he is doing it through his church. He has called all of us to this work. He makes no promises about our names being remembered or our seeing any success in this life. He just calls us over and over: trust him, be strong, and do the work, for he said, "I am with you always, to the very end of the age" (Matthew 28:20b).

Made in the USA
Lexington, KY
22 August 2017